The Right to Lifers

**Who They Are
How They Operate
Where They Get Their Money**

Connie Paige

SUMMIT BOOKS | New York

Copyright © 1983 by Connie Paige
All rights reserved
including the right of reproduction
in whole or in part in any form
Published by SUMMIT BOOKS
A Division of Simon & Schuster, Inc.
Simon & Schuster Building
Rockefeller Center
1230 Avenue of the Americas
New York, New York 10020
SUMMIT BOOKS and colophon are trademarks of Simon & Schuster, Inc.
Designed by Irving Perkins Associates
Manufactured in the United States of America

1 2 3 4 5 6 7 8 9 10

First Edition
Library of Congress Cataloging in Publication Data

Paige, Connie.
The right to lifers.

Includes bibliographical references and index.
1. Pro-life movement—United States. 2. Abortion—
United States. 3. Abortion—Political aspects—United
States. 4. Pro-life movement—United States—Finance.
I. Title.
HQ767.5.U5P34   1983   362.8'2   83-4795
ISBN 0-671-43180-3

TO MY SON

Contents

I.

The First Trial

The tap was bloody, a bad sign. The woman—actually a girl—on the operating table was a sixteen-year-old who had inadvertently gotten pregnant by her boyfriend. She had concealed the pregnancy as long as she could from her father, a West Indian immigrant with strict moral standards who might have reacted violently to the news. Finally, when she could deny her condition no longer, she confessed to her mother, who quickly brought her to Boston City Hospital for an abortion. The examining physician determined that she might be as far as twenty-four weeks along. The advanced state of her pregnancy meant that she would have to undergo a more complicated type of abortion than the usual scraping out of the uterine cavity.

Once she was admitted to the hospital, doctors tried twice to perform the delicate saline infusion. A saline, so called, is the injection of a salt solution by a long, thin needle into the amniotic sac, a procedure that for unknown reasons usually promotes labor. Before the injection, the doctor takes a sample, called a tap, to check

9

whether the needle has lodged in the right place. If the tap comes through bloody, that means the needle has probed either the placenta or a fetal or maternal blood vessel. Mistakenly introducing salt solution into either place could prove extremely dangerous to the woman, causing convulsions and even death. This, on October 3, 1973, was the third bloody tap.

The doctors had already decided that in the event of a third failure they would go ahead with a hysterotomy, a kind of early Caesarian section. After scrubbing, Dr. Kenneth Edelin took his place by the girl's side. Edelin had refused to do late-term abortions on younger women, particularly the thirteen- and fourteen-year-olds, because the physical strain on them was so great. He especially disliked doing hysterotomies, major surgery, which is always risky. In this case, he felt he had no choice. More taps could cause hazardous infection.

The operation began routinely enough. Edelin made a small incision about eight to ten centimeters, or about four inches, crosswise into the girl's abdomen just above the pubic hairline. Then he sliced through the skin and the subcutaneous tissues, clamping the blood vessels as he went along. He next cut through muscle, exposing the peritoneum, and screwed everything open and back with a retractor. He was working with an assistant unfamiliar with the operation, so the whole process, including explanations at each step, took about thirty minutes.

Underneath all the outer tissue was the uterus. For a number of reasons—because of the risks of substantial blood loss, complication to future pregnancies, or infection—Edelin decided on the smaller sideways rather than a vertical incision; this was later to slow him down considerably. He pierced the uterus, put his finger inside and then, balancing the scissors on the finger, cut each way until he had an opening about six to seven centimeters, or about three finger breadths, wide. The girl was finally ready for the last part of the abortion.

Steadying the uterus with his right hand, Edelin inserted two fingers of his left hand into the cavity. He swept them along the inside wall in order to peel the placenta from the uterus. Unfortunately, the effort broke the amniotic sac, which made the rest of the procedure more difficult. Edelin quickly felt with his fingers for the fetus and tried to grab the lower extremities. The wound was bleeding profusely by now, making the limbs slippery, and his groping inside the small incision was decidedly awkward. The extraction took him a long time, maybe two minutes or more.

In the split second after the fetus emerged, Edelin realized once again how uneasy these later abortions made him feel. He loved the work of an obstetrician, delivering a robust baby to a satisfied mother. These fetuses, while unnaturally tiny and obviously immature, still looked like infants. He always had to remind himself that if they had lived at that stage of development, which was highly unlikely, they would end up blind, retarded—vegetables, really. And without a mother, or with a mother who more often than not hated them. If they were black, like this one, they might have yet one more strike against them.

The hospital had a policy that any fetus born alive had to be taken immediately to the nursery for intensive care. This one had a faintly bluish color and a lack of tone to the muscles, indications that it was dead. Just to make sure, Edelin touched the chest wall and, feeling no heartbeat, deposited it in the stainless-steel basin the scrub nurse extended to him. The abortion had been altogether unremarkable, and he had only to sew the girl up quickly so that she wouldn't lose too much blood. He turned his attention back to her. That, he thought, was that.[1]

Six months later, Kenneth Edelin was indicted for the manslaughter of that premature, lifeless fetus. The charge caught Edelin, his superiors, the medical establishment, the women's movement, the press and much of the rest of the country and the world by surprise. The Supreme Court on January 22, 1973, had legalized abortion in the first two trimesters of pregnancy. Following the decision, the abortion rate had risen steadily, and it would soar to almost 900,000 by the end of 1974.[2] Public acceptance of abortion was widespread: an NBC News poll taken shortly after the indictment showed that 58 percent of the voters who were questioned (46 percent of the Roman Catholics) approved of laws permitting abortion in the first three months of pregnancy.[3] Certainly no one—not even the prosecutor—thought of this earnest young doctor as a murderer in the conventional sense of the word. But an accused murderer, for the time being, he became.

Directly responsible for this turn of events was a small group of dedicated anti-abortion activists who had been galvanized by the Supreme Court ruling. Without them, the authorities never would have discovered the evidence, nor even thought to look for it. Without them, the prosecutor never would have brought the charge, the witnesses given the testimony, nor the jury delivered the finding.

These activists intended to make the case the first test of the Supreme Court abortion decision. What made this possible was the ambitious prosecutor's discovery of a loophole in the law that allowed him to use the proceedings to examine the rights of a fetus born alive during the course of an abortion. The resulting trial became a modern-day morality play with the American public as the audience. It featured a cast of characters including the pro-choice doc and his civil-liberties lawyer on the one side and the politicians, prelates and honest idealists on the other who formed the first crude cadres of the emerging right-to-life movement. As such, the Edelin trial was a major attempt to get around the reproductive rights established by the highest court in the land.

Kenneth Edelin's background did not exactly prepare him for the role of victim, but more for that of crusading doctor. Edelin was born in Washington, D.C., into a family of modest circumstances. His father worked for the U.S. Post Office. His mother had two boys and a girl; he was the oldest. The Edelins are black, but to look at Kenneth, no one would know it. He was so light-skinned that new acquaintances invariably took him for Jewish or part of that great mass of indistinguishable white Americans. The inevitable confusion was a source of usually well-concealed insecurity, but also racial pride. In his youth the family lived in the ghetto, where he saw the scourges of poverty. When he was still a boy, Kenneth's mother died, a loss to which he attributes his physician's passion for healing women, particularly poor women.

Paying for his education largely through scholarships, Edelin attended a private prep school in Stockbridge, Massachusetts, and then Columbia University. Afterward he returned briefly to Stockbridge to teach high-school math and science. He went on to Meharry Medical School, the only private, almost exclusively black medical school in the country. Meharry is located in a poverty-stricken section of Nashville, Tennessee, and once again Edelin saw firsthand how cruelly poverty could undermine health. His medical-school experience stiffened his resolve to work with blacks and the poor. Doing abortions was a logical extension of that concern. "I've gone through the whole argument about when life begins," he explained in an interview just after his indictment. "I've seen too many women sick and sterile from hysterectomies and women who eventually die from abortions. That horrible picture of the women in a knee-chest position on the floor with blood spurting everywhere— I've seen that. The problem is, the women who die are poor women, and mainly black women."[4]

After four years in the Air Force, Edelin went to Boston City Hospital, a public institution, for his residency. In time, he became its first black chief resident in obstetrics and gynecology. Kenneth Edelin was widely acknowledged to be a competent physician, a dedicated worker and a congenial man.

That Edelin was the particular subject of this sensational trial was no accident. The hospital's omnipresence in the public eye allowed many of its internal affairs to become a matter of public record. As Edelin would remark after his indictment, "We're a real fishbowl." Then, too, because of his pro-choice convictions, he was doing most of the abortions there, and a lot of them. Before the Supreme Court decision, Boston City Hospital had accepted only about two to four abortion cases per week. After, the number rose tenfold, but the hospital's OB/GYN service was hardly equipped for the rush. Moreover, many residents refused to do abortions. For some it was a matter of moral conviction. For most it was just that they did not consider the operation challenging enough. By the time Edelin came to work there, he was one of only two residents performing the procedure, both of them together handling the astonishingly high case load of eighteen to twenty-four per week.[5]

It was no accident, either, that Boston was the scene of the trial. The city has a hundred-year-old history of antagonism between the Protestant Yankee settlers and the immigrant Irish. Around the turn of the century, the politically astute Irish made their mark by seizing control of local government. Up until very recently, almost all Boston public officials were white, male and Irish, and their dominant social institution, the Roman Catholic Church, exercised enormous moral authority over city affairs. Even so, the Irish appeared insecure. The foundations of church and state were no longer so comforting in a rapidly changing world. Newcomers were encroaching on their see. Blacks now made up one third of Boston's population,

and Hispanics constituted a growing minority. With their hegemony
slipping, some of the Irish started to shore up ethnic pride by opposing busing. Others chose abortion as their target.

The church, after all, had vociferously protested the Supreme
Court decision. The Archbishop in Boston had immediately promulgated his position. The largely Catholic community had long
since taken it to heart. The Catholic political infrastructure had
supported it. Police, prosecutor, prosecution witnesses, members of
the jury, almost all were Catholics themselves, and many of them
sympathetic to the church position. In this supremely amenable
environment, a small group of right-to-life activists had no trouble
manipulating the judicial process in an effort to challenge the law.
While the emerging right-to-lifers may have mystified outsiders, in
the context of Boston politics the Edelin trial made perfect sense.

The activist who actually prompted the series of events leading
up to the trial came out of the state's antiabortion organization,
Massachusetts Citizens for Life. Founded in 1970, MCL by four
years later was claiming a membership of forty thousand. Although
its officers maintained a low profile, not trusting the mass media to
report accurately on the cause, they had an active group of volunteers
who monitored local radio and TV shows, wrote letters-to-the-editor,
picketed abortion clinics and attempted to lobby politicians.[6] It was
one of their number, founding member and director Thomas Connelly, who discovered both the large numbers of abortions being
done at Boston City Hospital and what then seemed like the potentially spicier scandal, that fetal experimentation was being conducted
there. His efforts eventually prompted a public investigation of the
experiments, a grand-jury exploration of the abortions and, finally,
the indictment of Kenneth Edelin.

In January 1973, Connelly, the only right-to-lifer ever to take
credit for the Edelin case, contacted both the mayor's office and the
State Attorney General's criminal division to inform them of the
hospital's liberal abortion policies and of fetal experimentation taking
place right on the premises. Connelly provided proof of the charges
with an article he had unearthed from *The New England Journal
of Medicine*. According to the article, researchers at Boston City
Hospital had conducted a study in 1971 and 1972 looking into the
properties of the antibiotics Erythromycin and Clindamycin, giving
the drugs to pregnant women with dangerous congenital diseases

like syphilis who were planning to abort. The object was to find out whether the medicine reached the fetuses in sufficient quantities to prevent their contracting the diseases. If proven effective, the drugs could be prescribed for women allergic to penicillin. The studies were successful and established Clindamycin as the "drug of choice." Not long after the article appeared, Connelly called a press conference. Pointing to the evidence he now had in black and white, as a *Boston Globe* account detailed, he accused city and state officials of "dragging their feet."

The next month, after a Massachusetts Citizens for Life mailing on the subject, MCL members followed up on Connelly's appeal. Member John Day, for instance, a federal bank examiner, sent letters to Senators Edward Kennedy and Edward Brooke, among others, asking them to do something to stop the experiments. Although insisting that he was acting as an individual, Day anticipated by more than a year and a half a critical issue that was to come up at Edelin's trial: Day asked explicitly in the letters whether the appropriate birth and death certificates for the fetuses had been filed, as required by state law. He got little help from Kennedy and Brooke, the one maintaining relative silence on the issue and the other being actively pro-choice.

About the same time, two other Citizens for Life members got in touch with State Representative Raymond Flynn requesting his help. With him they had touched the right nerve.

Raymond Flynn comes from South Boston, an Irish-Catholic enclave that has supplied many local politicians. A modest but independent-minded man, Flynn has always had a kind of obsessive determination. As a youngster, he wanted to play professional basketball; he was so devoted to the game that he would practice in the local high-school gym in the dark. Early in his political career, Flynn made abortion his cause. Today his name is identified in the public mind with what is generally referred to as the Doyle-Flynn Amendment, a rider he and another state legislator attached to appropriations bills year after year to try to cut off state funds for abortion. Flynn was exactly the right man for the right-to-lifers to approach. He more than willingly forwarded the appeals from constituents to City Councilor Albert "Dapper" O'Neil.[7]

This was too good an opportunity for O'Neil to ignore. Dapper O'Neil is the quintessential Boston politician. An ample-waisted

Irishman, he is forever seeking higher office, to no avail. In the Council he perpetually rails against busing to promote school desegregation, against affirmative action—against anything that smacks of liberalism. He happily joined other councilors in posting giant letters in their City Hall office windows that together spelled out the acronym of the local anti-busing organization, Restore Our Alienated Rights, or ROAR. He also served as a delegate for George C. Wallace at the 1976 Democratic national convention. Shortly before the Edelin affair, O'Neil had launched a probe into the illegal carryings-on of the Suffolk County sheriff, who was stealing choice meats from the county jail kitchen. O'Neil's efforts finally chased the scoundrel from office. It just so happened that the office left thus vacant was one for which O'Neil wanted to run. He was campaigning for it when he heard about the fuss at Boston City Hospital.[8]

Fetal experimentation was an issue tailor-made for O'Neil, and he quickly got on the case. By September, he had initiated one of his famous hearings, with a roster of like-minded speakers. Packing the hearing were hundreds of right-to-life supporters. Ironically, among the spectators—one of the few who did not share the prevailing sentiment—was Kenneth Edelin, who had dropped by out of curiosity. The hearing lasted more than five and a half hours.

A good deal of the testimony had to do less with fetal experimentation than with abortion. The first to talk was an official of the Roman Catholic Church, Monsignor Paul Harrington, speaking on behalf of the Cardinal. The church had previously come out strongly against both abortion and fetal experimentation, but this was the first time that an official church representative had used a public forum to make the argument. Harrington testified at length about the propriety of allowing abortions at a public hospital. Additionally, he made a number of points, some of them in error, specifically about the experiments. He insisted, for instance, that the "babies" in question were born alive, that their delivery "was accomplished by violence" and that they were "being treated as experimental animals."[9]

Following the Monsignor came Dr. Mildred Jefferson, vice-president of Massachusetts Citizens for Life and a director of the National Right to Life Committee. Jefferson at the time was one of the few nationally recognized leaders of the right-to-life movement. This may have been because she had an excellent set of credentials, which made the press that much more likely to cover her. Jefferson was the first black ever to graduate from Harvard Medical School, and at a time when women doctors were also unusual. She is strikingly beautiful, and speaks in a precise, melodious contralto.

Jefferson had first gotten involved in the right-to-life movement in 1970, reportedly because, in her words, "the American Medical Association first considered bending its founding principles in such a way that a doctor would not be considered unethical" for doing an abortion. [10]

In her testimony, Jefferson questioned whether the women in the experiments had given truly informed consent. She also asserted that if she were governor she would fire the state's entire Department of Public Health for having written abortion guidelines of which she disapproved.

After Jefferson came Dr. Joseph Stanton, a member of a small MCL affiliate called the Value of Life Committee, who added another erroneous observation about the experiments, bolstering the Monsignor's charge. Stanton implied that in order for the doctors to get meaningful blood samples from the fetuses, the fetuses must have been born alive. He also stated gratuitously—and again mistakenly—that the fetuses, once dead, were "homogenized" in preparation for analysis. [*11]

The most sensational testimony was delivered by a nurse who had worked at Boston City from 1963 to 1971. She claimed that while on duty on the OB/GYN service, she had been asked to dispose of live fetuses. "I have taken live aborted babies to the nurseries during this time," she told the stunned audience, "and have gotten a lot of harassment from those people down there. 'Why are you bringing us these specimens, because now we have...to get rid of them?'" Although her charge was later refuted by Boston City's head nurse, it left its impression. [12]

These issues were to come up again. Indeed, in the midst of all the testimony, State Representative Raymond Flynn suggested—and Dapper O'Neil promptly agreed—that the minutes of the hearing should be passed along to the District Attorney for possible

---

*The *New England Journal of Medicine* article did use the unfortunate term "homogenized" to describe the process of preparing samples for tests, but these were fetal tissues, not, as Stanton implied, whole fetuses.

prosecutorial action. O'Neil subsequently hand-delivered those minutes to Assistant DA Newman Flanagan.[13]

If Kenneth Edelin was the archetypal crusading doc, and Raymond Flynn and Dapper O'Neil were the apodictical Boston pols,
then Newman Flanagan was an authentic fighting Irish Catholic
DA—the perfect prosecutor for the case. Newman Flanagan is another man with politics in his blood. His father had been a lawyer,
Boston's city treasurer and member of the important watchdog Finance Commission. Newman revered the man, whom he describes
with obvious admiration and occasional hyperbole. "My father had
a tremendous law practice—but not many paying clients," the son
explained in an interview in 1980. "He could have been a millionaire, but because of the type of man he was, he became a millionaire
not with money, but with friends. He went to Mass every day of his
life. There wasn't a better man who lived on this earth, except maybe
Christ Himself."

Religion and law were the dominant forces in the household. Two
of Newman's brothers entered the priesthood. One of them, showing
the Flanagan grit, started his own order, developing missions in
Central America and Africa. The other, showing the family gift for
disputation, became a Jesuit and chairman of the Boston College
philosophy department. Flanagan himself was an officer of the Knights
of Columbus, a Catholic fraternal organization which engages in
antiabortion activity. His mother and aunt worked in the Flanagan
law firm, but of the five children only he became a lawyer.

Flanagan worked his way through law school, having to labor
variously as a parking-lot attendant and a longshoreman. By the
early sixties he had secured a spot as assistant to the Suffolk County
District Attorney.[14] Over time, the short, scrappy young assistant
with the bouffant-style hairdo became known within the legal community as a brilliant trial attorney capable of charming a Catholic
jury into convicting a nun. The Edelin case, however, was the first
to bring him into the public eye.

Flanagan's conduct even before the Edelin hysterotomy indicated
that he was anxious to do something about abortion. A month earlier
he had assigned a law student to research all available state and
federal law and recent legal decisions regarding abortion and the
legal definitions of life, birth and fetal viability. The student discovered that the Supreme Court decision had not spelled out the

doctor's responsibility to a fetus born alive in the course of an abortion. That, anyway, was the story written up by respected court reporter Alan Sheehan for the *Boston Globe*. In the 1980 interview, however, Flanagan insisted that he did not remember the law student's work, and he denied the implication of the *Globe* story that he was preparing the legal groundwork so that when a late fetus had been found he would be ready to make the case. He did admit, however, that he had a "predisposition" that caused him to exercise his prosecutorial discretion in a certain fashion in the Edelin case.

Three months after the City Council hearing, in December, Flanagan convened a grand jury, which continued hearing evidence well into the following spring. In the beginning, Flanagan claims, he was looking into fetal experimentation with no thought to abortion, and happened upon the Edelin case by accident.

During the grand-jury hearings, as Flanagan tells the story, he received a couple of anonymous telephone calls insisting he investigate "two big babies" that someone alleged were in the Boston City Hospital morgue, the products of illegal abortions. Flanagan dispatched a police officer to the morgue and, corroborating the existence of two relatively well-developed fetuses, ordered the Suffolk County Medical Examiner to seize them. Neither had birth and death certificates. Checking the medical records, Flanagan then discovered that one of the fetuses had been delivered by saline infusion, which usually results in death, and the other by hysterotomy, which can result in a live birth. It is not known who originally put Flanagan onto the fetuses, and he would never say. Regardless, he claims he then realized that he might have a case even more explosive than anything involving fetal experimentation. Both of the fetuses had come from abortions Edelin had done.

Hot on the trail, Flanagan subpoenaed before the grand jury all the medical personnel who allegedly had attended the hysterotomy. Two of them turned out to be extremely useful. The first was a scrub nurse named Mamie Horner who contended that all live fetuses delivered of Catholics were baptized right on the spot after abortions. Horner later admitted to not having been present at the Edelin hysterotomy, and her information was proved incorrect. Still, she had led the grand jury to believe that Edelin had violated hospital policy, and the Catholics among them to suspect that the doctor had somehow deprived the fetus in question of the last rites.

Even more to the point was the testimony of Dr. Enrique Gimenez-Jimeno, another resident. Gimenez claimed that Edelin had
actually held the fetus inside the womb for a period of at least three
minutes, meanwhile watching the clock. Gimenez's charge was critical to the prosecutor. It was an eyewitness account, unusual in
medical cases. It implied that Edelin had purposefully deprived the
fetus of oxygen before delivery, thereby deliberately killing it.[15]

On April 11, 1974, the four doctors engaged in the fetal research
were indicted for "grave-robbing," the grisly charge unearthed out
of a 160-year-old statute originally designed to prevent medical students from exhuming cadavers. Kenneth Edelin was indicted for
manslaughter. The indictment stated chillingly that Edelin "did
assault and beat a certain person, to wit: a male child . . . and by
such assault and beating did kill the said person."[16]

The trial started on January 6, 1975, and was to last well past the
second anniversary of the Supreme Court decision. On one side of
the courtroom were lined up the prosecution forces, Newman Flanagan and a string of assistant district attorneys surnamed Mulligan,
Brennan and Dunne. At the defense table were Kenneth Edelin and
his attorney, William Homans, a respected criminal lawyer with
distinctly Boston Brahmin blood. Once having served as one of the
defense lawyers in the trial of Dr. Benjamin Spock for counseling
draft resistance, Homans has won more than the usual share of
socially and politically significant cases. He has never considered
himself a radical, however, but rather a civil libertarian.[17] Homans
was clearly the appropriate counsel to defend a black man who
himself had been defending a black woman's right to an abortion.

Prosecution and defense agreed early on that the trial had almost
nothing to do with abortion. What was at issue was the absence in
the Supreme Court decision legalizing abortion of any consideration
of a fetus born alive during the course of an abortion. The Supreme
Court decision had definitively stated that the fetus was not a person,
but Flanagan rested his legal argument on the presumption that it
became a person at the exact moment of birth—no matter how
premature or in what fashion—and thereby was subject to murder.
Flanagan's case was bolstered by an apparently calculated confusion
over precisely when and how Edelin was supposed to have committed

the crime. The state's bill of particulars in answer to defense questions about this very issue described the death only as occurring "when Baby Boy was within the mother, albeit detached from the mother and independent of the mother, and [sic]... when Baby Boy was partially expelled or removed from the body of the mother."[18]

How Flanagan coordinated the testimony to define birth, life and death, as well as a number of other critical concepts, transformed what ordinarily would have been considered a fetus into the putative "baby boy." Making those definitions were a string of witnesses associated with local or national right-to-life organizations who clearly had preconceived notions about the terminology and a definite stake in the outcome of the trial. Flanagan claims most of these volunteered their services, but one was a next-door neighbor of his, and at least another came by way of an assistant to the prosecutor who belonged to Massachusetts Citizens for Life.

MCL vice-president Mildred Jefferson, whom Flanagan called as an expert witness, gave the lead-off descriptions of embryonic development, abortion and birth. Jefferson was not necessarily the most qualified witness. She had never performed an abortion, although she claimed once to have "cleaned up" when a woman who had secured an illegal one required emergency care afterward. The part Jefferson played in the trial was all the more memorable because she was hardly an expert in the subject, having no experience in embryology, gynecology or perinatology. The last time she had even delivered a baby had been in 1951, twenty-four years earlier.

Jefferson did serve the prosecution in another way, however. She made her case resolutely, staying by her account even under stern cross-examination with all the ferocity of a bulldog. It was she who was the first in the proceedings to offer the critical opinion that a premature fetus, even if delivered by hysterotomy, could be considered "born" and therefore subject to murder.[19]

Another interested witness was Minnesota obstetrician Dr. Fred Mecklenburg. In an apparent effort to damage Edelin's credibility, Mecklenburg criticized the resident's manner of performing the operation as posing a possible danger to the girl. He also maintained that Edelin had erred in removing the placenta from the girl before the fetus, saying it "would be analogous to cutting the air hose on a salvage diver." Mecklenburg was a founder of Minnesota Citizens Concerned for Life—with his soon-to-be-prominent wife, Mar-

jory—and a former chairman of the National Right to Life Committee.[20]

Also criticizing the professionalism of the job was St. Louis obstetrician Dr. Denis Cavanagh, who claimed Edelin had engaged
in "bad medical practice" by attempting a hysterotomy in the first
place. The day Cavanagh took the stand, the second anniversary of
the Supreme Court decision legalizing abortion, his name appeared
in an advertisement in his hometown *St. Louis Globe-Democrat*
condemning the procedure with the words "Abortion degrades
women, our profession and our country."[21]

By the time the prosecution finished presenting its witnesses, the
jury had received a novel education. Abortion, according to Flanagan, was the termination of pregnancy in the twentieth week resulting in either a stillborn or a live-born infant. Hysterotomy was
appropriately carried out differently from the way Edelin had done
it: he had opened the abdominal cavity, separated the placenta from
the uterine wall and attempted to remove all the products of conception; the prosecution witnesses had the operation going the other
way, with the doctor first removing the fetus—as in a Caesarean—
and then separating the placenta from the uterine wall. With that
in mind, birth, they said, was a process which included the point
at which the placenta was separated from the wall during a hysterotomy. The fetus still inside the womb could at that moment be
considered a "person" or a "baby." That baby, the prosecution contended, could live, or be "viable" anytime after the twentieth week
of pregnancy.

Defense witnesses later attempted to refute all the definitions and
the appraisals of Edelin's work. They proved with data gleaned from
national and Boston City Hospital studies that, at that time, the
chance of the Edelin fetus living longer than a few moments was
nil. (Today younger fetuses are surviving.) Most importantly, they
emphasized the distinction between the purposes of abortion procedures and those to facilitate birth. This difference was lost on a
jury that had already accepted the concept that this fetus was a
human being.

Flanagan's was a clever and convincing case, made all the more
so by his own theatrics and the cooperation of other witnesses who
ordinarily might have been assumed to be more disinterested. One
interchange highlighted this well. It occurred on the second day on

the stand for Dr. George Curtis, Suffolk County medical examiner. Curtis has impeccable credentials—Berkeley, Boston University, Harvard. He speaks with the absolute authority of a Harvard man, in the mournful cadences of one used to talking about death. His voice sounds, in fact, as if it were echoing from a crypt. He was the coroner who the year before had taken into custody the fetus Edelin was charged with killing.[22]

Curtis had just testified that the fetus might have been alive after birth. This would later be the very information on which the jury's verdict turned. He was being cross-examined by defense attorney Homans. Homans was attempting to get the medical examiner to concede that what appeared on microscopic slides of the fetus's lung tissue to be signs of a possible gasp for air outside the womb could also indicate trauma-induced sucking of fluid before delivery, what Homans in passing referred to as a "phenomenon." Flanagan suddenly jumped up and objected to the word. The judge inquired if he could think of a better one, to which Flanagan replied coyly, with a pregnant pause for added effect, "The ... miracle?"[23]

The interchange—one of the few moments of mirth in this lengthy, exhausting and esoteric proceeding—was typical for Flanagan. Frequently depending upon the dramatic touch, he repeatedly used inflammatory rhetoric. Early in the trial he referred to the crime, for instance, as "suffocation," a characterization the judge would not permit. Flanagan also ignored another order to refrain from calling the fetus a "baby," always excusing himself afterward as if it were a slip of the tongue. To some, his behavior seemed flagrantly inappropriate. For his part, Flanagan maintained that he was simply exercising his conscience and his considerable courtroom talents.

Flanagan's acting effectively obscured the weakness of his case, which would later fall apart under judicial review. At issue was manslaughter, whether it had been committed, by whom and how. What made it seem initially as if Flanagan had a case at all was a crucial prosecution witness claiming that he had personally observed Kenneth Edelin deliberately killing a live fetus. Dr. Enrique Gimenez-Jimeno, Edelin's colleague at the hospital, testified truthfully that he had been present at the abortion in question. Then he asserted that he had seen Edelin at the end of the operation hold the fetus within the uterus for three minutes while watching the operating-room clock, presumably to time the fetus's demise. Gimenez was a nervous witness, forever contradicting himself and gnawing on his lip. Subsequent testimony revealed that the clock to which Gimenez referred—and on which so much of the prosecution case rested—was out of the operating room for repairs.[24]

Equally suspect was testimony about whether the fetus was really alive at the time of the abortion. Prosecution witness Dr. John Ward, a pathologist, stated baldly, on the basis of his microscopic examination of its lung tissue, that the fetus "did breathe outside the uterus." By comparison even with other more reserved prosecution witnesses, Ward's assertion was so blatantly wrong that it would move the three judges who would later write the appeals-court decision on the case to note, in typically muted judicial language, "in this he seemed to stand somewhat apart from other experts."[25] When the trial was over, the weight of the evidence indicated that the fetus had actually been dead by the time Edelin got to it, making the question of manslaughter moot.

On February 15, 1975, the jury convicted Edelin of manslaughter. Foreman Vincent Shea gave the verdict. Right-to-life sympathizers claim that Shea, unaccustomed to being in the public eye, was nervous. Pro-choice advocates say in contrast, that his voice sounded vengeful and almost pleased as he shouted out the jury's decision: "Guilty!"[26]

On February 18, Judge James McGuire gave Edelin a one year's suspended sentence, staying execution pending final determination of his appeal.

Kenneth Edelin believed from the moment he was indicted that he could never get a fair trial in Boston. Postmortems on the final jury deliberations indicate that he may very well have been correct. During the polling before the trial, the jurors—ten out of twelve of them Catholic—all swore that their personal opinions about abortion would not influence their verdict, but some admitted afterward that that might not have been so. According to an article in *Newsweek*, one juror revealed that among themselves they had always referred to the fetus as a "baby."[27]

Edelin called it a "witch-hunt." Expressing the sentiments aired by most of the media, *The New York Times* editorialized that "the case was an attempt to use a criminal jury to set social policy."[28] Even some of the jurors were troubled on afterthought. "I'm glad he got off without going to jail," commented juror Francis Mc-

Laughlin after hearing about the sentence. "I hope he wins his appeal. He hasn't done anything that a thousand other doctors haven't done. It's too bad to make an example out of him."[29]

The outcome of the trial seemed to have a ripple effect that would not stop. Hospitals across the country began announcing that they would no longer provide late-term abortions. A month after the conviction, doctors at West Pennsylvania Hospital in Pittsburgh decided to refuse to do abortions even after the twelfth week of pregnancy. A rash of Edelin-like cases started to appear. In March, New York's Nassau County District Attorney Denis Dillon launched an investigation into charges made by a Long Island right-to-life coalition that a doctor at the Nassau County Medical Center had allowed a fetus to die. Pregnant women went to court to challenge his colleagues' subsequent refusal to abort, also past twelve weeks, but a federal judge upheld the doctors' position on the grounds that they reasonably feared charges of murder.[30] Not surprisingly, the Los Angeles Planned Parenthood office reported in March to Newsweek a 10 percent rise in the number of women seeking their aid because doctors or hospitals to which they had gone first had denied them abortions in the seventeenth or eighteenth week.[31]

In Massachusetts, the state legislature revived previously abandoned attempts to stop abortion, and tried to outlaw the fetal experimentation that had prompted the whole affair. As with the Edelin trial, this new flurry of activity brought hitherto unknowns to the fore. Attorney William Delahunt, a state legislator from a Boston suburb who was just beginning his political career, was one of the sponsors of the bills. In an interview shortly afterward, Delahunt admitted that his interest in the subject of abortion came not so much from his Catholic background, nor from a desire to enhance his career, although those were important to him, as from direct self-interest. Delahunt's wife had been unable to conceive a child, and the couple had been unable to adopt the kind of children they wanted. Delahunt assumed that restrictions on abortion would, as he put it, increase the supply of white babies up for adoption.[32] As debate over the bills wore on, Delahunt made a name for himself negotiating with prominent Harvard physicians and researchers to change the bills so as to make them conform with standard medical practice and federal and state law.

In the midst of all the furor, a curious thing happened. The right-to-lifers in Boston began establishing ties with the city's primary anti-busing organizations. As William Safire noted in an op-ed article in *The New York Times*, busing and abortion were linked in the sense that they were both an expression of the resistance of local people to changes made at the national level over which they had no control.[33] The outreach was the first sign of a coalition around what would come to be known as the "social issues," a cluster of concerns not traditionally the province of politics that affected people's day-to-day lives. This kind of alliance would one day prove vital to the strategy most likely to stop abortion, packing Congress with right-to-life votes. Once having been noticed, the coalition closed its ranks, and it would be a long time before it emerged publicly again.

The conviction was the first stroke of luck for the right-to-life movement. Before Edelin, no one had perceived the volatility of the issue of abortion. After Edelin, it was recognized as having a potential for enormous political significance in the right place at the right time. As a Chicago right-to-life activist remarked to a reporter a month after the verdict, "A year ago I would have said we didn't have a chance. But today I think we're making progress."[34]

Indeed, the right-to-life movement would go on to astounding victories. Right-to-lifers would eventually achieve significant legislative, political and electoral gains, giving the pro-choice movement a hard run for its money. Right-to-life groups throughout the country got laws restricting abortion enacted. Nationally, they were able to pass the "Hyde Amendment" cutting off federal funding for abortions for the poor. They elected a number of anti-abortion politicians to office, and even ran two candidates for President of the United States on a right-to-life ticket. Perhaps most important, by giving credibility—if not legitimacy—to the idea that the fetus had a "right to life," they undercut the force of the Supreme Court decision giving women a right to abortion.

These triumphs would prompt *Time* magazine to characterize the right-to-life movement as causing the country's greatest controversy since slavery.[35] Advocates of reproductive choice would condemn the right-to-lifers as unconscionable violators of human rights. As Planned Parenthood president Faye Wattleton would put it, "The self-appointed moralists believe that an unwanted pregnancy—with all its implications and potential complications—is the penalty that must be exacted from a woman in exchange for an act of love. Because, after all, isn't punishment due—aren't women to blame for stirring up sinful thoughts in the hearts of men? It is a vision of the Dark Ages, of the Inquisition, of a time no person—man or woman—should have to face."[36] Joining the chorus, legal scholars would excoriate the right-to-lifers for endangering democracy. "Our constitution," former Watergate special prosecutor Archibald Cox would assert, "is under siege."[37] From a handful of believers in Boston—some underhanded, some ambitious, some merely following their lights—the right-to-lifers would grow to become one of the quintessentially American populist movements of our time.

The right-to-lifers who participated in the Edelin trial subsequently went their separate ways, none of them apparently chastened by the uproar, and some of them helped by it. Raymond Flynn joined Dapper O'Neil on the Boston City Council, where they both attempted to pass an ordinance requiring a prohibitively large licensing fee of $1,000 for all abortion clinics. Flynn went on to make a name for himself championing the poor and middle-class residents of the city of Boston, black and white alike, in matters having to do with housing and city services. O'Neil lost his bid for sheriff and made an attempt for United States marshal, to no avail. William Delahunt successfully ran for district attorney in 1978 in his county, where he set up a crack unit to deal with white-collar crime. Newman Flanagan handily won the race for DA in his county in the same year. From the new post, he finally dismissed charges against the "grave-robbers," for reasons which neither he nor their defense counsel will disclose.

What happened to those on the other side of the case is a little more surprising, and shows the emotionalism abortion can elicit. On the strength of the publicity around the trial, Kenneth Edelin became a figure of international renown, his opinions on medical matters, particularly with respect to abortion, widely sought after. Still firm in his convictions, Edelin willingly made public appearances on behalf of the pro-choice movement. His lawyer, William Homans, however, was widely credited with spurring on Newman Flanagan's

victory at the polls. Pro-choice, too, Homans backed the controversial assistant DA because he felt that the only other candidate,
Flanagan's boss, was becoming too much of a publicity hound,
bringing indictments in sensational cases with minimal evidence to
support them. Meanwhile, the girl who had had the abortion in the
first place ended up regretting it. Had she to do it all over again,
she told attorney Homans, she probably would consider other alternatives.[38]

II.

The Politicization of Abortion

Nobody likes abortion. It is bloody. It is a last resort. It is so close to the onset of birth that some have called it murder. Churches have condemned it. Governments have outlawed it. People have vilified the women who have tried to get it. Still, abortion has persisted in almost every time and place, regardless of the stigma, an heroic feminine protest signaling women's determination to control their own fertility. What is more, the authorities have often quietly allowed it to go on.

This bizarre exercise in mass self-deception is one of the great unrecorded ironies of history. As a matter of fact, irony surrounds this jarring human experience at every turn. It is strange indeed that many women feel ambivalent about abortion and yet, like the girl in the Edelin case, go ahead with it anyway. It is stranger still that the prevalence of abortion did not cause its acceptance sooner. Perhaps strangest of all is that such a private matter did finally become the subject of such a very public dispute.

The key to all of this lies in the religious scruples, dim in origin, that have put sexuality into perpetual moral twilight. Indisputably, human beings have always considered sex a crucial part of life. As Macaulay once observed, "The mutual relations of the two sexes seem to us to be at least as important as the mutual relations of any two governments in the world." Just as we have not been able to devise the perfect diplomacy, however, so we cannot seem to resolve the nagging conflict between religious belief about sex and actual practice. It is no wonder, then, that abortion, the fail-safe method of eliminating any unwanted consequence of sex, has assumed an ambiguous social status. This very ambiguity has allowed abortion to become a symbolic issue, indicating something about a society's sexual mores. Abortion policy has reflected this correlation, wavering according to the relative interest of the authorities in controlling sexual behavior, and their relative power to do so.

Complicating matters further is the dual nature of abortion, by definition involving more than a single being. Western religion, for reasons again obscured by time, developed the unshakable conviction that both woman and fetus were human, sacred and worthy of the same regard. This in effect gave the fetus a "right to life" and the woman the responsibility for its protection from the moment of conception up through birth. Theologians within the Judeo-Christian tradition came to presume abortion to be a violation of natural law, and thus murder.

The modern world brought to these classic judgments a new and stunning dimension: feminism. Feminists declared for the first time that women should have rights equal to those of men. Feminists argued additionally that their freedom depended on a sanctioned ability to control their fertility. In making the case for reproductive rights, the feminists laid bare the hypocrisy that had kept belief about sex and the practice of sex apart, and challenged the notion of absolute fetal rights. They made the private public, in the process transforming abortion, once considered just a moral issue, into a political issue as well.

The politicization of abortion outraged traditionalists—principally Roman Catholics—who could not or would not sit by idly and witness this profound overturning of their most cherished religious values. Always disapproving of abortion, the Papacy rededicated the offices of the church to combating the notion of reproductive rights. In America as nowhere else the campaign took on a unique

guise. Here, with significant wealth at its disposal, the hierarchy of
the church started right-to-life organizations and dominated their
early growth, fashioning their philosophy, political base and strategy,
and paying their way. Because of the country's democratic traditions
and a history of populist revolt, it was only a short step from the
church's initial creations to the development of a full-fledged, partially independent movement with a life of its own.

If the church was responsible for the right-to-life movement, it
was also, ironically, its greatest barrier to success. Many outside the
faith bitterly resented what they perceived as religious interference
in secular affairs. The right-to-life movement would not obtain credibility until it could discard this baggage. Eventually the right-to-
lifers appeared to shed their clerical garbs and adapt to the demands
of the times. Their next task was to convince a majority of the
American people to agree with them and vote-in a Congress that
would vote-out abortion rights. Alternatively, the right-to-lifers had
to figure out a way to engage in the political process themselves.

The architects of their eventual strategy would turn out to be the
ultraconservative heirs to the Goldwater legacy, principally Richard
Viguerie. Where there was confusion, Viguerie brought efficiency;
where doubt, expediency; where a meager allowance, big bucks. Of
equal importance, this prince of public relations delivered the media.
Viguerie and his New Right colleagues would consciously and carefully shape what they called a "winning coalition" out of the right-
to-lifers and fundamentalist Protestants for whom abortion had formerly been of little concern. The alliance would grant the movement
the kind of cash it had never seen. Before, right-to-lifers' finances,
such as they were, had been the function of the depth of feeling of
the local parish priest. Now the movement would have indirect
support from the various sources to which the New Right and the
fundamentalists had some access: the Republican Party, the independent conservative political-action committees and the fabulously
wealthy eccentrics who were interested mostly in creating a Christian
Republic on earth. The "social issues," abortion chief among them,
would become part of everyday discourse and take their place on
the nightly news.

In time, it would be difficult for the casual outsider to discern
much if any difference between the original right-to-lifers and the
New Right, although the former did try to maintain their autonomy.

Certainly the media would not often make the distinction. As a practical matter, most of the quantum leaps forward for the movement—the election of right-to-life members of Congress, congressional consideration of a right-to-life constitutional amendment banning abortion, President Reagan's support for the cause—would come as a result of their combined pressure. Although many within the right-to-life movement remained uncertain about or unsympathetic to the rest of the New Right program, they would allow its leadership to call the shots.

But there always was that annoying other agenda. From then on, it was not simply a constitutional amendment banning abortion that they were after. The particularly aggressive breed of politicos that was the New Right was interested in a full radical conservative program that went way beyond the concerns of the original right-to-lifers. The youthful right-wing zealots wanted to bolster free-market capitalism, slash government spending, stop Communism, revitalize the military and, in the process, restore the preeminence of the United States to make it the most powerful nation in the world. Their messianic mission would help establish "right to life" as code words signifying a conservative attempt to take over America.

Abortion has probably not always been a moral issue. Anthropological findings suggest, on the contrary, that early peoples may have dealt with it matter-of-factly. Experts used to think that ancient societies were stable in size because their high mortality rates more than matched high fertility rates. Recent discoveries indicate instead that some preindustrial peoples may even have consciously practiced contraception, abortion and infanticide as a means of population control. The Melanesian island people of today, for instance, engage in a practice, which may have come from ancient times, of deliberately encouraging abortion when the number of sons reaches a certain quota, in order that they will have enough property to inherit. In the same way, prehistoric people may have appreciated abortion in times of resource scarcity as a help in reducing the size of the tribe, village or parish. Alternatively, when survival demanded greater numbers, they may have celebrated birth as the advent of a potential human recruit.

Whatever the motivation, evidence from contemporary primitive tribes suggests that almost all the modern forms of contraception were known to early peoples, including coitus interruptus, condoms, the rhythm method and prolonged suckling of infants. One of the most effective was the pessary, or vaginal suppository, frequently a mixture of some part dung. Ancient techniques were often quite sophisticated, even by contemporary standards. An anthropologist visiting Java in 1897 discovered midwives using external manipulations to tip the uterus of women who did not want to conceive. Some primitive people even performed surgical sterilizations consisting of widening the vaginal entrance or cutting open the cervix. When these failed, according to Linda Gordon, the foremost authority on the subject, women opted for abortion.

The most common type of abortion was most likely the taking of a potion, now considered only 7 to 14 percent likely to work, and that possibly correlating with the normal rate of spontaneous miscarriage. If potions did succeed, it could have been because they so irritated or poisoned the woman that her reactions brought on the desired result. German folk medicine probably originating in prehistory recommended marjoram, thyme, parsley, brake and lavender to help dislodge the fetus. The French favored the also likely ancient remedy of the root of the worm fern, otherwise known as "prostitute root." Certain Hungarians used a concoction of gunpowder dissolved in vinegar. Other known abortifacients included a paste of mashed ants, foam from a camel's mouth and tails of the blackhair deer.

By far the most effective type of abortion, although probably often dangerous, was the use of probes into the uterus. An early Persian physician recommended inserting root of mallow into the womb "until the menses do appear," and Eskimo tribes in Greenland used a walrus rib sharpened and covered with the animal's skin. Women also lifted heavy objects, climbed trees, took hot baths, jumped from high places and shook themselves. Certain societies poured hot water over the belly, or arranged for the woman to be bitten by large ants. In some places, a helper would grasp the uterus through the abdominal wall and twist it, hoping to dislodge the fetus.[1]

The origins of moral compunctions about abortion are shrouded in mystery. The first recorded condemnation appears in ancient Jewish texts, and the Christians carried it forward into their tradition. Jewish law considered marriage and the exercise of sexuality a *mitzvah*, or religious duty and blessing. Traditionally, nothing was supposed to interfere with the spilling of the male seed. The Talmud gives a variety of possible origins for this superstition. It may have had to do with a dislike of interrupting coitus, a horror of onanism or even the mystic sense that interference with the seed was somehow wrong. Whatever the reason, Jews did not necessarily link sexuality with sin* or abortion with murder.

Jewish law on the relationship of marriage and sexuality to procreation allowed for a relatively understanding approach to fertility control. The assumption was that when a couple entered marriage, they would certainly have children, which was also a *mitzvah*, but they could separate marriage from procreation in some extreme cases. When pregnancy might endanger the woman's health or life, contraception and even abortion were acceptable. As the famous rabbi Moses Sofer elucidated it, no woman "is required to build the world by destroying herself." Later rabbinical interpretations held the even more permissive view that women could use contraception of a nonabortifacient sort in some situations to save themselves from shame or pain. The pill, for instance, according to Jewish scholar David Feldman, is still "a very live subject."

The status of the fetus was also not particularly elevated. The early Jews believed that the fetus was not a separate person until it came into the world. Accordingly, the punishment for feticide was less severe than for homicide, the usual compensation being monetary.

Although Jews did condemn abortion, it was the Christians who were to make it anathema throughout the Western world. Christian notions about abortion have been tied in with a decidedly more

---

*The same parts of the Old Testament that were later used by Christians to condemn sex were found by Jews to be open to entirely different interpretation. The germane passage on the subject appears in the Book of Psalms: "Behold, I was brought forth in iniquity; in sin did my mother conceive me." The Talmud, according to one Jewish scholar, David Feldman, does not even elaborate on the passage, and the single reference to it connects it not with the sex act but with the monthly cycle of the woman. Even at that, Feldman says, the reference is remarkably "tongue-in-cheek." "Iniquity" is taken to mean near the time of iniquity, or menses, when sexual intercourse was not allowed; "sin" refers to the time of purification after the menses, about 16 days later. Taken as a whole, instead of being a profound statement on the nature of sin, as in Christian thought, the passage is a simple lesson for Jews on the rhythms of the woman's body, explaining that conception takes place about 16 days after the onset of menstruation.

negative attitude toward women. Early Christians may have shared the positive Jewish outlook, but abandoned it for contemporary Greek asceticism. In the third century, one of Christianity's more misogynist theologians, Tertullian, called women "the devil's gateway" and proposed sourly, "Above all, it seems right that we turn away from the sight of women." Tertullian elaborated on this theme by developing his scorn for marriage in three treatises, the last of which insisted that celibacy was the true mark of virtue. [2]

This prejudice persisted for centuries to come with only minor modifications. In the fifth century, Augustine, Bishop of Hippo, developed the notion of original sin, the stain thereafter associated with all sex. Thomas Aquinas in the thirteenth century added to this his conviction that the single possible moral justification for sex was procreation. Theologians also implicitly established the "personhood" of the fetus by introducing the concept of "ensoulment," a process considered to happen at what was then called "quickening," the point at which the fetus started to move, or about forty days after conception. Following this line of reasoning, contraception, as the implicit acknowledgment of the practice of sex for pleasure, and abortion, as both the relief from its consequences and the killing of a being with a soul, were violations of the laws of God. The woman's needs—or, for that matter, the man's—did not even come into the picture.

While finding its roots in moral theology, however, the Christian ban on abortion had a decidedly practical element to it as well. Politically well-established popes down through the ages prohibited abortion, according to authority John Noonan, but then weaker ones vacillated. Pope Innocent XI, for instance, ruling over a deeply divided church and reacting to the obvious and widespread flouting of a ban on abortion then in force, adopted a remarkably lax position that would remain in force for two centuries. Two of sixty-five propositions he promulgated in 1679 overturned the ban, one explicitly allowing abortion before quickening, and the other stating that even afterward "no abortion is homicide," because "the fetus . . . lacks a rational soul and begins first to have one when it is born." Pope Pius IX instituted his ban in 1869 at least in part as a response to contemporary conditions, to encourage the growth and solidarity of a flock then dispersing over distant and sometimes hostile continents. [3]

The Catholic position would remain essentially the same up through modern times. In the turbulent 1960s, the extraordinary ecumenical council known as Vatican II did take a major step in conceding that sexual pleasure could properly help renew conjugal bonds, but would go no further. It was not sexuality, however, that the church stressed when condemning abortion, but rather its issue. As Pope Paul VI reminded an audience of Catholic jurists in 1972, quoting from his predecessor Pius XII, the fetus had an inalienable "right to life":

> [T]here is no man, no human authority, no science, no medical, eugenic, social, economic or moral "indication," which can show or give a valid juridical title for a *direct* deliberate disposing of an innocent human life—which is to say, a disposition that aims at its destruction either as an end in itself or as the means of attaining another end that is, perhaps, in no way unlawful in itself.

Paul also spoke directly to the many women who were beginning to chaff under the church's stern proscriptions. To those who felt themselves already burdened by a double standard, the Pope added a third responsibility. In her primary "vocation" as a mother, the Pope saw the woman as having the fundamental duty to consider not only her own salvation, and that of her future child, but also the "common good."[4]

From these basic premises, modern Catholic prelates developed a profile of the "humanity" of the fetus described by John Cardinal Krol, Archbishop of Philadelphia, in this way to the Subcommittee on Constitutional Amendments of the U.S. Senate in 1974:

> Before a woman ordinarily knows that she is pregnant, the new human being has developed thousands of cells, a heart which began beating within twenty-five days from conception, veins and circulating blood, a backbone and skeletal system, a brain with traceable brain waves, rudimentary organs, arms and legs, fingers and toes, eyes and ears and a mouth. At the very moment of fertilization, all of the unique genetic characteristics of an individual are determined: eye, skin and hair coloring, height and bone structure, intellectual potential, inherited emotional makeup, etc. From conception on, forty-six chromosomes are

present, twenty-three from each parent. This is the chromosomal content defined by biologists as that of a normal human being. Furthermore, this new individual's chromosomal pattern is utterly unique, absolutely its own and unlike that of any other human being in the world, including either of its parents. The scientific evidence points to only one possible conclusion: this is a new, unique, human individual. When this individual is killed, human life is destroyed.[5]

The church also considered society's readiness to perform abortions as part of a mentality that considered life meaningful only insofar as it measured up to ill-defined standards of usefulness and productivity. This "abortion mentality," so called, was supposed to be a dangerous first slide down the slippery slope to finding all life cheap. Any government that did not guarantee protection to the unborn, went the thinking, threatened the lives of all, particularly the ill, weak, mentally or physically incapacitated, old or ostracized. Furthermore, any government that used abortion in the service of some other goal, such as population control, was participating in nothing less than genocide. Civil law was inconsequential when matched against these moral convictions.

The Catholic Church, however, did not express the views of all Christians. The Reformation had a profound effect on Christian thinking about sexuality and abortion. Martin Luther did regard sex as shameful, but John Calvin found not only marriage but even sexual enjoyment a positive good, and that one of the wife's duties was to satisfy her husband's sexual desires. Early Protestants also felt more relaxed about contraception and abortion. Along with their feisty individualism, Protestants brought this permissiveness with them to the New World.

Toleration for abortion lasted for some time on American soil, and even the drive to ban it came actually not so much out of religious scruples as from mercenary greed. Indeed, abortion politics would continue to take bizarre twists and turns, with some of the same forces that mounted the effort toward prohibition in the nineteenth century taking exactly the opposite position a hundred years later.

All the evidence points to widespread acceptance of abortion in colonial days. Linda Gordon cites the case, for instance, of "prominent citizen" Captain Mitchell who impregnated Suzanna Warren, a single woman from Maryland, in 1652. In order to bring about miscarriage, Mitchell administered to her a "potion of Phisick." When the remedy didn't work Warren actually brought charges against her lover.[6]

An additional indication of indifference about abortion comes as late as the nineteenth century from notices of the evidently booming business of the providers of the day. A *New York Times* exposé found a certain Madame Restell, for instance, a notorious New York–based abortifacient dealer with branches in Boston and Philadelphia, spending $60,000 a year, then a princely sum, on advertising alone. Not just the lower classes but also women of substance were apparently snatching up her wares. According to the feminist publication *Revolution*, "Restellism" was "fashionable in the American *dress circle.*"

Even the law reflected this nonchalance. According to James Mohr's authoritative *Abortion in America*, American laws on the subject had derived from English common law, which condemned abortion only after quickening. In the early part of the nineteenth century, a number of states passed more involved measures, but these were an attempt to protect women from unscrupulous practitioners and harmful practices, chiefly poisoning. Connecticut's omnibus crime act of 1821 mentioned for the first time a prohibition on poisoning to bring about miscarriage, but did not even mention abortion. A revision in 1830 had a section on abortion separate from the poisoning decrees, but the penalties were less severe than for "killing." Likewise, Ohio (1834), Indiana and Missouri (1835), Arkansas (1837), Mississippi and the territory of Iowa (1839), and Alabama and Maine (1840) all passed laws similarly controlling the administration of dangerous abortifacients, but not abortion itself.

The first impulse for drastic change of the law actually came out of this concern for the protection of women. In 1844, in the city of Boston, Maria Aldrich, an unmarried woman from Rhode Island, died an agonizing death in an anonymous boardinghouse from massive uterine infection, the complication of an attempted abortion. Fenner Ballou, the man who had gotten her pregnant, and Dr.

Alexander Butler, the physician who did the abortion, were both indicted—Ballou for setting up and paying for the abortion, and Butler for committing murder. Ballou and Butler were acquitted, principally because the chief witness in the case, the boardinghouse owner, was paid off and absconded to avoid testifying at the trial. The case received sensationalistic treatment in the newspapers of the day—not, as might be expected, because the two got off, but instead because they were brought before a jury in the first place. Since Aldrich's pregnancy had not yet reached "quickening," people did not consider the abortion a crime.

Five days after the acquittal, state legislator William Bradbury introduced a measure to reduce the likelihood of this sort of thing ever happening again. Within a week, Massachusetts had the country's first law effectively banning abortion. The law mandated that any doctor attempting an abortion would be guilty of a misdemeanor and subject to a $2,000 fine and one to seven years in jail. If the woman died, the crime would be considered a felony. The statute was almost completely ignored. Between 1849 and 1857, the state had only thirty-two trials related to the offense, and not a single conviction. Massachusetts had, however, provided the opening wedge.

The revision of the law had come at an opportune moment in history, when society was becoming more prudish about sex. Linda Gordon attributes the gradually more repressed attitudes to the complex forces impinging on the American family as a result of the Industrial Revolution. Whatever the cause, they imposed a double burden on women. Unlike men, if women violated the sexual taboos their pregnancy revealed it to the rest of the world, yet they were also begrudged the abortion that might save them shame.

Recognizing the implications of this new social trend were the first wave of feminists, who were beginning to organize for the first time around a number of issues exclusively relating to the rights of women. The feminists understood immediately the importance of reproductive rights to their efforts. Without the ability to control fertility, women were virtual slaves to their families. With a means of limiting family size, they could plan their lives, participate more easily in the affairs of the world and possibly gain previously elusive economic independence. Once the momentum toward limiting access to abortion began, the feminists considered a counterassault. They soon realized that their numbers were too small and the roots of the issue too deep for them to win, and they abandoned the attempt.*

In the absence of a strong drive to save abortion, the crusade to ban it became a movement in its own right. Interestingly, those who took up the prohibition campaign most fervently were physicians who had as their real motive neither morals nor rights, but regularization and regulation of their own kind. Mohr describes doctors of the day as more often than not viewed virtually as a menace to society. Ill-trained and out for profit, they frequently wreaked great damage on their patients. Their objective in having abortion outlawed was both professional and pecuniary, Mohr shows, a way of safeguarding women but at the same time putting midwives out of business.

The crusade against abortion was not especially popular at the start. Doctors went to great lengths to win the endorsement of other more established professionals, but without much success. One group they failed to interest was the clergy. This was peculiar, since some traditionalist denominations had embraced highly restrictive views. The tendency of the clergy to back away from the controversy was

---

*One feminist quoted by James Mohr wrote to *Revolution* from the mill town of Androscoggin, Maine, where there was apparently an extremely high abortion rate. A previous letter-writer had likened this to mass murder. The feminist responded by writing back that the aborters' cry was "Liberty or Death," and that all that would keep American women from abortion would be "liberty to women, freedom entire." She signed herself "Conspirator."

By far the more usual reaction, however, was gnawing ambivalence, as in another woman's response to a survey asking how she felt after an abortion:

I consulted a woman, a friend in whom I trusted. I found that she had perpetrated that outrage on herself and on others. She told me it was not murder to kill a child any time before its birth. Of this she labored to convince me, and called in the aid of her "family physician," to give force to her arguments. He argued that it was right and just for wives thus to protect themselves against the results of their husband's sensualism,—told me that God and human laws would approve of killing children before they were born, rather than curse them with an undesired existence. My only trouble was, with God's view of the case, I could not get rid of the feeling that it was an outrage on my body and soul, and on my unconscious babe. He argued that my child, at five months (which was the time), had no life, and where there was no life, no life could be taken. Though I determined to do the deed, or get the "family physician" to do it, my womanly instincts, my reason, my conscience, my self-respect, my entire nature, revolted against my decision. My Womanhood rose up in withering condemnation.

all the more remarkable since some of its members were engaged in something of an attempted resurgence themselves.*7

This was the age of religious revivalism that saw the rise of the National Reform Association, one of the most powerful constituent groups of the time. Foreshadowing later such drives, the NRA at one convention demanded a constitutional amendment declaring God as the nation's source of authority, Jesus as its ruler and His revealed will as its creed. They also proposed that only "God-fearing men" should be elected to public office, and sought another constitutional amendment to establish "moral and religious" qualifications for officeholders. They advocated laws requiring Bible reading in the public schools and outlawing, among other things, Sabbath-breaking. Their political strategy was that of the modern-day fundamentalists in reverse: they admonished followers to refuse to vote or run for office.[8]

Abortion, however, was not a pressing issue for the NRA. More than likely, it was not so much that they cared one way or the other as that the clergy of the time were just as happy not to rock the boat. Long after some of the more restrictive laws had already been passed, the Reverend Morgan Smith candidly told the Michigan Board of Health that one of the primary reasons that men of the cloth were ignoring the doctors' crusade was self-interest:

> We are willing to state to our congregations what we think to be right. Were we certain always of the course to take upon this and other things we should do as requested. There are obvious reasons why the pulpit should not always be used to denounce crimes of this nature. To do it continually would be to turn the pulpit and church into a place that many people would not like to visit.

---

*In 1868, the Maine Congregational Church did assemble a committee to study "the alleged prevalence of pre-infanticide" and praised doctors for their vigilance on the subject. Connecticut's Congregationalists and the Old School Presbyterians also condemned the practice, the Presbyterians calling it "the destruction by parents of their own offspring, before birth . . . a crime against God and against nature . . ." However, these did not at all represent the vast body of Protestants in America. The next year, the influential Bishop of Baltimore also came out against abortion—but this was hardly the kind of support the doctors needed. Catholics being then only about 10 percent of the population, and unpopular at that, their opinions did not carry much weight.

Regardless of the snub by the clergy, the doctors ultimately achieved their objective. By 1877, forty states or territories had statutes on the books, thirteen of them outlawing abortion for the first time and twenty-one revising the old "poisoning" code. Most of these mandated that interruption of pregnancy at any time was a crime. Some of the more stringent added provisions putting not only the doctor but also the woman in jeopardy, and criminalizing the advertising of abortion services as well. By the turn of the century, every state except Kansas had outlawed abortion, and it was associated in the public mind, in Mohr's words, with "the poor, the socially desperate, and the unwed—usually seduced or misled—girl."[9]

The turnabout in abortion policy, remarkable in itself, had extraordinarily little impact. The Wisconsin Medical Society had claimed in 1879 that the abortion rate was as high as two abortions for every child born. In 1881, the Michigan Board of Health estimated that 100,000 abortions were still being done per year across the country. A much more authoritative study done at Stanford University in 1921 would find an average of one out of every 1.7 to 2.3 pregnancies nationwide ending in abortion. Birth rates may have reflected the same phenomenon. In the eighteenth century, the United States had had one of the highest birth rates in the world, but the rate plummeted in the next century to the lowest but for France. From 1800 to 1960, the average number of births per woman would fall from 7.04 to 3.52. Many historians feel that the drop was due in large measure to the widespread use of abortion.[10]

It took another hundred years for the conditions to be right for the second wave of feminists to be able to overturn the laws. The continuing practice of abortion coupled with more open attitudes toward sex created a more favorable climate for reconsideration of reproductive rights. This time around, too, feminism found wider appeal, and feminist activists mounted a more effective political struggle. Moreover, they had powerful allies to help them get their message across, among them the advocates of population control and members of some of the very professions, ironically, that a century earlier had condemned them—especially physicians and clergy. Starting in the 1960s and up through the following decade, the feminists and their allies would begin to convince the American public to accept abortion.

Planned Parenthood became one of the primary protagonists in favor of reproductive rights during the 1960s, at a time when its major focus, population control, was in high vogue. The widespread alarm caused by the publication of Paul and Ann Erlich's *Population Bomb* in 1968 and the MIT-sponsored *Limits to Growth* in 1972 made population control a hot topic. Agencies like Planned Parenthood undertook surveys of women's conditions all over the world, which began to reveal the links between fertility, childbearing and health. Ten to fifteen percent of all births worldwide—or about twelve to eighteen million per year—were from teenage mothers. These youngsters were much more likely than older women, surveys were showing, to die in childbirth, and their infants were at even greater risk, more likely to suffer from prematurity, low birth weight and possibly death. This was true even for the United States and even during the supposedly chaste 1950s, when three quarters of the teenage brides, according to statistics, were already pregnant when they married. Moreover, population experts were beginning to discover that having too many babies could also adversely affect a woman's health, with any beyond four carrying a significantly higher probability of maternal death, stillbirth and infant and childhood disease.[11] Increasingly, government money began to flow toward providing contraception and abortion services at home and abroad.

Another persuasive force that gave the incipient reproductive-rights movement an almost immediate boost were reform-minded clergy. Organized religion came out early in support of liberalizing the laws. Although Catholics remained adamantly opposed, many of the Protestant denominations—even some considered conservative on other doctrinal or political questions—began to reconsider their value system and favor change. One of the first religious groups to take a stand was the Jews. In 1967, the Association of Reform Rabbis and the United Synagogue of America, New York Unit, had criticized the Catholic Church for its opposition to reform as "harsh and unbending" and its use of terms such as "murder" as inappropriate. That same year, the American Baptist Convention urged legalization of abortion in cases of rape, incest, mental incompetence or when the health of the mother was endangered by pregnancy. Not long afterward, twenty-one rabbis and ministers formed the Clergy Consultation Service on Abortion to aid women in finding doctors who would do abortions despite the law. In the next two years, the conservative Southern Baptist Convention, the Southern

Presbyterians and the United Presbyterians affirmed a position similar to that of the Baptists. The United Church of Christ subsequently voted to take abortion out of the realm of penal law altogether.

Probably even more influential were the members of the medical profession. The defiance of perfectly respectable doctors who risked their reputations and practices to perform abortions helped convince the general public that the prohibitions were archaic. Just as in the previous century, some of these doctors had the double motivation of wanting not only to save women from unscrupulous practitioners but also to control their own profession—the latter concern a reaction to feminist suggestions that abortion was so simple that it could easily be performed by nonprofessionals. The charge was even made that some doctors who wanted to legalize abortion were profiteers anxious for the extra business—an allegation that may have been true of a few. At any rate, a poll taken by *Modern Medicine* in 1967 found that of forty thousand American doctors surveyed, an astounding 86.9% favored more liberal laws. The American Medical Association's House of Delegates backed the idea, the first change in its policy since 1871. Then, in 1970, the delegates voted in favor of allowing doctors to perform abortions for social and economic as well as medical reasons and endorsed a draft statute to that effect. They made sure to insist that doctors doing these abortions be properly licensed, that the operation be performed in an accredited hospital and that two other doctors be called in for consultation, but this was still a big step. [12]

All this prepared the ground, but it was the lawyers, of course, who finally changed everything. On January 22, 1973, Supreme Court Justice Harry Blackmun delivered the historic decision striking down the restrictive abortion laws of every state in the nation. The legal establishment had already indicated its displeasure with the state of things, the American Bar Association having endorsed the AMA's proposed statute. Blackmun arrived at his opinion not so much because of that, however, according to the insiders who revealed his thoughts on the matter in Bob Woodward and Scott Armstrong's *The Brethren*. The urgings of his wife and three daughters had some influence. Even more important was his past experience. Blackmun had been the counsel for the Mayo Clinic for the decade before Richard Nixon appointed him to the Court in 1970. The justice had consorted with the physicians, rejoicing at their triumphs and mourning their losses, and remembered those as the best years of his life. It was apparently his fascination with the now supportive medical profession that convinced him to write such a strong opinion in the abortion cases.

The cases involved a Texas law dating back to 1854 which banned abortion except when the mother's life was in danger, and a Georgia law dating to 1876 which allowed exceptions for life, health, rape or when the child would be physically or mentally defective. Sarah Weddington argued the Texas case, *Roe v. Wade*, and Margie Pitts Hames the Georgia case, *Doe v. Bolton*. Their basic theme was that pregnant women had a constitutional right to abortion which superseded the rights, if any, of the fetus.

Blackmun was originally expected to base his decision on a slew of earlier findings that laid out a constitutional right to privacy in the sphere of marriage, procreation and the upbringing of children. In 1965 the Court had struck down as unconstitutional a Connecticut law banning the use of contraceptives, because it invaded "the sacred precincts of the marital bedroom." That right was extended to individuals in a 1972 Massachusetts decision exonerating reproductive-rights champion Bill Baird for distributing birth-control devices without a license.

Blackmun reportedly worked prodigiously on the decision. Of particular concern to him was the point at which the fetus became "viable," or able to live outside the womb. His first draft of the decision, in fact, did not even address the question of privacy, but concentrated instead on a seesaw of balanced values, attempting to delineate the time in pregnancy at which the state's interest in protecting fetal life began. Blackmun fixed it at the end of the second trimester, or about six months.

After he circulated a draft of his opinion in the fall of 1972, the other justices criticized its weaknesses. Justice William Brennan pointed out that since "viability" could be expected to shift with advances in medicine, any decision depending on it would be on shaky grounds. Furthermore, while Blackmun had discussed the rights of the doctor and the fetus, he had neglected those of the woman, and particularly her right to privacy. Moreover, Chief Justice Warren Burger objected to allowing unrestricted abortions beyond the first trimester. This conflicted with the strong feelings of Justice Thurgood Marshall, a black who recognized that many poor women would not get in touch with a doctor in time to secure an abortion by the end of the first trimester.

Blackmun obligingly incorporated all of this into his next draft and came up with the following formula: (1) for the stage up to "approximately" the end of the first trimester, abortions would be left to the medical judgment of the doctor; (2) for the stage after "approximately" the end of the first trimester, abortion procedures could be regulated or even prohibited, to protect the mother; (3) for the stage after "viability," abortions could be regulated or even prohibited, to protect the fetus. Blackmun made only one substantive change after that, at the request of Justice Potter Stewart, who asked him to state more clearly what he thought about whether the fetus was a person. That was the essence of the decision which finally went through by a vote of seven to two.[13]

The decision received almost immediate ridicule within the legal community. Blackmun had avoided the issue of fetal rights by claiming that the fetus was not a person in the eyes of the law because no one—neither theologians nor doctors nor lawyers—could agree on when life began. At the same time, the justice had also failed to elucidate the case for privacy in terms strong enough to make the woman's right to abortion absolute. In the absence of this, he had spelled out conditions under which abortion was and was not legal— essentially drafting law rather than delivering an opinion on it. Former Watergate special prosecutor Archibald Cox characterized Blackmun's decision in less than congratulatory tones by saying, "The failure to confront the issue in principled terms leaves the opinion to read like a set of hospital rules and regulations... Neither historian, nor layman, nor lawyer will be persuaded that all the prescriptions of Justice Blackmun are part of the Constitution." Yale Law School Professor Alexander Bickel wryly described the ruling as a "model statute."[14]

Regardless of its limitations, feminists and their allies had finally succeeded in securing reproductive rights. To all appearances, the battle was over. Not so. Blackmun's sloppiness had left the right to abortion open to attack, not only in the way that Newman Flanagan recognized, but also from other angles. On the federal level, a constitutional amendment could simply contradict it by stating that the fetus was a person and had rights. On the state level, a law could countermand at least part of it by putting restrictions on early abortions and prohibiting late ones altogether. The state of Texas even petitioned for a rehearing, ultimately denied, using in its argument a comparison between Blackmun's decision specifying that the fetus was not a person and the Court's 1857 *Dred Scott* decision denying personhood to slaves.

The decision was vulnerable not just legally but, even more importantly, politically. The Supreme Court had ruled before feminists had been able to develop a nationwide consensus on the issue, leaving them weak in the face of legislative assault. While the numbers of anti-abortion activists were small, they had the advantage of the fact that the majority of Americans had not really made up their minds yet about the rightness of abortion in every instance, or even thought about it much. In short, the feminists had effectively politicized abortion, but it was now for the other side to take the initiative.

III.

Our Father

"Urgent, urgent, eMERRRRRgency..." The words to the popular tune were echoing through the open pavilion for the teen pool party, one of the special events planned into the 1982 National Right to Life annual convention. Despite the insistent music, the party was noticeably quiet. At one end of the pool, over the music console, stood five boys talking among themselves. Three or four girls clustered chastely in the shallow water.

Chaperoning was forty-year-old Phyllis Deroian, the youth co-ordinator of the New Jersey right-to-life movement. "Mrs. D.," as the kids call her, is the wife of a dockworker and the mother of five. Talkative and animated, she was delighted to have the opportunity to show off several teenagers who have been active in her area, Manalapan-Englishtown, and suggested her motel room as a good place for an interview. "They've worked so hard," she chattered away while ascending the steps to the room. "They'll just be thrilled to get the recognition." Inside, the music provided a subliminal beat to the conversation.

The three teenagers who soon arrived had been involved in right-to-life activities for a number of years. All of them Catholic, they were Chuck Benke, eighteen, tall and clean-shaven, a recent graduate of the local Catholic high school; Marie Damiano, seventeen, plump and quiet, just graduated, too, but from the public high school; and one of Mrs. D.'s daughters, Andra, fifteen, dark-skinned and pert, who also went to the public school.

The group is under the firm direction of Mrs. D., who sets policy and directs the programs. She had first gotten interested in the movement early on, when New Yorkers were considering changing the law restricting abortion. As she tells the story, she encountered a man in the Port Authority Bus Terminal in New York City trying to get passersby to sign a petition to keep the old law intact. He challenged her into taking a stand with the goading remark that he had never seen a woman sign a petition. Now aroused, Mrs. D. argued with the activist until they had attracted an audience. Another woman stepped out of the crowd and put her signature on the paper. Not to be outdone, Mrs. D. followed. "Now there's two of us!" she exclaimed to the onlookers, and marched off in all her glory. That was the start of an involvement that today takes up a significant portion of her time.

The teenagers came to the movement in a more organized fashion. One of the ways in which Mrs. D. got recruits was to give lectures at meetings of the Catholic Youth Organization and the parish's religious-education program. She made right to life such a part of the social life of Catholics in the town that Marie Damiano found herself nagging her older sister before an organizing meeting, "Why can't I come, too?" Their group is small, varying in size from seven to fifteen youngsters. They have consistently had no luck trying to attract non-Catholics. They are reluctant to admit to this, however. As Chuck put it, "We try to stay away from this. They always try to stick in, 'Look, it's a Catholic issue.' And it makes it very hard, because they can say, 'Well, every member of your group is Catholic.'"

Mrs. D. is a resourceful organizer. One of her techniques for acclimating the kids to frequent speaking engagements and demonstrations is to have them critique each other's work and do role-playing. As a result, the teenagers accept whatever negative reactions they receive as part of the perils of organizing, and keep on trying. Chuck, for instance, now likes doing it, because he feels that he is "educating" his peers. "The biggest argument I get from my friends," he explained, "is, 'It's my body. It's my choice.' The selfish kind of attitudes. What I always try to do is say, 'Stop thinking about yourself. Look at the baby.'"

Andra's experience is a little different, possibly because she is younger than the other two. "We don't usually get into discussions about abortion. A lot of people I know think it's disgusting."

Sex among teenagers in their area apparently is rampant, but not as promiscuous as might be expected. "Everybody likes to put a stereotype on teenagers that they're oversexed, overdrugged and always drinking. It's not true," Andra said. "I think most teenagers just have sex with someone they really care about."

The youngsters feel that the best way to avoid problem pregnancies is to make birth control available. "I don't think there's anything wrong with birth control," Marie asserted flatly.

"I think birth control is the beginning to the 'abortion mentality,'" Mrs. D. countered, "because birth-control methods—which most of them are very unsafe—free women up. I'm a feminist in many ways, but I think once a woman is free to look at all these choices, then children become a commodity, no longer a blessing, and then it's only another step to destroying them."

At the same time, Mrs. D. appeared to have some regrets about not having had a life of her own. "The problem is that when I was growing up, unlike these kids, I lived in the city and there weren't a lot of options. So I didn't go to college and I took a secretarial course. For me, secretarial work is not a career. It was a dull, daily routine. Raising a family was much more enjoyable." Mrs. D. plans to study interior decorating when her children have left home. She has the school all picked out.

The girls both feel comfortable about the prospect of women limiting their family size to pursue career goals. Chuck, on the other hand, unashamedly calling himself a "male chauvinist," thinks women should work only until they have children and should then stay home until the children are grown. None of them had ever considered the prospect of the father remaining at home with the children, or sharing child care, and they couldn't even conceive of how it could be done. When asked what they thought of the idea, they were for the first time speechless.[1]

•   •   •

Phyllis Deroian and the young people she has drawn in are eminently representative right-to-lifers, the majority of whom are Catholic. While their opinions may differ on many other subjects, those on abortion uniformly reflect their background in the church. As Roy White, then executive director of the National Right to Life Committee, asserted in 1975, "The only reason we have a pro-life movement in this country is because of the Catholic people and the Catholic Church."[2] And this is exactly the way the hierarchy would have it.

The Roman Catholic Church created the right-to-life movement. Without the church, the movement would not exist as such today. The church provided from the start the organizational infrastructure, the communications network, the logistical support, the resources, the ideology and the people, as well as a ready-made nationwide political machine otherwise impossible to duplicate. Always, the church contributed money, a great deal of it, either through its own organizations or through direct grants to independent but related groups.

The church's presence has had so profound an impact on the movement that almost all the events, even if organized by lay people, are imbued with Catholic ritual and symbolism. Conferences have mass scheduled into them, sometimes twice and three times a day. One National Right to Life convention was timed for the same weekend in the same city practically across the street from an annual convocation of priests. The yearly march on Washington on the anniversary of the Supreme Court decision always has a noticeable checkering of clerical collars, banners draped with rosary beads and earnest young men carrying crosses.

The church started the movement as part of an effort to deal with a world rapidly becoming more secular. For the hierarchy, such a movement served a number of purposes. One of the primary goals—although outsiders did not always see it this way—was to establish the church as a leader in the movement for social justice. It was also an attempt to reinvolve a straying flock. Along the way, it gave some individual Catholics a sense of solidarity that helped allay their feeling of nonacceptance into modern society.

What made the church's right-to-life effort significant was that this was the first time in American history that Catholics had made that kind of all-out bid to influence national policy. In force in almost every state, and everywhere well organized, the church made it possible for this compelling single issue to dominate for a time the democratic process.

The movement accomplished some of what the hierarchy set out to do, but it had a serious problem. Paradoxically, the very issue that was supposed to unite Catholics ended up driving them apart. Some church leaders, finally recognizing the implications of an anti-abortion policy, began tentatively to voice their concerns. But it was too late. The Roman Catholic Church had irrevocably committed itself to the right-to-life campaign. In doing so, it had also unloosed, albeit unwittingly, a generation of evangelical Catholic fanatics.

The Roman Catholic Church is one of the oldest institutions in the Western world. It has miraculously survived the rise and fall of cultures, nations, potentates, princes and presidents, economic orders, ideologies, scientific discoveries, religious reformations, revivals and fads, internal disputation, schism, purge, evangelical excess and savage war. These have left the church stronger and all the more certain of its rightful mission. The church does not question itself, and, as for others who do, it can responsibly claim its place in history: for all its conservatism, the church has been a humanizing force through the ages; for all its repression, it has stabilized whole societies and provided one strand in the web holding civilization together. It has a majestic, if not always proud, past, but one that is slowly being undone. The Roman Catholic Church is in trouble, rift by forces inside and out.

In the latter half of the twentieth century, the church has undergone a vast transformation in order to respond to the changes taking place in the modern world. The democratization of society promoted by liberation movements in underdeveloped countries and the civil-rights movements in the more developed countries have called into question some of the most basic tenets of Catholicism. Catholics inside and outside the hierarchy have been reexamining the place and purpose of the church, many of them scoffing at the theological and moral basis for what theologian Mary Daly called "patriarchal authoritarianism" and the rituals that upheld it.[3] On their own, individual Catholics have been defying church dogma by pursuing their own lifestyles without regard to the classic teachings.

This decline in moral values has torn at the very fabric of Catholic social life. In the United States, the numbers of young men from Catholic families choosing to become priests, and the women nuns, have dropped precipitously. At the same time, Catholic women have been agitating for the right to enter the priesthood. Attendance at Catholic schools has dwindled to the point where many buildings have been unceremoniously shut. It has almost seemed as if the dangers of the diaspora which Catholics had feared in the nineteenth century were finally coming to pass.

As part of this turmoil came the challenge from the women's movement testing the theology, moral authority and day-to-day practice of the world's millions of Catholics. Feminists were making the case that the church as a social institution oppressed them perhaps more than any other, standing for a metaphysic and a culture based on the superiority, indeed the divinity, of the male and the necessity of female allegiance to him. Sexuality was the main instrument through which the church maintained this control. Reproductive rights were a major form of rebellion. For Catholic women, these began as theoretical arguments, but very quickly took on very real flesh. These women were not only accepting unorthodox views about birth control and abortion, but acting on them.

This tendency was highly threatening to the Catholic hierarchy, striking at the very core of Catholic theological, moral, social and economic life. Women's liberation within the church could mean a complete reordering of the governing-power structure, as well as certain diminution of the large Catholic family upon which much of the institution's financial base depended—not necessarily a happy prospect.

The church coped with the dilemma by liberalizing its politics with respect to the outside world, but leaving sexual politics within intact. The impetus for this change came from the ecumenical council usually referred to as Vatican II. Vatican II started in 1962, to extend for several years. Out of it developed the concept of the "Social Gospel" as described in a call to action drafted by the body and delivered in 1965:

> By preaching the truth of the Gospel and shedding light on all areas of human activity through her teaching and the example of the faithful, she [the church] shows respect for the political

freedom and responsibility of citizens and fosters these values.
She also has the right to pass moral judgments, even on matters
touching the political order, whenever basic personal rights of
the salvation of souls make such judgment necessary.[4]

Translated into a program, this Social Gospel would include organizing efforts around peace, poverty, human rights and economic
development in the Third World, some of them markedly radical.

The revolutionary new teaching also established a different relationship between the individual and the church. The outward sign
of this was the modernization of the church liturgy. Of more importance was the church's encouragement to Catholics to think more
for themselves than in the past. No longer was a priestly class of
clerics to dictate morals to a quiescent lay flock, but rather priests
were to function more as guides to the faithful who acted on their
own "enlightened conscience." This was enormously liberating, especially for Catholic women. As one of the women in the church
interviewed by Mary Hanna, who did an authoritative study on the
subject, explained, "Vatican II hit religious women as it did no other
group. Once the documents encouraged a reexamination of our
lives, freeing us, opening our eyes, there was a real blossoming, a
real development of religious women."[5] Or, as Mary Daly was to
phrase it bluntly, "The very existence of a hierarchy seems like a
dead remnant of an earlier stage of human evolution."[6]

One of the most pressing questions that all of this raised was the
handling of sexuality. In March 1963, as part of Vatican II, Pope
John XXIII convened a group to study the question of birth control,
which was enlarged the following year after his death by his suc-
cessor, Pope Paul VI, a much more traditional prelate. Indeed, had
John XXIII lived, the course of reproductive rights might have been
much easier.

The commission took three years to do its work and made its final
report in June 1966. The majority of the delegates recognized that
sexuality was "proper to man," and called for the church to allow
"decent and human means of contraception," including artificial
birth-control devices. The next year, the third-world Lay Apostolate
Delegation, under the influence of Vatican II, endorsed what the
birth-control commission had done. By a vote of sixty-seven to twenty-
one, these lay Catholics approved another proposal in favor of al-

lowing Catholics to use contraception. Neither of these liberal opinions, however, was destined to make its way into church law.

Disregarding both, Pope Paul chose instead to adopt a traditionalist minority report that the birth-control commission had also produced, giving his reasons in an encyclical called *Humanae Vitae* issued in July 1968. The encyclical firmly reiterated the positions that had survived more or less intact from the Middle Ages.[7]

The pronouncement hardly quieted the debate on sexuality within the church, if anything causing the dissidents greater distress.*[8] But the word of the Pontiff was final. Opposition to, first, birth control and then abortion took its place on the Social Gospel agenda. The irony of this was lost on a hierarchy that was still apparently too insular to understand that many non-Catholics regarded the anti-abortion element as reactionary and thus vastly different from the rest of the liberal program.

Following Vatican II, the church went into action. The main

---

*The respected theologian Bernard Häring, who had helped write the majority report, called for a more factual approach to theology than the encyclical. Häring claimed that the Pope was ill-informed about the question of birth control because he was under undue influence from his advisers, who wanted to use this as a test case to break the power of the bishops generated by Vatican II and reestablish the Pontiff's primacy. Häring also pointed out the difficulty of determining the precise moment at which human life begins. His thoughts were widely reported within the Catholic community and the mass media.

Ethicist Daniel Callahan took another tack, arguing that the debate over fetal personhood obscured many other equally important, and theologically significant, considerations, including "the mother's duty towards her children, her psychological state and freedom, her economic situation."

Theologian John Wright advanced the argument still further. Wright observed that nature had long ago separated sex from conception by insuring fertilization in only 5 percent of the instances of intercourse. In addition, Wright pointed out, the church had already recognized this separation by allowing Catholics to select infertile periods in which to engage in sex. Wright then introduced the concept of considering sex with conception as an "obligatory ideal" that need not always be realized, much like the Catholic prohibition against oaths or lying. Elaborating on this, he wrote:

> It is only if we suppose a kind of sacred structure to the physical act itself, a divine purpose in this particular activity that renders any attempt to control or interfere with it immoral, that we would have to judge that no departures from the ideal are possible. If it were possible to show that every particular fertile period were a direct result of a positive divine determination then this would indeed be the case. But short of such a demonstration there seems no way to invest this activity with a sacredness not found in all natural processes necessary for the life and survival of the person and the species.

body responsible for the drive against contraception and abortion
was the United States Catholic Conference and its subordinate National Conference of Catholic Bishops, headquartered in Washington, D.C. In response to the 1965 Supreme Court decision
overturning a Connecticut law prohibiting the sale of contraceptive
devices, the USCC earmarked $50,000 for a propaganda campaign
by something it called the Family Life Division, administered by
the NCCB.[9] After the abortion ruling, the Family Life Division
would make abortion its primary thrust, although its early work went
virtually unnoticed. The most significant church activity around
abortion actually occurred first at the local level, and it took a while
before the bishops realized that they would have to take advantage
of the USCC's centralized authority to increase the campaign's impact.

California was the place where the early demand for abortion
rights was the most insistent and attracted the most vehement local
Catholic opposition. In 1967, when pro-choice forces were mobilizing for a third try at liberalizing the law, the Los Angeles diocese
hired Spencer-Roberts Associates, the advertising agency that handled then Governor Ronald Reagan, to organize "Right to Life
Leagues" across the state. These opposition groups were flown to
Sacramento in chartered planes in order to testify against the bill.
The bill did finally pass. Afterward, communicants in Los Angeles
inaugurated on the Feast of the Holy Innocents a special annual
mass with obvious anti-abortion overtones.

The campaign in New York, another state that liberalized early,
was equally frenzied. During the second and eventually successful
attempt at repeal in 1970, the church urged parishioners to apply
pressure on assemblymen, and particularly the Catholics among
them. Typical was the experience of Anthony Mercorella, a Bronx
Democrat who previously had voted for liberalization. Polls of his
district showed his constituents supporting the repeal bill three to
one, including 60 percent of the almost exclusively Catholic Italians
who comprised the largest bloc of voters. On a Sunday in April,
when Mercorella went to church with his family his priest singled
him out by name and accused him of promoting "murder." The
accusation set his wife and children to weeping and his twelve-year-old daughter to asking him repeatedly whether he really had committed murder. Later that day, three priests visited him at home to

try to persuade him to change his vote. Laymen within his parish also barraged him with phone calls, and six hundred people signed petitions distributed to children in the parochial schools in an effort to sway him. Mercorella ultimately voted again in favor of liberalization, and was subsequently voted out of office.[10]

As a result of the movement to repeal anti-abortion laws, New York State, Alaska, Hawaii and Washington State voted in quite permissive reforms, and fifteen other states relaxed their standards considerably, but few people expected total nationwide repeal. The Supreme Court ruling came as a surprise to both sides. For the church, it was a signal to step up its activities, both official and unofficial. The highest court in the land having ruled that abortion was a constitutional right, the only remedy for it was to get Congress to change the Constitution. Accordingly, the hierarchy began putting together a variety of secular organizations that could work on electoral and legislative politics, and then proceeded to try to dissociate itself from their activities.

Soon after the Court's decision, the Family Life Division spun off a group calling itself the National Right to Life Committee. This is the same group that is currently associated in the public mind with the right-to-life cause. NRLC remained separate from the church from then on, but continued to receive unofficial support. This is, understandably, a sensitive area for both NRLC and the church. Too close a tie with the church opens NRLC up to criticism about its independence; the church stands to lose even more from an overt affiliation which would jeopardize its tax-exempt status. Still, the relationship is clearly there.

A 1973 memorandum written by Monsignor James McHugh, an official of the Family Life Division, says outright that the National Right to Life Committee "originated with the assistance of the Family Life Division as a small coordinating unit for local right to life or pro-life groups." The memo explains that NRLC members voted to become independent from the USCC in June 1973. McHugh then went on to make the case for the church helping to finance NRLC anyway. Describing the organization as being in a state of "impending financial crisis," he suggested a penny-per-person tithe based on state population.[11]

Documentation is not available for how successfully this arrangement worked, but there is evidence that at least some individual state organizations did their part. The New York State Catholic Conference, for instance, organized special collections throughout the state on "Respect Life" Sundays and divided the proceeds with the national and state right-to-life organizations. The generosity of parishioners increased year after year. *[12]

Meanwhile, the church was putting astounding resources behind the effort although much did not appear on the public record. The annual budget of the bishops' committee was relatively small—starting at about $200,000—but this did not begin to approach the actual amount the church contributed. Furniture, office supplies, meeting spaces, advertising, transportation and free volunteer labor—all courtesy of the national offices in conjunction with state offices, dioceses and local parishes and schools—added additional support to the movement. Catholic newspapers became saturated with abortion coverage, the kind of publicity that elsewhere only money could buy. †[13]

Enhancing official institutional efforts were a number of individual priests and nuns who took it upon themselves to assume particularly active roles within the right-to-life organizing effort. One such is Father Paul Marx. The white-haired Marx, standing barely five feet tall, is one of the more influential among the right-to-lifers with his fervent advocacy of "natural family planning," a system of measuring temperature changes and mucus buildup within the woman so as to keep track of her fertile periods. Even outside Catholic circles, NFP has become popular as a way to avoid the hazards of the pill and the interuterine device (IUD). For his early promotion

---

*According to information gathered for the lawsuit against the Hyde Amendment, detailed in McRae v. U.S. Dept. of Health, Education and Welfare (1980), the New York State Right to Life Committee collected a total of $62,458 from the effort in 1974, for example, and the money just kept on coming. In the fiscal year ending September 30, 1976, the state committee took in $60,932 from Respect Life collections and an additional $27,828 from an annual spring "Save-a-Baby" raffle. For the ten months ending in July 31, 1977, the state committee received $77,656 from Respect Life and $25,569 from the raffle.

†The National Abortion Rights Action League did a study showing that from January 1977 to January 1978 the national Catholic weekly magazine Our Sunday Visitor carried 87 news articles or signed commentaries and 15 editorials on abortion. The diocesan newspaper of Rockville Center, New York, The Long Island Catholic, that winter carried 16 items on abortion.

of it, Marx has become something of a folk hero. "They used to call me Father Rhythm," he chuckles of his notoriety. "Then they called me Father Temperature. I hope they never call me Father Mucus." Marx has received a great deal of direct and indirect support from other individual Catholics and from the church, which is very interested in this modernist version of the "rhythm" method of contraception. Marx was given space for his Human Life Center, one of seven hundred such places around the country propagating information on NFP, by St. John's University in Collegeville, Minnesota, a Catholic institution.[14] He was able to keep the operation going with the help of the largesse of Harry G. John, the reclusive Catholic heir to the Miller Beer fortune.[*][15] Marx has apparently gotten the highest praise of all that a Catholic can receive for his work. In an audience with Pope John Paul II not long ago, the priest claims the Pontiff told him, "'You're doing one of the most important things on earth.'"

Along with individual preachments such as those of Marx, the church used its considerable institutional moral clout, further advancing its position on abortion by quite literally putting the fear of God into its people. Barely a month after the Supreme Court decision, the bishops in a pastoral message publicly proclaimed the ruling "erroneous, unjust and immoral" and advocated civil disobedience to "any civil law that may require abortion." They warned Catholics who underwent or were party to abortion that they would be subject to automatic excommunication. Simply advocating abortion could lead to other disciplinary measures.[16]

This turned out to be no idle threat. In September 1974, the provincial supervisor of the Jesuits of the West Side of Manhattan in New York City dismissed a priest, the Reverend Joseph O'Rourke, who baptized the son of a Massachusetts woman, Carol Morreale, after several local priests had refused to do so. The reason for the boycott was that Morreale had been quoted in the newspaper as believing in the woman's right to choose abortion. In announcing the dismissal, the Very Reverend Eamon Taylor, O'Rourke's superior, claimed it was due to "differences of understanding and

---

*According to foundation records, John has lavished money on NFP through the De Rance Foundation, reportedly one of the 50 largest in the country, giving in 1979, for example, $439,280.

judgment" between himself and the priest, but admitted that the priest was "told not to go" to the baptism. [17]

Similarly, some church fathers also punished errant individual Catholics. The Most Reverend Leo Maher, Bishop of San Diego, for instance, at one point announced that he would bar from participating in Holy Communion any woman admitting to membership in the National Organization of Women (NOW) or other organizations supporting abortion rights. The Sunday in question, the local NOW chapter gathered women together to protest. Catholic women all over the city went to mass wearing NOW buttons and attempted to participate in Communion. According to a report in *The New York Times*, at St. Brigid's Church in Pacific Beach, about twenty-five women were turned away by Monsignor Donald Doxie, the pastor, and five priests who stood at the altar watching for buttons. Wendy D'Addario, a local NOW officer, was one of those who was asked by a smiling young priest whether she believed in abortion. "I told him," she reportedly recalled, "that like other members of NOW I was not a pro-abortionist, but that I strongly believed every woman should have a free choice, that she should be master of her own body and that every child that is born should be wanted and loved." The priest replied that he could not "in good conscience" administer the sacrament and asked her to move down the rail. [18]

The church did not just concentrate on its own people, but also tried to exercise more widespread influence by controlling the nation's airwaves. The first attempt of this sort had occurred in August 1973 when the USCC distributed a statement to priests all over the country directing them to get their parishioners to exert pressure on the Columbia Broadcasting System and its relevant on-air advertisers in an effort to stop reruns of two programs about abortion in the popular series *Maude*. The call was so effective that twenty-five affiliates decided against airing the shows, among them those in Boston, Albany, Milwaukee, New Orleans, Rochester, Indianapolis, South Bend, Salt Lake, Omaha and Seattle. Norman Lear, producer of the show, announced publicly that while all the other *Maude* reruns were sold out, the ad time for the two concerning abortion amounted to only thirty seconds instead of three minutes, with one of the principal defecting advertisers being Pepsi-Cola. Lear labeled the blitz "censorship." Bishop James Rausch, then USCC general secretary, retorted that CBS's decision to offer the shows to other affiliates despite the pressure was "a breach of good faith." [19]

A much more effective tactic even than that was having prestigious members of the clergy testify before Congress. When a Senate Judiciary Committee subcommittee chaired by Senator Birch Bayh held hearings on the subject of abortion in 1974, the USCC submitted its testimony and four prominent cardinals traveled to Washington to add their personal views. It was at this hearing that the hierarchy made its position on abortion unalterably clear and gave a hint of what was to come.

Humberto Cardinal Medeiros of Boston announced the church's intention of continuing to push for a constitutional amendment banning abortion, but disdained one then under consideration in Congress that would have allowed the various states to draft their own laws. Medeiros also ruled out an amendment that would have permitted abortion in exceptional circumstances, such as when a woman's life was threatened. He stated flatly that the church would settle for nothing less than an absolute national prohibition, and he outlined the three elements such an amendment would have to contain:

1. The constitutional amendment should clearly establish that, from conception onward, the unborn child is a human person in the terms of the Constitution.
2. The Constitution should express a commitment to the preservation of all human life. Therefore the prohibition against the direct and intentional taking of innocent human life should be universal and without exception.
3. The right to life is described in the Declaration of Independence as "unalienable" and as a right with which all men are endowed by the Creator. The constitutional amendment should restore the basic protection for this human right to the unborn, just as it is provided to all other persons in the United States.

Anticipating that the long-standing criticism of church interference in state affairs would come up again, Philadelphia's Archbishop John Cardinal Krol in his testimony asserted that Catholics had no intention—indeed, no right—to "advocate sectarian doctrine." He was speaking, however, not only for Catholics, he said, but also for "many Americans who are members of other faiths and of no faith."

> ...We reject any suggestion that we are attempting to impose "our" morality on others. First, it is not true. The right to life is

not an invention of the Catholic Church or any other church. It is a basic human right which must undergird any civilized society. Second, either we all have the same right to speak out on public policy or no one does. We do not have to check our consciences at the door before we argue for what we think is best for society. We speak as American citizens who are free to express our views and whose freedom, under our system of government, carries with it a corresponding obligation to advocate positions which we believe will best serve the good of our nation. Third, in our free country, decisions concerning issues such as the one before this subcommittee are made by legislators who themselves are free to act according to their own best judgment. We dare not forget, however, that to separate political judgment from moral judgment leads to disorder and disaster.[20]

Regardless of Krol's disclaimer, the sight of four cardinals expressing such absolutist views before a congressional committee caused more furor than ever before. It was one thing to try to bring Catholics around, but quite another to attempt to impose Catholic values on the rest of the country. In the shocked tones characteristic of most of the rest of the press, the *New Republic* editorialized: "When any religious denomination, however powerful . . . , demands that private doctrine be made into public law, more than the ecumenical spirit is strained: the whole fabric of mutual toleration may be ripped apart."[21]

The criticism hardly deterred the hierarchy. Several of them arrived not long afterward to testify against the confirmation of Nelson A. Rockefeller as Vice-President because of his stand on abortion, and then again on specific right-to-life bills and amendments to the Constitution.

Feminists trying to diminish this sort of influence went to court in 1974 to challenge the church's tax-exempt status. The now defunct Women's Lobby sued both the USCC and the National Right to Life Committee for violating the rules prohibiting political activities by non-profit organizations. The suit was dismissed by Judge Aubrey Robinson, Jr., of the United States District Court for the District of Columbia. His ruling did not turn on the issue of whether the USCC should be forced to register as a lobbying organization, thereby changing its tax status, but rather, according to a *New York Times* account, on the technical question of whether lobbying was the conference's "principal purpose."[22]

The threat of another such challenge made the church's win something of a Pyrrhic victory. From then on, the bishops would do their lobbying through yet another organization, the National Committee for a Human Life Amendment. Like the National Right to Life Committee, NCHLA was supposed to have no official connection with the church. Its affiliation, however, was obvious from public records showing where it got the better part of its money, a good deal of it coming from Catholic communicants across the country. *[23] The link was also widely acknowledged within the right-to-life movement, where activists unhesitatingly referred to NCHLA as "the bishops' outfit." Yet another connection was through the person of the Reverend Edward Bryce, who was once head of NCHLA and now directs right-to-life activities for the National Conference of Catholic Bishops.

The Reverend Edward Bryce has presided over the transformation of the church into a right-to-life political machine. He is representative of the mainstream of the hierarchy in feeling absolutely comfortable with this new interpretation of the church's place in American society, a position he expressed forthrightly in an interview. Tall but unassuming, with a big toothy smile, Bryce has an anxious strain around the neck as if he didn't quite fit in the clerical collar. He speaks in circumlocutions that seem to peter out rather than end.

Bryce does not feel that the church unduly stresses abortion. "We do not accept the notion that all issues are equal. That's a bit naïve. We conceived of abortion as a paragon issue." Nor does he think the church squanders too many of its resources on the right-to-life campaign. He does admit that the expenditures on abortion are much larger than the records show, and that most of this is buried in bishops' discretionary funds and individual diocesan ledgers. Still, he does not think that, whatever the sum, it is disproportionate. "Actually, it's embarrassing the minimal amount we spend on an issue that's so important. You have to appreciate the Catholic Church as a total budget item. We're the second largest phone customer in this country." Nor does he hesitate to reveal the underlying motives

---

*According to the obligatory statements filed with the clerk of the United States House of Representatives, for example, NCHLA received $459,403 in contributions of $500 or more from January 1, 1976, through March 31, 1977, from separate dioceses or archdioceses across the country.

of the right-to-life campaign. "People who avoided social issues—
abortion has given them an opportunity to understand the relatedness
of many issues. But you don't teach relatedness in a kaleidoscopic
fashion, by saying, 'Here are *all* the issues.' I find most people's
sense of *all* is usually three or four. Abortion is not the only issue
that we could develop as a model, but this happens to be the one
that has gotten the people out. With them, we are creating political
cells."[24]

Strategy for creating cells comes from men in the hierarchy like
Bryce, but ironically it is the Catholic laywomen who are the back-
bone of the right-to-life movement. In scores of interviews with
them, they revealed a surprising diversity, but the most striking thing
about them is their commitment—or in some cases recommit-
ment—to Catholicism. In one discussion between a middle-aged
mother and a youthful feminist during the course of a joint interview,
the younger woman explained that she felt that choices about sexual
expression should be left up to the individual, and that premarital
sex was not necessarily wrong. The older woman was plainly shocked.
"How can you say that?" she replied scornfully. "That's just sex
for . . ." and she searched about for the right word, concluding finally
with a snort, "sex for *pleasure!*" Despite these sometime disagreements, the youthful Catholics especially find the movement helping
them to get back to their roots. As the same young woman put it
when surrounded by Catholic artifacts at a right-to-life event, "I
went to a lot of feminist meetings, and they were very cold. It was
all rich, professional women who wanted to get ahead. Here—just
look at it!" She gestured at all the people. "Babies! The elderly!
These are my people! This is where I belong!"
    Patricia Driscoll, for instance, is a vivacious and attractive Cali-
fornian. She is one of the right-to-lifers whose intellect and imagination are dominated by church imagery. She and her husband,
an attorney, have eleven children. When she was pregnant with her
fourth, she had a mystical vision of the pregnant Virgin Mary that
so inspired her that she created her own right-to-life organization.
Driscoll came to believe that the pregnant Virgin might be a "mi-
crocosm of the Christian mission" because "our Christian purpose
is to let Jesus Christ grow to fullness within us." Driscoll then felt

a calling as a poet and sculptress and, upon seeing the vision, wrote a prayer using birthing images ("Pray for us now/And at the hour of our delivery") and fashioned a ceramic statuette of Mary looking about five months along.[25]

Driscoll sought Vatican approval of this as yet unapproved form of worship and was rebuffed, she says, "on the grounds of indelicacy." A cardinal whom she asked to intercede for her with the Pope wrote her a long, thoughtful letter which pointed out: ". . . in view of all the commotion about the use of recent forms of contraception, it wouldn't be prudent to launch the devotion. Ridicule would be cast on our method of defence of our Catholic doctrine and of our combating the great evil."[26]

Undaunted, Driscoll continued what she calls her "apostolate," concentrating, as time went on, more and more on the theme of sexual abstinence. She developed an entire line of pamphlets, slide shows and buttons about sexuality, particularly for teenagers. The message is always simple and direct, a variation on the theme "Be a square with flair; stay virgin." In 1975, her bishop, the head of the Oakland diocese, started giving her a donation which amounts to about one quarter of her operating expenses, and office space in the church's Family Life Center in Pleasant Hill. By 1982, Driscoll was working with a staff of anywhere from six to twelve volunteers and had inspired programs on, as she put it, "God, sex and the family" in San José, Florida and Maryland. She had also distributed hundreds of thousands of pamphlets, and had planned a seminar on sexual abstinence that was supposed to be accredited for nurses.

Complementing right-to-lifers like Driscoll who have their own personal fascination with abortion are others for whom reflection upon their experiences led them to use the movement as sort of an expiation of guilt. Susan Brindle, for instance, was raped, an experience that set off a chain of events that finally brought her to the cause.

Brindle is thirty-three years old. She has an attractive, wide smile, and her broad shoulders and amply muscled frame betray her upbringing as a farm girl from Tennessee. Brindle is a searcher who took a long time to discover her identity. Ever since the age of thirteen, she had wanted to be a nun, and she entered a cloistered order of Carmelites in St. Louis, in 1972. "To me the convent was like marriage," she explained in an interview. "As a child I used to

say to God, 'If you don't want me in the convent, send me the right
guy.'" A year after entering, she left, realizing that the contemplative
life was not her true calling after all.

Barely a year out of the convent, and still a virgin, she was brutally
raped on her way home from work. The experience horrified her
so that to this day she cannot utter the word "rape" to describe it
and refers to it only obliquely. Some time afterward, she realized
she must be pregnant, and came to terms with it in a way that only
a Catholic would. She felt guilty, but that God had sent her this
baby, as she put it, "to help me grow and become a better person.
I was thrilled. It gave my life purpose."

Interestingly, Brindle's mother, a nurse, was not as sure as her
daughter that the rape had actually caused a pregnancy, and urged
her to get tested. Brindle insisted in the interview that she tried to
do so at the local public-health clinic and was refused. Brindle never
sought out another place and consequently never discovered whether
she was pregnant, her behavior after the first try appearing almost
like avoidance of the truth. In any event, under the assumption that
she was going to give birth, she got ready for it. She started a reading
campaign to learn all she could about babies. She took vitamins.
After struggling with the moral ramifications of living a lie, and
getting the endorsement of her local parish priest, she had her name
legally changed, told her father and brothers that her "husband" had
died in an accident, and made preparations to move to Canada, all
in an effort to conceal the nature of her impregnation from her
future child.

All the plans came to naught. "I miscarried," Brindle explained
simply. "I *know* I miscarried."

Four years ago, she married David Brindle, an engineer who has
his own business constructing gas chromatographs. They have two
towheaded children, and at the time of the interview Susan was
pregnant with a third. She wanted to have "as many children as
possible."

The skirmish with the clinic had drawn the attention of a local
right-to-life group, which recruited her. Now she does what right-
to-lifers call "sidewalk counseling," essentially trying to convince
women who are on their way into an abortion clinic to reconsider. [27]

Pat Driscoll and Susan Brindle are clearly traditionalists, but right-
to-lifers span the political spectrum from right to left on other issues.

Among those out of the mainstream are the "progressive" Catholics who listened very carefully to the message of Vatican II. Many of them initially shied away from the right-to-life movement, some because they agreed enough with feminism not to accept church teachings on contraception and abortion, others, standing with the church on the reproductive issues, because they could not abide the movement's initial taint of racism.

Among these is Pam Cira, who eventually abandoned her scruples and became part of the movement's radical left. Cira is representative of those radicals who recommitted themselves to Catholicism and the right-to-life cause to bring their perspective to it. In the end, they may have changed the church and the movement, but the church and the movement also changed them.

Cira is thirty-one years old and hails from Milwaukee. With long, straight hair and a face bare of makeup, she explained in an interview that she used to be pro-abortion in high school, a Catholic girls' academy. She was the only one in her class to defend abortion rights when they studied *Humanae Vitae*, because she "was very concerned about women's rights." One summer she took a course in logic while attending Marian College in Indianapolis. "After that, I found I couldn't logically defend my feminist position," she recalled. She discovered that she felt not only that the fetus was a person, but also that her views seemed to correspond with other notions about social justice that she was developing. But what really influenced her was her own life experience. As yet unmarried, Cira inadvertently got pregnant. She found that no matter what her feelings about feminism, she could not bring herself to get an abortion. She carried to term, and gave the baby up for adoption.

Cira, who now works as a counselor for sexual-assault victims in the Milwaukee District Attorney's office, has formed a group called Feminists for Life. She finds no irony in the difference between her and the classic feminist. "I think the feminist movement has sold women out. They say we have to have abortion rights so that women can have options. Nobody ever said to an expectant father, 'Listen, buddy, you know, your career's in jeopardy here.' Men never had to make those choices."[28]

Another like Cira is Juli Loesch. Loesch may be in the new wave of Catholic "progressivism," embodying as she does not only right-to-life sympathies but anti-nuclear ones as well. Juli Loesch is thirty years old, rotund and full of girlish enthusiasms, with an easy laugh and a quick wit. She attended high school in Erie, Pennsylvania, where she was, as she described it in an interview, "an ardent anti-war kid who wanted to grow up to be an organizer." She went to Antioch College, but stayed only a few months. Her lust for adventure and her desire to become involved in some socially significant cause prompted her to make a pilgrimage to California in 1969 to work with the United Farm Workers in their campaign to obtain recognition as a union.

She boarded with a farmworker family for six months, then journeying to Detroit to live with a lover, Michael, for another six months. After that she returned to California, where she got a job as a live-in baby-sitter for a woman whom she describes as a "nouveau lesbian," an instructor at the women's-studies program at Sacramento State University, recently and "bitterly" divorced. Loesch's participation with her hostess in a radical lesbian consciousness-raising group was her first brush with the women's movement. She didn't stay for long, however, soon going back to Erie.

Her next formative experience was the most compelling to date. In 1972 she was taking some classes at nearby Mercersburg Academy when she met a nun on leave of absence from her convent who was starting what she called the Pax Christi Center. Loesch has now lived and worked at the center for nine years. Housed in an inner-city convent with the basement and the first floor occupied by nuns, the center comprises thirteen people, all of them Catholic, and serves as a nonviolent meditation and action group. As Loesch explained it, "Anybody that could tolerate our prayer life is welcome to move in. We're sort of the sidekicks of the sidekicks of God."

Although she considers herself a feminist, Loesch was not entirely comfortable with the feminist movement. "The feminists are so thoroughly absorbed by the masculine ideal that they denigrate things that are biologically female. Pregnancy—all of a sudden, it's being seen as a high-risk occupation. They talk about the battle of the sexes. It seems to me that the radical demand, to change the whole system, lost out. The woman has to say, 'I have to get fixed. If I get myself fixed, then I can fit in.' You've got doctored sex, altered vaginas. Evacuate the uterus, and I can be just like the guys. A wombless male.

"It's funny. The pro-abortionists call themselves the women's movement, making all the rest of us nonwomen, when in actual fact the pro-abortionist career women identify fully with the ideal of the bourgeois male with his individualistic, atomized, carefree sex and his no responsibility."

Loesch was impressed early in life with the dimensions of the Social Gospel. Long before members of the hierarchy were publicly doing so, Loesch was making the intellectual connections that she very strongly feels exist between abortion and war. Her affinity for the right-to-life cause developed, in fact, out of her horror of nuclear war. "I was doing house meetings against nukes. I was showing those charts of how radiation hurts the unborn, how it can go through the placenta. And I always used the word 'baby.' I always said things like 'Your unborn son or daughter could be damaged by radiation.' Then one time I was talking to a group of right-to-life women about radiation, and this lady stopped me cold and said, 'What do you think about abortion?' I said, 'I don't know.' And she said, 'How can you say it's wrong to kill those kids accidentally when you don't know whether it's wrong to kill them deliberately?' And I thought, Wow, those right-to-life people are going to be a great constituency for anti-nukes."

In 1971, she organized Prolifers for Survival, which to her way of thinking has been enormously successful. "We work both sides of the aisle. We preach no nukes to the pro-life movement and anti-abortion to the peace movement. We have dues-paying members all over the United States, in just about every state."

For trespassing at abortion clinics and nuclear facilities, Loesch has been arrested four times, convicted once and spent a total of six hours in jail. She travels constantly, delivering her message all over the country, usually living hand to mouth. "To this day," she asserted, "I never have made enough annual income to pay taxes." Indeed, the evening of the interview, she had not eaten, had no money for food and eagerly accepted the offer of the interviewer to pay for her dinner. She refers to herself as a "fetus-loving peacenik"; a sympathetic observer on the fringes of the movement calls her a "modern-day saint." In a sense, the label does convey something of her uncompromising spirit.

As she described her work, "I find myself today organizing simply by preaching Catholic moral doctrine to Catholics. People like Cardinal Krol say that unless the United States and the Soviet Union

make political progress toward disarmament, it is almost certain that
the Holy Father will condemn the possession as well as the use of
nuclear arms, and when he does—I say when, not if—there's a lot
of American Catholics who are going to have to jump one way or
the other. It's going to be very hard, just like when *Humanae Vitae*
came out. People are going to have to decide whether they want
the Pope out of the bedroom and out of the war room."[29]

The church's right-to-life campaign started fairly quickly to bring
some loyal Catholics like Loesch back into the fold, but the bishops
were nowhere near to accomplishing their paramount goal. Abortion, after all, was still legal. Moreover, right-to-life activism was
proving divisive within the church. Accordingly, the hierarchy made
its most decisive move to date, entering the political process with a
plan to elect right-to-lifers to Congress. However, because of the
never-ceasing charges of interference in politics, the church fathers
moved circumspectly.

The bishops made the decision to enter politics at a confused time
in church history, which right-to-life questions only muddied further. Optimists like Mary Hanna continued to believe that the right-
to-life effort was good for the church. As she saw it, Vatican II had
deeply divided Catholics, and right to life was bringing them back
together. Others like the Reverend Andrew Greeley were not so sure.
Greeley, the sociologist and author, felt that the church's adamance
about birth control and abortion was the cause rather than the effect
of its declining membership. Greeley had good reason for his sus-
picions, since he was among those conducting the polls surveying
Catholic attitudes on the subject. His observations suggested that
the right-to-life thrust was attracting those Catholics who wanted to
maintain a spiritual home in the church, but alienating those who
no longer felt comfortable there.

Certainly the polls indicated that Catholics as a group were beginning to accept abortion as a fact of life in America. Surveys done
by Greeley's outfit, the National Opinion Research Center in Chicago, from 1972 to 1975 showed that 86 percent of white Catholics
of European descent* favored legal abortion when the mother's life

---

*For Spanish-speaking Catholics, the percentages were smaller: in the life-threat-
ening situation, they favored abortion by 86.9 percent; for rape, 67.2 percent; and

was threatened, 79.1 percent when the pregnancy resulted from rape, and 76.5 percent when the fetus was severely damaged. †[30] By 1975, the views of Catholic women on family size were also changing, and changing more quickly than those of women from other backgrounds, with a clear trend toward a desire for fewer children. ‡[31]

Another Gallup poll, in 1978, showed that Catholics with a college degree were more likely to question church teachings on a number of issues, 44 percent of the respondents holding that the church should "relax its standards forbidding all abortions under any circumstances."[32]

If all of this was discouraging to the Catholic hierarchy, there were also some hopeful signs. The Catholic population of the United States, now amounting to about one quarter of all Americans, had grown to the point where it was potentially the largest voting bloc in the nation. Moreover, Catholics had worked their way up the social scale, achieving ever higher political office in ever larger numbers until their representation in the United States Congress began to approximate that in the population at large. The church was no longer a minority institution, and it was time to capitalize on the new status by developing a new strategy. Thus, the Pastoral Plan.

The Pastoral Plan for Pro-Life Activities was developed by the National Conference of Catholic Bishops, and was presented to the public in November 1975. According to the plan, every Catholic in all the eighteen thousand parishes of the 160 dioceses across the

---

in the case of the damaged fetus, 75.4 percent. In less serious circumstances, all Catholics did retain an aversion to abortion. When the family could not afford any more children, white Catholics of European descent accepted abortion by 43 percent and Spanish-speaking by only 29.1 percent; when the woman was unmarried, whites by 39.7 percent and Spanish-speaking by 23.7 percent; and when the woman was married but wanted no more children, whites by 35.6 percent and Spanish-speaking by 21.2 percent.

†These polls reflected feelings not just about hypothetical cases involving other people, but about the Catholics themselves. According to another National Opinion Research Center survey of 1977, 66 percent of the Catholics polled said they would have an abortion themselves or urge it on their wives if there were a "serious threat of a defective child," and 76 percent said they would do so if pregnancy threatened the mother's health.

‡Non-Catholic women in the age group twenty to twenty-four wanted 9 percent fewer children (an average of 2.35 children in 1975 as compared to 2.57 in 1970), but Catholic women wanted 20 percent fewer (an average of 2.45 as compared to 2.75). Moreover, while non-Catholics were actually having 32 percent fewer unwanted babies, Catholic women were cutting down their intended family size by 45 percent (57 percent for the college-educated).

country was considered under its jurisdiction. Its purpose was to thrust these millions of believers into an instantaneous and formidable pressure group to mobilize for the election of representatives to the United States Congress who would pass a constitutional amendment banning abortion. It was a masterful touch, the ultimate in creating the "political cells" that the Reverend Edward Bryce talks about.

The plan was amazingly thorough, outlining three ways in which Catholics were to work on the abortion issue. The first was an educational and public-information effort directed both at the general public and at Catholics. As a pamphlet explaining it stated, "the primary and ultimately most compelling arguments must be theological and moral." The second was a pastoral effort to help women with the problems associated with unplanned pregnancy and to redeem those who actually obtain abortions. The final element was a legislative and public-policy effort. The pamphlet was explicit on how to go about it, outlining a three-tiered pyramidal approach to political action. A "state coordinating committee" functioning under the State Catholic Conference, including bishops' representatives from each diocese, was supposed to monitor trends in the state, coordinate efforts of the various dioceses and evaluate progress in the diocese and the congressional districts with an eye to giving direction and support on all their mutual interrelationships. At the next level down, "diocesan pro-life committees" would coordinate activities within the diocese, providing the educational and counseling help, encouraging the development of grass-roots political-action organizations, and maintaining a close relationship with the media and with each senator or representative. It was also at this diocesan level that the right-to-life group was to keep in touch with the Washington office of the bishops. Finally, and most important, there were the parish right-to-life committees. Their responsibility was to sponsor the actual educational and counseling programs, create or join the political-action organizations and do media- and congressional-liaison work.

Key to success was the formation of the political-action committees in congressional districts. The task of the PACs was to organize Catholics and non-Catholics to help persuade elected representatives to pass the constitutional amendment banning abortion. If elected representatives were unresponsive to persuasion, the PAC was charged with identifying, supporting and ultimately electing another representative. The Pastoral Plan described in detail how to do this—right down to phone banks, voter files and the need for individual members to join or coordinate with local political-party organizations.

The plan was explicit in directing that the PAC be bipartisan, nonsectarian and, above all, completely separate from the church. "It is not an agency of the Church, nor is it operated, controlled or financed by the Church," stated the pamphlet in no uncertain terms. [33]

The Pastoral Plan was a brilliant blueprint, essentially combining in a legal way the efforts of the already existing right-to-life offices of the National Conference of Catholic Bishops and the National Committee for a Human Life Amendment. This peekaboo public presence allowed the church to maintain for tax purposes the pretense of staying pretty much out of the abortion controversy and yet still exercise some control. The message of the plan was absolutely clear: Move over, Caddell, Garth, Spencer and Marttila; the Roman Catholic Church was getting into the business of electoral campaigns in a big way. It was as if the bishops had switched on an enormously powerful political engine that then appeared to run on its own. But the perpetual-motion machine is a thing of the imagination. A closer look at the right-to-life machine revealed that fuel and labor costs, maintenance, body work, lubrication, and replacement parts right down to the last screw all remained very much under firm pastoral guidance.

The machine went into high gear. NCHLA organizers created and developed grass-roots right-to-life PACs, which they called "congressional district action committees," in almost half of the country's 435 congressional districts. The CDACs involved thousands of sympathetic Catholics in right-to-life activity, including letter-writing, meeting with elected officials, conducting candidate and voter education projects and developing efficient phone networks. [34]

Despite all this activity, the church still had a problem. Theoretically, the agenda of the Pastoral Plan was supposed to include all the concerns relevant to the Social Gospel. The bishops, in their literature on the program, gave nominal support to full employment, maintenance of social services, the right of every citizen, including the economically disadvantaged, to an education, domestic and international food aid programs, housing as a basic human right, an

end to torture as a weapon of political repression, and arms limitation. The item first on the list, however, was always abortion. As
a practical matter, that was where almost all of the efforts went. This
tendency aggravated the ideological split within the church, the
conservatives favoring the concentration on abortion, the liberals
appalled by it.

The wholesale entry into politics alarmed even some members of
the church whose credentials were beyond reproach. Their criticism
did not necessarily deal with the church's right-to-life commitment,
which many of them supported. In fact, they often avoided grappling
with that subject altogether. They voiced concern instead that the
original intent of the plan was being ignored. Monsignor George
Higgins, recently retired from the NCCB himself, reiterated the
point with passionate alarm in an article in the influential Jesuit
publication *America:*

> We cannot concern ourselves strictly with abortions and subor-
> dinate our other concerns until we have stopped abortion. We
> cannot wait until a Human Life Amendment is passed to face
> the problems of massive poverty and starvation, of high unem-
> ployment and severely inadequate housing. While some threats
> to human life are obviously more serious than others, none can
> be adequately dealt with in isolation. To suggest otherwise is to
> promote the kind of moral and political naïveté that will ulti-
> mately hinder the struggle for human dignity.[35]

Higgins contended as well that the right-to-life movement was so
clearly identified in the public mind with the church that Catholics
would do well to monitor it better. Specifically, he warned against
allowing it to fall under the control of conservatives attempting "to
transform prolife sentiment into a right-wing political movement."

Moderates like the Reverend Edward Bryce didn't believe this
could happen. "The Catholic church has a pretty clear sense that
it's going to be here forever," he insisted in an interview. "If the
church is secure enough in its goal, and understands where it's going
and why it's going there, then it will go through sometimes very
narrow paths, knowing full well that an organization that wants to
go with you today will be against you tomorrow. I think all of this
is blown out of proportion."[36]

Bryce's faith in the church notwithstanding, the right-to-life movement was becoming a haven for traditionalist radicals, the kind of people who were easily manipulable and often mistaken for the mainstream. These adamant supporters of the church would eventually prove almost as embarrassing as the feminists once were. They took very seriously the hierarchy's admonition to do anything—even civil disobedience—to enforce church teachings on original sin, sexuality, contraception and abortion.

These Catholic radicals made the Social Gospel into a weapon, using it as the justification for reviving the medieval mentality of the Crusades. These were the Catholics who believed the church should reign supreme, and they set about establishing their particular heaven on earth. This was the *enfant terrible* the church had loosed— once out, very difficult to control.

It was eight o'clock on a Saturday morning in May 1981, in Walnut Creek, California, a part of the suburban sprawl near Fresno. Tony Mendoza, a twenty-four-year-old college student, and René Emery, nineteen, entered the waiting room of the Planned Parenthood abortion clinic, ostensibly to ask for information. A few minutes later, two more young people, Jack Pelikan and Marguerite Stearns, sneaked in behind them unnoticed. Pelikan opened the door to the surgery area and, meeting an employee, asked, "Are you killing babies here today?"

The employee, surprised, demanded that Pelikan leave. At that, a priest held back the waiting-room door to let in five more demonstrators and then sat down in front of the doorway. Stearns and another woman squatted down as well, blocking the way to the surgery area. A Planned Parenthood employee tried to shove Stearns out of the way, to which Pelikan cried out in alarm, "You're going to break her back!" The group meanwhile kept murmuring the rosary: "Hail Mary, Mother of God . . ."

Meanwhile Mendoza and Emery, mistaken for clients by the clinic staff, were isolated with women awaiting abortions, all the time trying to persuade them to reconsider. When the staff realized what was going on, they moved the patients to another room. Mendoza and Emery followed, knelt outside the door and pleaded with the women not to "murder your babies."

Alerted beforehand by the group, the crew from the local TV

station arrived along with police officers in five separate cars. When asked whether he would leave on his own accord, demonstrator Mark Drogin, bearded and striking-looking, answered, "As long as I'm here, they can't use these machines to kill babies again, and as soon as I leave they will start murdering babies again, and there will be no one to baptize or even bury the innocent babies." On his left breast pocket, Drogin had had embroidered a large cross inside a sunburst, the design the same as that worn by the Crusaders of the Middle Ages.

The first arrest was of Raul Gomez, middle-aged and burly. Gomez had in his pockets several hundred dollars in cash that he had brought along to offer as assistance to the needy women who might have been there, in order to persuade them to cancel their scheduled abortions. "We are targeting Planned Parenthood," Gomez told reporters, "because their real objective is to carry out a program of worldwide genocide against our Hispanic people."

Altogether, eight demonstrators, including the priest, were arrested, the prosecutions being handled by Assistant District Attorney Robert Ring. At the trial, the demonstrators insisted on interviewing over one hundred potential jurors in order to weed out those who might be biased. The defendants decided to attempt what they called the "defense of necessity," the argument—used without great success by protestors against the war in Vietnam and nuclear installations—that a given action, even if unlawful, has the validity of higher moral law.

One year later, all eight were convicted of illegal entry and obstruction, the maximum penalty for which was six months in jail. They were not happy with the handling of their trial. They accused the prosecutor, a Catholic himself, of exhibiting "Judas-like behavior," comparable to that of "'respectable' professionals" in Nazi Germany. "One wonders," speculated one of the defendants in a printed handout, "if Mr. Ring ever heard of the Nuremburg [sic] Trials." Of their own efforts, Mark Drogin announced, deliberately using biblical imagery, "We are like dead men. Exhausted and spit on by everyone."[37]

The demonstrators were part of Catholics United for Life, a small group who see themselves as carrying out a lifelong mission to stop abortion, primarily through nonviolent direct action at clinics like the one at Walnut Creek. These naïve zealots have helped establish a tone for the right-to-life movement that is way beyond what the church fathers originally intended. They also so distorted the debate on abortion as to open the way—as Monsignor George Higgins suggested such a group might—for a conservative bid for power.

The Catholics United for Life live communally in a single ramshackle adobe building, once a dude ranch, on five acres of land in Coarsegold, California. The community was started by nine pilgrims from the Midwest and their five children. The nucleus of the group was Elasah Drogin, Mark's wife, mother of seven. Elasah Drogin was actually born Elasah Engel, the daughter of a wealthy Ohio Jewish family. In 1968, Engel, then twenty-one and not married, became pregnant and decided to get an abortion. A friend drove her down to Mexico, where a doctor performed the operation safely and painlessly. Even so, Engel afterward experienced a deep depression which convinced her that she had no longer than two years to live. She began reading the Bible and converted to Christianity and then Catholicism, largely because of the church's stand on abortion. By this time she had married, and she and Mark had their marriage blessed by the church in 1974. About six months after the Drogins converted, everyone else in the community did so also. By 1982, the community would number twenty adults, all but two of whom were converts to Catholicism. They had all taken to heart the biblical charge to be fruitful and multiply, having among them twenty-three children. [38]

The entire community picked up and moved to Oregon and then California, part of the back-to-the-land migration that was occurring among the young all over the country. "There was a great longing for people wanting to have freedom to do what they wanted to do," explained one member of the community, "and not all of them were hippies."[39] Gradually, over time, the group became more and more devoted to religious rather than just social change.

They refer to themselves as a "lay monastery" with the official name "the Third Order of Penance Dominican Community," a title having special significance for them. The Dominicans are named after Dominic de Guzmán, a priest, later sainted, who led a small band of followers on a Crusade in 1217 to convert the Cathars of northern Italy and southern France. The members of the CUL community believe that these Cathars—otherwise known as the Albigensians or the Manicheans—held suicide to be the highest

form of devotion. The Cathars supposedly also indulged in what
CUL members find an especially loathsome form of debauchery,
consisting of the ritual offering of ejaculated semen and menstrual
blood to God. CUL members believe as well that the Cathars practiced contraception and abortion so rigorously "that they turned
many villages in southern France into ghost towns," according to a
CUL booklet on the subject. Dominic is said to have conquered
the Cathars by using the rosary as a weapon. They were subsequently
tried and executed under the jurisdiction of Grand Inquisitor Juan
de Torquemada, to whom the CUL booklet refers as "a very fair
man." The CUL members see themselves in a direct historical line
with the early crusaders like Dominic and the Grand Inquisitor.
"Jim Jones," CUL members like to say, with no apparent irony, "is
nothing compared to what the Albigensians did, and people don't
realize that this is what Planned Parenthood is for."

"Third Order" refers to a system of religious orders of particularly
pious men and women. As the CUL booklet describes their concept
of their mission, the First Order is any social or religious institution
at the top of a hierarchy, such as a father, a President or a Pope.
The Second Order consists of those institutions that help enforce
the general wishes of the leader, such as a mother, a police force
or the laity. The Third Order constitutes more of a "mystery" than
the other two, but does have its own special characteristics. As the
booklet portrays it:

> Surely this social institution would have many childish traits
> about it—it would be naïve, inquisitive and highly experimental.
> Its works would be of a rather rudimentary and temporary nature,
> and the best thing one would find to say about it is that it would
> be obedient to the First and Second Orders. Like obedient chil-
> dren the Third Order would develop and play in an orderly
> fashion under the protection of its parents.[40]

CUL members have protested at abortion clinics—or what they
call "abortuaries," "abortoriums" or "murderatoriums"—almost from
the start. They take great pride in the mothers they have helped
persuade not to have abortions. One of their prize cases, described
in their newsletter, was "Maria," mother of eleven children. Maria,
her husband and the children were very poor, living in two small
rooms and often without food. When Maria became pregnant again,
she was frightened because she had a heart condition that she had

been told could be fatal if she carried another baby to term. Though the couple spoke no English, they heard an ad for a family planning clinic on the local Spanish-speaking radio station and decided to procure an abortion. One of the Spanish-speaking counselors for Catholics United for Life dissuaded them by promising to take care of their medical expenses if they went ahead with having the child. "Please pray for the safe delivery of Maria's baby," the newsletter beseeched. With the story was printed a picture of Maria and her husband surrounded by the eleven children, the youngest a toddler.[41]

In May 1981, CUL officially "declared war" on Planned Parenthood. May 9 was proclaimed a "National Day of Rescue" in which they planned to raid the Walnut Creek clinic. The clinic circumspectly closed to avoid confrontation, so the group waited a few days. A year later, after several such actions, they decided to export the technique to other cities. Traveling in an old school bus, several members of the community went to Albuquerque, New Mexico, where they stayed with Brother Mathias Barrett, founder of the Little Brothers of the Good Shepherd, an order that maintains soup kitchens and homes for the homeless in Florida and California as well as in Albuquerque. CUL members view Mathias as "the Mother Theresa of New Mexico." They timed their visit to coincide with the scheduled space-shuttle landing at Albuquerque and garnered some attention from the press gathered for that event. The CUL demonstration consisted of "sidewalk counseling sessions" outside Albuquerque's Presybterian Hospital, which performs abortions. Aided by Barrett and the local Knights of Columbus, Jack Pelikan set up a more permanent "Center of Concern" to continue the work.[42]

Pelikan is typical of CUL members in his religiosity and dedication to the cause. Thin and excitable, he has been arrested nine times and has spent over fifty days in jail, much of it fasting. Pelikan explained in an interview that he has always wanted to do this kind of work. "I told my parents I wanted to be a preacher, I wanted to talk to people about God. They said, 'You can't do that. People will hit you and they'll hurt you.' I've almost had my arm broken at abortion clinics."

Pelikan is deeply religious, with a mystical bent to his nature. In 1976, during one demonstration, he had a vision of the Virgin Mary outside the abortion clinic window. Later, another demonstrator was thumbing through an art-history book and happened to open to a page with a picture of the Virgin. "And I knew," Pelikan concluded, "that it was my inspiration, my mother, saying, 'This is what I want you to do.'"

Two years later, he experienced another coincidence that reinforced his convictions. Pelikan's "patron" is Joan of Arc, whose symbol he has had sewn on the back of his jacket. Once he was arrested on her feast day. Ordinarily, during these arrests, according to Pelikan, the police were quite brutal, often dragging his "face in the dust." This time, the officer was unusually gentle. In conversation with him, Pelikan discovered what he considered a significant deterrent—that the policeman had made a pilgrimage himself to the shrine of Joan of Arc on a recent visit to Europe.

"We don't want abortionists to think the flesh is bad," Pelikan explained. "It's not. It's good. We're not Puritans." Indeed, their particular form of worship incorporates an almost sensual appreciation of the flesh, but always in terms of its proper fecundity. Not long after he made this remark, Pelikan also stated in no uncertain terms, "We do not want a Human Life Amendment that lets babies die, that's not going to defeat this devil, abortion, that would leave too many loopholes. Many people are involved in contraception, and sex out of marriage. They're committing sins. We're against contraception not only because it's sinful, but also because it promotes sex among youth."

Like other CUL members, Pelikan does not understand the reluctance of the right-to-life movement to admit to its Catholicism. He is also not certain of the wisdom of waging this war alongside Protestants, even fundamentalist Protestants. "The problem with Protestants is that there are so many different kinds of them. Give me two Protestants, and they'll have two different sets of ideas. We Catholics have to be of one faith. For us black is black and white is white. Abortion is murder, and that's all there is to it."

Above all, Pelikan is convinced he will prevail. "When abortions go underground, I'm going to do the same kind of work. It'll be a little harder, but we'll have the police on our side. But then when we're trying to save a life, we'll be the good guys, not the bad guys."

Stopping abortion, however, is not all he's after. Speaking of the Third Order, Pelikan announced unabashedly, "Our principal objective is to create a Catholic world."[43]

IV.

Cutting the Cord

The leadership of the right-to-life movement was as eager to separate from the church as the bishops were to see them go. Indeed, the hierarchy—perhaps inadvertently—had set the movement up well for the secularization process, having permitted these strong, independent lay leaders, some of them not even Catholics. Once severed, the leaders developed a serviceable infrastructure of organizations, with the primary one, the National Right to Life Committee, establishing branches in almost every state in the country. This put them in a good position to launch their offensive against abortion rights.

Even so, in the face of general, if not universal, acceptance of abortion, the movement still had to prove itself a legitimate cause. Achieving this kind of credibility was no easy matter and required overcoming several stereotypes, some of them at least partially accurate. The inception of the movement within the church had rightfully branded it as little more than the secular branch of the local parish. Moreover, the movement's objection to what had been the primary focus of feminism made it seem anti-woman, which was also uncomfortably close to the truth. Additionally, a complex matrix of forces gave it the stigma of being racist. Finally, the insistence of many right-to-lifers that abortion was the paramount single issue that mattered in modern society gave them the appearance of fanaticism.

In order to rectify all this, the leadership systematically set out to change their image by tolerating—indeed, often encouraging—a varied membership and broadening their ideological outlook. Their efforts helped convince, even more than outsiders, their own kind, who could appreciate being part of something that they felt was a positive step forward.

Success, however, brought its own problems. The inevitable leadership squabbles began to slow down momentum. Ideological differences began to emerge. The closer the movement got to its goal, the more elusive it began to seem. Still, by the end of the decade, right to life had become a formidable, much more heterogeneous movement with a truly dedicated following.

California was the place where the state leaders were most anxious early on to assert their independence from the church. Even before the Supreme Court decision, in 1970, they had begun calling informal gatherings of right-to-lifers from all over the country. At first they all met in the basement of a private home to put together what onetime National Right to Life Committee president Carolyn Gerster called "essentially an informal debating society." Later, it was more catch-as-catch-can, often in airport lounges. Once the ruling had come down, it became apparent that they would have to formalize their activities. A week afterward, Marjory Mecklenburg called around the country to the various state directors to see if they would be willing to meet at Chicago's O'Hare Airport every couple of weeks or so and get the thing going.

Mecklenburg's timing was perfect, and she was successful in arousing the troops. That June in Detroit they held their first convention, which included both secular and clerical representation. A struggle developed almost immediately between Monsignor James McHugh, then the Catholic Church's chief of right-to-life activities, and the state leaders. McHugh was in favor of having an organization with strong, centralized leadership, an opinion reflecting the position the church had held so far within the movement. The state leaders preferred to preserve their autonomy and recognized that this movement would best draw its strength from independent, lay grass roots. After much deliberation, the National Right to Life Committee voted to sever its overt affiliation with the church. From then on, the church and the lay right-to-life organizations moved on separate though parallel courses, both still drawing their strength from the Catholic people.

This kind of lingering identification with the church was potentially catastrophic for the movement. It opened up the National Right to Life Committee and its state affiliates to the persistent charges of attempting to impose church dogma on others who did not share the faith. Too close a tie also continued to jeopardize the church's tax-exempt status. Moreover, the most effective rendering of the Social Gospel, as the more astute clerics now understood, was to popularize Catholic principles without necessarily imposing dogma.

The NRLC solution was the election for several years running of executives who would present an entirely different image to the public. The first of these was Marjory Mecklenburg, chairwoman of the board in 1973. Marjory's husband, Dr. Fred Mecklenburg, the obstetrician-gynecologist who had testified at the Edelin trial, had actually served as an officer of the NRLC even before the break with the church. Marjory, who was to become the more prominent of the two, is a pleasant, motherly sort of woman with four grown children. A former home-economics teacher, she brought to the NRLC her own history of interest in setting up support services for adolescent pregnant girls.

The Mecklenburgs were both highly respected within the movement. They had started Minnesota Citizens Concerned for Life, which had been perhaps the most successful of any state group. MCCL produced one of the more professional-looking newspapers in the movement, a speakers' bureau, a resource library with an audiovisual-aid lending service, quantities of printed material on how best to perform right-to-life activities, and a number of creative suggestions for attracting attention to the cause. One of its most celebrated techniques was the use of the "Lifemobile," a twenty-five-foot mobile trailer with its own generator unit and a complete display of educational materials to be trucked free of charge to any

interested group in the state. MCCL also originated what was called
"Mission Possible," a well-endowed fund and political consultation
service that gave contributions to right-to-life candidates across the
country and provided expertise in conducting campaigns. One of its
budding activists, David O'Steen, would even provide the movement's ultimate legislative strategy.

As a Methodist, Mecklenburg by her very presence helped rid the
NRLC of its faintly clerical air. She also tried to institutionalize her
concerns for alternatives to abortion, although NRLC would ultimately leave that sort of problem up to outside service organizations
and independent homes for unwed mothers.

The organizational structure adopted at that first convention under
her leadership was along the federalist model, with a board of directors consisting of one representative from each state, the District
of Columbia and, at least theoretically, Guam and Puerto Rico, as
well as several delegates at large, all of them with a single vote
apiece. The organization was to be headed by a chairman who was
the chief executive officer and a president who was to carry out the
will of the board. Decisions were made by majority vote, and any
state organization could back out of the national or dissent from any
of its policies. Its stated purpose was to overturn the Supreme Court
decision allowing abortion—if necessary, by constitutional amendment.[1]

The founders also drafted their desired constitutional amendment,
reading as follows:

> With respect to the right to life, the word person as used in
> this article and in the Fifth and Fourteenth Article[s] of the
> Amendment to the Constitution of the United States applies to
> all human beings irrespective of age, health, function or con-
> dition of dependency, including their unborn offspring at every
> stage of their biological development.
>
> No unborn person shall be deprived of life by any person;
> provided, however, that nothing in this article shall prohibit a
> law permitting only those medical procedures required to prevent
> the death of the mother.
>
> The Congress and the several states shall have power to enforce
> this article by appropriate legislation.[2]

Mecklenburg's liberalism, particularly her support for the idea of
distributing contraceptive devices to teenagers, ultimately proved too

much for the rest of the movement. She remained with NRLC only a short time before she went off to form her own national group, American Citizens Concerned for Life. Her leavetaking was not an altogether happy one, and her relationship with the others deteriorated afterward.

The next executive, who would present a quite different impression, was Dr. Mildred Jefferson, also a Methodist, as well as a surgeon and a black. The superbly composed witness at the Edelin trial, Jefferson was the ideal candidate to shatter stereotypes. She had the professional credentials and the social outlook to disarm the most adamant critic. Always stylishly dressed, Jefferson lived a life of impeccable purity. She drank neither alcohol nor coffee, nor did she smoke. Jefferson had been married thirteen years, but she and her husband were childless. "Determine what you wish to do" was her motto, "and then set out to do it." Serving as president from 1975 to 1978, Jefferson set out to make the NRLC a viable, nationally recognized force.

Jefferson offered the NRLC several attributes. As another Protestant, she continued the tradition of non-Catholic leaders. Indeed, she was quite militant about it. "The Catholic Church is not leading the Right to Life Committee," Jefferson once told a *New York Times* reporter. "I am." As a woman and a black, she was also able to fend off charges of anti-feminism and racism. Jefferson made two more critical contributions to the organization—the first in the person of Judie Brown, whom Jefferson hired as her right-hand woman.[3]

If any single person is responsible for the growth of the right-to-life movement, that person is Judie Brown, who worked at NRLC from 1976 to 1979 doing mailings, soliciting members and keeping membership lists. One of her first acts was to coordinate information. At the time, NRLC was simply mailing out flyers to the directors of the fifty related state organizations. Brown began sending information out to all the independent groups as well. She eventually developed five different kinds of mailings: general educational material; updates on legislative matters; a medical backgrounder about developments in the field; a media alert about how to handle the press; and miscellaneous tidbits. "Every three months, we tried to give people something good or bad. It didn't matter," she explained in an interview in 1981. She has since written a book on the subject. As a result of her skill at public relations, NRLC started becoming more influential, both with its own members and with the outside world.

Instinctively, Judie Brown also knew how to handle the delicate task of organization-building, which for any group always includes one part hard work and one part hype. For all its powerful backing, the movement itself was relatively small in numbers, a grave strategic disadvantage. It was Brown who inflated the NRLC membership lists to make the movement seem much bigger than it really was. "I know that they say that they represent twelve million people. I made that up," was Brown's admission in the interview. "Somebody called and asked after I took over there, so we came up with a formula. If you took the two thousand groups and figured the average group has a five-member family, you multiply that all out to twelve million. It was a total lie." Judie Brown's lie, repeated over and over to the media, finally convinced the general public and the politicians that the right-to-life movement was a force to be reckoned with.[4]

Eventually Judie Brown and her husband, Paul, would become so visible that a *Washington Star* reporter would see fit to dub them "Mr. and Mrs. Anti-Abortion America." But that would not happen for a little while.[5]

Mildred Jefferson's second accomplishment was to recognize, in view of the right-to-lifers' weaknesses, the importance of their seeking out political alliances. From her point of view, these did not necessarily have to accommodate any particular ideological leanings, since anti-abortion activists did span the spectrum from right to left. However, Jefferson's choice of allies was limited. The politics of the 1960s had grouped together the left, liberals, Democrats and feminists in something of a coalition to which Jefferson obviously could not look for help. Her only alternative was the right wing. Accordingly, she sent Judie Brown to the very first gatherings of conservatives who would ultimately determine so much about the fate of the right-to-life movement. But that too would not happen until later.

Jefferson eventually was ousted from her presidency in a coup that ostensibly had to do with her imperious personality, her mismanagement of money, and power struggles within the leadership. Both Paul and Judie Brown feel that there were people within the movement who simply wanted to get rid of her, particularly future president Dr. Jack Willke. At the time, the organization was in chronic debt running as high as $25,000. Jefferson also had a tendency toward monopolizing the spotlight, and many within the NRLC resented her visibility. "I didn't realize how bad it was," Judie Brown recalls, "but it was hate." Eventually, two longtime board members, Mary Hunt and Jack Willke, hired a lawyer. "One day poor Mildred was in Washington" is the way Paul Brown explained it in an interview also in 1981, "and Jack told Mildred that she had totally screwed up and there was chaos going on and that if she would resign he would, quote, reluctantly become president, unquote. And, mind you, they spent over fifty or sixty thousand dollars just on attorney's fees."

Judie Brown tried to get Jefferson to answer her accusers at the next board meeting, even drawing up a letter of explanation. Jefferson refused. At the meeting, the charges were repeated. "I won't say who led the fight against her, but it was the most satanic thing I had ever seen," Judie Brown recalled. "The man who did it is an awfully good Catholic. I was just appalled. She just sat there while they were attacking her, smiling at them. And then she got up to the microphone and said, 'I simply don't have time for this!' and sat down." Jefferson resigned gracefully after a negative vote.[6]

The woman who took over after her from 1978 to 1980 was Carolyn Gerster, a statuesque blond doctor from Arizona. Gerster, like Jefferson, is highly intelligent. Her mind moves so quickly that her conversation is sometimes hard to follow. Curiously, her life paralleled Jefferson's in many ways. They are both Protestants. Each was an only child. Each grew up in a home which the father had abandoned when she was very young.

Gerster's mother was the seventh of twelve children from a Danish immigrant background and married before completing school. She desperately wanted her daughter to succeed as she had not been able to. She insisted on having her tested at an early age. As a result, Carolyn entered school at the second-grade level, skipped another year, and started high school when she was only twelve. The accelerated grades and the fact that she was always tall for her age fooled her classmates into thinking she was their age. Gerster feels that the premature advancement may have put her at a social disadvantage, but from it she learned to push herself all the time. She worked her way through college and medical school, in jobs as a press operator, a long-distance telephone operator and then a carhop—a job in which she got sixty-five cents an hour in wages, plus ample tips (probably because the place where she hoisted hamburgers, the Tick Tock restaurant, had all five feet ten inches of her dressed up in black tights and a short red jacket).

Gerster graduated from the University of Oregon Medical School at age twenty-one, too young to get a narcotics license to write prescriptions. After interning in Hawaii, she joined the Army and in 1957 was the only woman among 250 military physicians at Fort Sam Houston in Texas. In time, she was stationed in Paris and then Frankfurt, where she met her future husband, Josef, also a doctor. After a whirlwind courtship, they married.[7]

Today, the Gersters are in private practice together. They reside in Paradise Valley, Arizona, a prosperous community that boasts swank modernistic homes. With their medical practice among the affluent, the two doctors live quite well. Carolyn Gerster refers to their elegant home as "early Castle—all that's missing is a moat." Reportedly she takes breakfast on a tray in the "fantasy bathroom" containing a sunken tub, an antique telephone and an oil painting of a bare-breasted Mexican.[8]

Gerster has had three miscarriages, about which she candidly testified before congressional committees. The third time, she was three and a half months pregnant. Her husband had gone to the hospital to read EKGs and left her alone in the office. She started to cramp, rushed for the bathroom and got there just in time to catch the flow of blood in a basin. Once she had recovered, she let water run over the bloody tissue and retrieved the "baby," which, she recalled, was three and a half inches from crown to rump. It was one of those eye-opening moments of stark reality. "All of a sudden I realized," she explained, "my God, I've lost a baby." Gerster claimed that this experience awakened her right-to-life sympathies.

The Gersters now have five boys. Two of them were arrested for picketing abortion clinics—escapades whose planning Carolyn Gerster says was unbeknownst to her. Gerster travels frequently throughout the United States and abroad in connection with right-to-life organizing, keeping her away from home an average of two days out of seven. When she's gone, her mother baby-sits.[9]

Under Gerster, the right-to-life movement finally developed enough sophistication to be taken seriously. If Mecklenburg severed the connection with the church, and Jefferson gave the movement an organizational machine, then Gerster got the apparatus finally oiled and ready for the most difficult challenge, entering the political process. It was she who would help make the critical transition from an educational outlet to a political juggernaut. Before that could happen, however, the movement had to have in place an explanation for what they did and why they did it—an explanation that would filter down to even the youngest among them.

"Having a baby," the little girl intoned solemnly, "is the most precious feeling in the world. You shouldn't have to get an abortion."

She was dressed neatly in a white sunsuit edged in pink and sandals decorated with a yellow plastic Snoopy. Her name tag read "Maggie Gans." She was nine years old, the youngest of seven children from Monmouth Beach, New Jersey. Behind her was her twenty-three-year-old sister, Olivia, an aspiring actress outfitted provocatively in a frilly sundress which showed off her ample bosom. The entire Gans family had been active in right-to-life affairs for some years, Olivia being the most recent convert after her own unplanned pregnancy not long before.

Around them were gathered a crowd of about fifteen, all of them participants in the 1982 National Right to Life convention at the Hyatt Hotel in Cherry Hill, New Jersey. Outside was a pro-choice rally from which a lone demonstrator, Naomi Braine, had strayed into the lobby away from the stifling summer heat. Braine, a New Yorker about Olivia's age, was a study in contrast with the Gans sisters, wearing as she did loose-fitting army fatigues with an American-flag bandana around her head. Maggie was engaged in heated debate with Braine, who at this moment was appealing to the younger girl to the sounds of whirring tape recorders thrust in their faces by reporters.

"Legalized abortion does not mean that every woman will have to have an abortion," Braine explained slowly and patiently. "If it did—"

"I know that," Maggie interrupted excitedly.

"—then," Braine continued, "something would be very wrong with our society, because—"

"I know that," Maggie repeated.

"—because it would mean that women would feel there was no need or purpose to having children."

"Yes, I know that. But the people who are for abortion, and the women who are for abortion, will have them, and then there will be only a few people around the world left, and even less people who are pro-life."

At that, big sister Olivia joined in, asking accusingly, "Do you realize that a woman can have an abortion up until the day of birth?"

Braine paused, considered the point carefully, and then replied that, no, she didn't.

"Where would you draw the line? At what age?"

"I have not researched the matter fully enough," Braine, clearly beginning to feel outnumbered, answered.

"Have you ever been a mother?" Olivia went on unrelentingly. "Have you ever had an abortion? Have you ever felt that life moving within you?"

"Have *you* ever been a mother?" Braine shot back. "Have *you* ever had an abortion?"

"Yes, I have, and it was a horrible, horrible, *horrible* experience which I will never, never, *never* forget."

The two young women glared at each other, debate momentarily stilled by their rage. During this interlude, Maggie had been shifting from foot to foot and repeatedly raising her hand, as if she were in class. Finally she got her chance to talk. "If a fetus is not alive before it is born, then how come it comes out alive when it is born?" The right-to-life activists crowding around her beamed at this bit of precocity.

"Would you consider the seed of a plant to be a full-grown plant?" Braine countered.

"Botanically, it is," broke in another young woman, "as a matter of scientific fact."

"Perhaps, I don't know about that," Braine responded, and then she tried another tack. "What about the many women who will get abortions, even if they are outlawed, who will get them in back alleys with coat hangers, who will get infected, who may even die? Do you think it's right to force those women, because they have no other resource, they can't get jobs, they have no choice, and they cannot support the child? Do you feel it's better for them to have a child that will be born into such terrible circumstances?"

"If they do abort," Maggie answered, "then that is murder. If it is only an egg, and you say it's not life—"

"*I say I don't know and I don't think you know any better than I do!*" By this time, Braine was practically yelling in frustration.

"There are millions of people waiting on line to adopt babies," Maggie persisted. "You don't have to have an abortion."

"What about all the little black babies who are left at adoption centers and bounced from one foster home to another and don't have parents who care about them?"

"It's not true."

"It is true. It is true."

"Well, I would adopt them," Maggie replied smugly. "I'd adopt all of them."

Up until this point, Maggie had been an unselfconscious partisan. Here the little girl stopped, looked around to make sure of her audience, and then advanced her very best argument. "I don't want abortion to be legal," she said simply, "because I want to have friends."[10]

Every movement needs an ideology. The right-to-lifers borrowed theirs from the church. Just as they needed their own organizational infrastructure, however, they also had to differentiate their thinking from that of the bishops. If anything, their views became more extreme than the hierarchy's, made many more diversions into philosophical limbo and took on meaning way beyond the community that Catholic doctrine was supposed to cover. The right-to-lifers effectively transformed the Social Gospel into a rigid prescription of how the world should work.

The basic right-to-life line, like that of the church, avoids the issue of sexuality and concentrates instead on the Christian concept of the personhood of the fetus and its putative rights—above all, of course, its right to life. The very words "right to life" appeared in Catholic teachings long before even the word "movement" had entered the language in its current usage. In his 1972 address to Catholic jurists recalling the message of Pius XII, Pope Paul VI had repeated his predecessor's use of the term. "Every human being," went the papal pronouncement, "even the infant in its mother's womb, has the right to life immediately from God, not from the parents or any human society or authority."[11]

Right-to-life literature reflects this same Catholic leaning. "The Diary of an Unborn Child," for instance, an early piece of propaganda often read aloud at public hearings, presents the visage of the fetus as martyrlike—a tendency not uncommon to the movement.

"Diary" begins on "October 5" when the putative fetus's life begins. It is a girl, who, as she informs the audience, will have blond hair and blue eyes. She goes through each stage of her development, on "October 23" describing how her mouth is opening and she believes her first word will be "Mama." By "December 13" she claims she can almost see, and asks, "How do you look, mom?" The entry for December 28 is the startling conclusion: "Today my mother killed me."[12]

Beyond this, many right-to-lifers expanded the slippery-slope argument to suggest that the same kind of ethic that led to the atrocities in Nazi Germany had allowed the widespread practice of abortion in this country. An essay that received wide attention among them makes this case. The essay was written by Dr. Leo Alexander, a physician who was one of the medical examiners at the Nüremberg Trials, and was originally published in *The New England Journal of Medicine* in 1949, long before abortion became controversial. Alexander contends in the piece that medical science under dictatorship has always been subordinated to the guiding philosophy of the dictator. In modern times, that has meant the replacement of ethical and religious values by utilitarianism. In Nazi Germany, doctors accepted the prevailing ethic, which led them to collaborate in the mass exterminations. This gruesome behavior, according to Alexander, was purposeful, with a practical end in mind, and was based on the philosophical premise that what is useful is right. Alexander originally wrote the article because he worried that American medicine might be heading in the same direction.*[13]

The right-to-lifers called this the "abortion mentality" and feared it would eventually result in euthanasia of the ill, the weak, the mentally or physically incapacitated, the old or the ostracized. Significantly, the pro-choice movement in the past had tried to make

---

*A peculiar aspect to all this is what became of Dr. Leo Alexander. A psychiatrist himself by training, Alexander eventually set up a psychiatric hospital in the Boston area. His interests drifted into the area of electroshock therapy for depression, a course of treatment he began to adopt with more and more regularity. In time, his hospital became notorious for the frequency with which electroshock was used, the sloppiness of the medical staff in its administration of it, and the doctor's almost careless prescription of it for arguably inappropriate cases. Ultimately the hospital, dubbed a "shock shop" by the press, was closed by the state. Apparently, Alexander's postwar observations were prophetic. The essay concludes: "The destructive principle, once unleashed, is bound to engulf the whole personality and to occupy all its relationships."

the case that, if anything, the tendency toward banning abortions was far more Nazilike than otherwise, since abortion was forbidden under the Third Reich. Carolyn Gerster disagreed. Using as her authority her husband Josef, who grew up under Hitler and even joined the Hitler Youth, Gerster tried to refute this argument by maintaining that the Nazis banned abortion only for Aryans, not for Jews or "misfits."

By way of illustration of her thesis, Gerster pointed to the situation of Maria von Trapp, the woman on whose life *The Sound of Music* was based. When Trapp was pregnant with her last child and subject to kidney infections, she traveled to Munich to consult with a famous specialist, who urged her to abort. Trapp refused, and the boy was later born in America after the family fled the Nazis. (Trapp, incidentally, subsequently became secretary of the Vermont right-to-life group.) As Gerster wrote in an editorial in the March 1980 *National Right to Life News*:

> There are, of course, significant differences in the German and American abortion and euthanasia policy. The government and circumstances differed. What was basically a totalitarian regime in Germany was rendered even more authoritarian by the war. Adolph Hitler never ran for re-election.
>
> In America the abortion and euthanasia proponents must operate within a democratic framework. Our ultimate guilt, for this reason, will be greater if we fail, through apathy, to utilize the legislative means to effect change. . . .
>
> The question to be decided now, as it was in the 1930's, is whether the right to life is truly inalienable or whether it may be set aside to satisfy the social or economic movements of society. Are only the wanted, the perfect, and the productive to be issued a license to live? Will we—as Santyana [sic] warned—having failed the lessons of history, be forced to repeat it.[14]

Perhaps the most skillful of all the right-to-life proponents was John Noonan, a distinguished constitutional scholar who wrote an entire book devoted to the subject, called *A Private Choice.* Noonan avoided ecclesiastical arguments, except to mention them in passing, but pursued the same logic. Following up on people like Archibald Cox, Noonan found the Supreme Court decision, simply, wrong, embodying "multiple errors of history, medicine, constitutional law, political psychology, and biology. . ." Worse yet, he reasoned, the government required those who in all good conscience disagreed with the ruling to pay for abortion with their tax money. Noonan maintained that the Court had engaged in "an act of raw judicial power" with frightening implications for the possible expansion of state powers. "If it becomes settled that it is the Supreme Court's will that confers personhood and existence," Noonan declared, "no one is safe."[15]

Right-to-lifers eventually went still further, to contend that the threat of overpopulation was a hoax. The principal apostle of this view was Robert Sassone of Santa Ana, California. Sassone, a slight man with rapid-fire speech, claims to have "10 years of college credits, including degrees in Physics from the University of Michigan, and Law from Loyola University." Sassone has developed many of his theories from the work of Colin Clark, who had apparently wrangled as far back as 1957 with the director general of the United Nations World Food and Agriculture Organization over that agency's contention that two thirds of the world went to bed hungry every night. When Clark asked for evidence of this, as he put it, "I received the astonishing reply that they had made the statement first, and were going to look for the evidence afterwards."[16] Clark's trumpeting of this piece of supposedly irresponsible scholarship gradually had its impact on some members of the population establishment, who ceased to try to link hunger and overpopulation questions so closely. Clark's book, published in 1975 by Sassone, had the provocative title of *Population Growth: The Advantages.*

Sassone's argument, developed from Clark's pioneering work, had a germ of truth to it, although his conclusions were pointedly partisan. The problem with the traditional approach to the population explosion, Sassone contended, was threefold. First of all, he established correctly that there was no evidence of a population bomb ticking away, or at least not one of the magnitude the Erlichs had proposed. Secondly, and also accurately, to the extent that population was outstripping resources, particularly in the Third World, the solution lay not in conservation but in distribution. Finally, in those countries in which the poor were multiplying rapidly, their zeal at producing children came from a perception—often true— that large families meant economic security.

The peculiar organization of his book gave away some of the carelessness with which Sassone had put it together. It was not so much a reasoned argument as a series of 806 questions and answers, some of them downright silly, for instance: "405. How big an area would be required for all the people in the world to stand, lay [sic] down, or have a big card game?" The answer given was that, standing, they could all fit into one quarter of the area of Jacksonville, Florida, and have "plenty of room left over." Sassone did not reveal how much room it would take to play a game of cards.

Sassone concluded that the best means of alleviating the world's dilemma was not population control but rather population growth. He pointed out rightfully that an aging population was soon to overwhelm the young. "A generation which aborts 10, 20 or 30 percent of its young," Sassone insisted, "cannot reasonably expect a great deal of mercy from the survivors." Yet he assumed without any substantiation of the facts that humankind would somehow find answers to all the contemporary problems of mineral depletion, waste disposal and generation of power, as well as the crowding in some of the more overtaxed countries.* Sassone then offered a $1,000 reward to anyone "proving the validity of any reason why population must be limited within the next century."[17]

Such arguments eventually led the movement to examine the tenets of one of the primary forces advocating the maintenance of liberalized abortion laws, Planned Parenthood. One of those who did a great deal of research on the subject was Export, Pennsylvania housewife Randy Engel. Engel produced three massive, painstak-

---

*On the question of mineral depletion, for instance, he wrote:

First, please note that we're not going to run out of anything. Except in the rare case of atomic energy, matter can neither be destroyed nor created. Matter can, however, be rearranged into more convenient forms. The resources that are presently used are not destroyed, they are put into a more convenient form . . . All of these materials can be recycled . . .
The sum total of human scientific knowledge has doubled approximately every 20 years. This means that at least as much scientific knowledge has been discovered between 1950 and 1970 as was discovered in all the years of human existance [sic] before 1950. As much more new knowledge will be discovered between 1970 and 1990 as was known prior to 1970. With what we know about science today, we can extract enough of every needed resource to supply ourselves for many years into the future. By the year 2500 A.D., if present trends . . . continue, the human race will know one million times as much about science as it does today. If resources are any problem, they will by that time know how to tap essentially all of the resources available in the earth.

ingly documented reports that she presented yearly to the National Right to Life conventions. In her reports, she came to three basic conclusions. In brief, she alleged that the original projections on world population had been overestimated, and that Planned Parenthood depended for its survival on continuing to provide abortion-related services. Engel also made the inflammatory charge that the population-control lobby was dominated by the interests of the Rockefellers and other wealthy families seeking to benefit economically from promoting family planning in the United States and overseas. In the florid language of many right-to-lifers, Engel's conclusions sounded like so much conspiracy theory, but, stated with some sophistication, they had the ring of truth.[18]

Indeed, the right-to-lifers had hit on a partial verity. Many population experts were in the process of revising their estimates of growth downward, although very few were discounting the problem altogether. The Club of Rome, which had initiated *Limits to Growth*, partially repudiated its findings. On the occasion of the turnabout, however, the club's founder, Italian industrialist Aurelio Peccei, explained that even with disaster not looming quite so menacingly on the horizon, it was still important to seek ways to close the widening gap between rich and poor caused in part by overcrowding.

Arguments about population helped right-to-lifers feel they were dispelling the Catholic image, but they needed other arguments to counter charges of sexism and racism. The movement went about changing these disagreeable stereotypes by developing an ideology that made being anti-abortion also mean—to their way of thinking—being pro-woman and pro-black.

Their strategy for appearing feminist was to produce materials purportedly showing that abortion was harmful to a woman's health. This ran directly counter to the conventional wisdom that most people had picked up from the pro-choice movement, and thus, when successful, it was doubly so, giving the right-to-lifers not only a kinder visage but also one leg up on the opposition.

Soon after the Supreme Court decision, abortion advocates had started arguing, on the basis of authoritative reports, that, particularly in the early stages of pregnancy, abortion was both physically and psychologically safer than carrying a child to term. They based their analysis largely on estimates of what the maternal mortality rate might have been had there been no legal abortion.

In May 1975, for instance, a National Academy of Sciences report noted a sharp decline in maternal deaths and injuries related to abortion. The study pointed out that admissions to New York City's municipal hospitals as a result of septic and incomplete abortions had dropped by about half from 1969, the year before the state's liberalization of the abortion law, to 1973. Moreover, the Center for Disease Control consistently reported that while the number of legal abortions was increasing, abortion-related deaths were declining.[19]

The psychiatric case had come from two classic studies, one published in Sweden in 1966 and another in Britain in 1972. Both concluded that to refuse abortions could have dire consequences. The Swedish study had involved a comparison of women who had had abortions with those who had been refused. The children of the women who had been refused were followed up for twenty years and were found to have significant social problems, including delinquency, poor school performance and psychiatric referrals. The British study had compared two groups, one of 186 "controls" who were refused abortion and 123 others who had them. Finding that the incidence of psychiatric problems for the mothers was about the same in the two groups, the study concluded that abortion presented no greater risk than pregnancy.[20] Later American research had been even more definitive. Scientists from the Center for Social Studies in Human Reproduction of the prestigious Johns Hopkins Hospital reported in 1974 that their study of the psychological effects of abortion on women indicated that abortion was no more traumatic, and might be less so, than giving birth. Early abortion by the vacuum aspiration method, according to the study, might even be "more therapeutic than carrying pregnancy to term."[21]

Right-to-lifers went about trying to change the public mind about this by gathering huge quantities of material that appeared to show that abortion hurt women. Tom Hilgers, a physician, and David Mall and Dennis Horan, lawyers, all of them associated with the movement, collaborated on a book of essays, *New Perspectives on Human Abortion*, sold widely among activists. While some of the material suffers from exaggeration or bias, much is authoritative, offering up the collected medical wisdom on the hazards of abortion.

An essay by Polish physician Stanislaw Lembrych, for instance, is an anecdotal account of the fertility problems of fifty-two women hospitalized ten to fifteen years earlier for abortions who later sought treatment at the Hospital of Obstetrics and Gynecology in Opole, Poland, where he was chief physician. Lembrych had the advantage of viewing the situation in a country that, like others in Eastern Europe, had had legalized abortion for twenty years. In the essay, Lembrych discussed how six of his patients at first failed to conceive, although two eventually did; and how eleven at first failed to carry to term, although seven eventually did, three of them having two children. Lembrych admitted that the number of abortion complications possibly causing fertility problems "depends on the experience of the operator [and] the patient's adherence to the doctor's recommendations," rather than simply the operation itself. "Such things as an inadequate gynecological examination prior to the operation, the inattention of the operator (e.g., in cases of a perforated uterus), or the retention of fetal and placental tissue (e.g., in cases of hemorrhage) may also bring on complications."[22]

Another essay detailed just how horrifying some of these complications could be. Richard Watson, assistant chief of the Urology Service at the Letterman Army Medical Center of the San Francisco Presidio, reviewed all the literature that had been accumulating on the subject of urologic complications. Watson reported that for the third-trimester hysterotomy, the literature had revealed "well-established" risks, including death from cardiac arrest, pulmonary emboli, peritonitis and massive hemorrhage. The second-trimester techniques of saline infusion and abortion by prostaglandin carried dangers as well, with six reported deaths from the latter, previously thought safe. Even first-trimester abortions by dilation and curettage or vacuum aspiration presented problems, some of them "life-threatening."

Watson described two particularly gruesome cases. In one, Russian physicians reported that a 3 percent solution of liquid ammonia was mistakenly introduced during an abortion; the error was not discovered until seven days later, when the woman complained of painful, frequent urination and passed dead tissue out of her vagina. Subsequent examinations revealed that her vaginal and bladder walls had deteriorated to the point where they formed a common cavity inside her body and caused total urinary incontinence. Eventually, the physicians were able to repair the damage to the urinary tract. The second case involved a twenty-seven-year-old woman who underwent an abortion by vacuum aspiration in which the vacurette was passed twice unsuccessfully and two subsequent attempts at forceps extraction were required to finally bring about delivery of the fetus. Soon afterward, the patient went into shock. Closer examination revealed a large perforation in her uterus and a two-centimeter hole and two smaller rents in her bladder. The patient required an emergency hysterectomy. Watson theorized that what had happened was that the physician had inadvertently perforated the uterus while dilating the cervix in preparation for the aspiration, and the vacuette had then ripped the bladder and sucked out its contents.[23]

A third essay was written by Matthew Bulfin, a gynecologist in private practice, whose own personal observations, reinforced by a review of the literature, gave a sense of how wide-ranging complications could be. Bulfin kept a log of 802 cases that came to him after abortion, in 159 (or 19.9 percent) of which the women "suffered mental or physical complications of such magnitude or duration as to be considered significantly disabling." In order to prevent or at least help remedy all this, Bulfin made two suggestions: first, that women should be given information about the possibly damaging side effects of abortion, and, second, that clinics should be required to document and report on mortality and morbidity rates and complications of abortions.[24]

An even more impassioned argument was advanced by Myre Sim, the clinical director of the Forensic Psychiatry Clinic in Victoria, British Columbia. Sim reviewed the literature in his field, to find a 1979 British study that showed only four out of 311 postpartum patients as compared to twenty-eight out of fifty-six postabortion patients developing psychoses. Sim also made an effort at refuting the two classical studies in the psychology of abortion. The Swedish one, he reasoned, had failed to match its samples for social class, and the findings, he concluded, represented no more than the normal problems of the Swedish lower class. The British one, according to Sim, used too small a sample.[25]

All of these essays clearly were written by partisans, and suffered from a medical person's trying to impart complex information to the lay public, which is more than likely to find it sensationalistic. Moreover, as Lembrych pointed out, many of the putative problems arose from incompetence rather than any intrinsic hazard of abortion. Also, the anecdotal nature of much of the material failed to ground it in statistical significance.

Hilgers also wrote his own essay attempting to refute the pro-choice arguments by undercutting their statistical base. Re-analyzing the original CDC data, Hilgers came up with two startling conclusions: first, that even before the Supreme Court decision maternal mortality had already been on the decline, and there was actually no significant change in the pattern that could be accounted for by the legalization of abortion; and, second, that while maternal deaths related to criminal abortion were decreasing, they were being replaced one for one by maternal deaths due to legalized abortion. Natural pregnancy, Hilgers concluded, was therefore safer than abortion after all.[26]

Hilgers' methodology would not be accepted by the experts. In July 1982, reiterating the previous findings, CDC investigators would find that deaths after abortion fell from 3.2 per 100,000 for the years 1972–75 to 0.9 per 100,000 for the years 1976–78, whereas maternal deaths fell from 12.6 to 9.3 per 100,000 live births during the same period. "The risk of a healthy woman's dying from elective abortion is extremely rare," said the study, which was published in *The Journal of the American Medical Association.*[27]

Whether or not the medical evidence was convincing, right-to-lifers required another approach to alter the appearance of racism. The movement's negative image in that regard had come about for a variety of reasons. The white ethnic Catholics who formed the bulk of the movement were perceived, however incorrectly, to be racist themselves, especially after their alliance with anti-busing forces. Moreover, black women did receive more abortions proportional to their numbers than white women, and the right-to-life movement was seen as trying to deny them that access. Also, the movement's drive to stop government payment for abortion would, if successful, burden blacks most.

The movement went about attempting to rid itself of this onus by shifting the turf of the argument. Mildred Jefferson argued that abortion performed on blacks was simply a polite form of genocide. "Abortion is a class war against the poor" was the way she put it. "People who are fewer will disappear soonest and fastest, especially people who have a background of neglect. If people think their problems result from being a minority, why should they become more minor?"[28]

Jefferson was backed up in this contention by a number of well-known figures, including a dissenter from the 1972 Rockefeller Commission population report, Grace Olivarez, a Chicano, who wrote:

> To talk about the "wanted" and the "unwanted" child smacks too much of bigotry and prejudice. Many of us have experienced the sting of being "unwanted" by certain segments of our society. . . . One usually wants objects and if they turn out to be unsatisfactory, they are returnable. . . . Human beings are not returnable items. . . . Those with power in our society cannot be allowed to "want" and "unwant" people at will. . . .
> The poor cry out for justice and equality, and we respond with legalized abortion.[29]

Jesse Jackson, the president of PUSH (People United to Save Humanity), agreed. In a talk before the American Student Association reprinted in *The National Right to Life News*, Jackson explained that the reason he personally abhorred abortion was that it was only at the intercession of his grandmother, who offered to raise him, that his mother decided not to abort him. Jackson took the argument a step further than Olivarez, lecturing his audience on the divine nature of procreation:

> The idea that says it's all right to conceive a baby, but unpolitical to have it—there's something shallow about that. I'm contending that unless we put human life second only to God in our lives, we're becoming a Sodom and Gomorrah–ethic oriented people. . . . [The decision that] I didn't want the most precious gift that life has to offer—which is more life—to me, there is something weak about it. . . . I'm thinking that we have an obligation to take sex and life as a far more sacred event than we do now.[30]

The right-to-lifers' desire to make their campaign against abortion appear less racist led them to compare the unborn fetus to the slave, an analogy that lent itself well to the movement's insistence that the unborn fetus, like the pre-emancipation slave, was a person, regardless of its legal status. The putative arguments for slavery and for abortion were paired graphically on a chart that received wide currency within the movement.

These arguments began to be accepted by right-to-lifers all over the country as part of their world view, and they became integral to the accepted right-to-life litany. The right-to-lifers' ideology, however, had its variations on the main theme, including fringe-group arguments. Under Mecklenburg, Jefferson and Gerster, particularly, other lines of reasoning developed with which some but not all members of the movement agreed. The new philosophy came both from "progressive" right-to-lifers like Pam Cira of Feminists for Life and Juli Loesch of Prolifers for Survival and from other less predictable sources.

Margot Hentoff, for instance, wrote an article in *The Village Voice* with the general theme that "one did not have to be Catholic to understand that what abortion entailed was the slaughter of innocents."[31] Similarly, Marshall McLuhan condemned abortion as a crude turn backward for humanity, a generalized "way-of-death."[32] Another who took up the argument from a slightly different angle was the playwright Eugène Ionesco. In an essay condemning the death penalty, Ionesco suggested that a society that could bring itself to institute capital punishment or euthanasia for the terminally ill would not be able to stop there, and in fact might not know where to draw the line. "After the hopelessly sick and the unborn," he asked, "would we consider terminating cripples, the aged, the insane, misfits, and drifters? And then red-haired children...?"[33]

Many of those who sympathized with the movement never actually joined it, but one who did was Richard Neuhaus, once described as "the most influential Lutheran in America." As onetime pastor of a church in Harlem, Neuhaus had been a leading activist in the civil-rights and peace movements. His right-to-life sympathies apparently extended a long way back. He had begun to feel uncomfortable about the growing movement for abortion rights as early as 1967, according to his account of it during an interview. By the end of the 1970s he had clearly lined himself up with the movement and was the keynote speaker at a National Right to Life annual convention. His theme then was the apparent conflict between life and liberty. "The first and most urgent business of government," Neuhaus contended, "is the protection of human life." To illustrate his point that this should not have to conflict with the protection of liberty, he told a parable:

Six months after Gettysburg, Lincoln spoke in Baltimore. He said this: "The shepherd drives the wolf from the sheep's throat,

for which the sheep thanks the shepherd as his liberator, while
the wolf denounces him for the same action. Plainly, the sheep
and the wolf are not agreed on a definition of liberty."[34]

The primary organizational vehicle for the "progressives" in the
movement was the National Youth Pro-Life Coalition, which developed concurrently with the National Right to Life Committee
and joined in virtually all its activities. As part of its statement of
purpose, NYPLC put itself squarely in favor of peace, prison reform
and an end to capital punishment—what it called the "consistency"
approach. Although their numbers would remain small, the "progressives" would ultimately challenge the much more hidebound
NRLC leadership and would inadvertently cause real problems for
the movement. But that would come later. In the beginning, they
helped the movement's image-making by voicing with more conviction than the average right-to-lifer their views on matters other
than abortion.

The kickoff event for the "progressives" had been a rally at the
Washington Monument on Labor Day in 1972. Among the speakers
there had been Richard Neuhaus, then head of Clergy and Laity
Concerned About the War in Vietnam. Long-distance greetings
arrived from Jesse Jackson and Cesar Chavez. Right-to-lifers at an
appointed time burned their birth certificates, and the rally ended
with a candlelight vigil in which they all sang a slightly reworded
version of the old peace song with the refrain "Give life a chance."
Participants called the event the Woodstock of the right-to-life movement.[35]

Clearly these "progressives" had some impact on the movement.
In 1978, Feminists for Life endorsed the boycott against Nestlé, the
company that was distributing in Third World countries an infant
formula that, many believe, was resulting in widespread and serious
infant malnutrition and even death. At the group's urging, the board
of directors of the NRLC a couple of years later adopted a similar
resolution condemning Nestlé.[36]

Then, too, the unlikely keynote speaker at the National Right to
Life convention in Omaha, Nebraska, in 1981 would be Jeremy
Rifkin, one of the founders of the People's Business Commission,
a vaguely leftist group critical of unchecked capitalism. Rifkin comes
straight out of the antiwar movement, the Woodstock generation.
As part of an ambitious quartet of volumes elucidating his philos-

ophy, Rifkin wrote one book on genetic engineering which he called *Who Shall Play God?* His message to right-to-lifers at the convention would be about the same as that in the book.

Rifkin hypothesizes that society is moving into an Age of Biology in which there is a choice between two methods of organizing the culture. One is an ecological approach in which people learn to live with "creation," and the other is an engineering approach in which people try to manipulate everything into the image they think they might like—and for the profit of a few. Rifkin's worry is that people are fast adopting the second approach without realizing it. The danger is that not enough is yet known to make the right decisions about that sort of manipulation, and some grave and irreversible mistakes may be made. "Where do you draw the line," he asked the hushed audience of right-to-lifers, "between the sacred and the profane; between what can be engineered and what is off limits? If you believe that life has no intrinsic value, that living things are subject to utilitarian goals to satisfy greed, then you have no purpose. If you believe that there is a creation with order and purpose which must be accepted and nurtured, then it is impossible to accept [this engineering] on any level."

Rifkin summed up his thoughts with a simple moral: "Single-issue movements are fighting the same thing, defending the sanctity and sacredness of life. The difference is the timetable, at what stage you take up the banner. The answer is to fight for human rights for all those powerless to speak for themselves." This was a not-at-all-disguised plea to the right-to-lifers to recognize a common interest with the radicals among them and on the outside who were promoting protection of the environment and of the poor. The applause from the 1,500 participants at the convention was sustained and deafening. [37]

The "progressives" were not always sanguine about their acceptance by the larger movement. As Juli Loesch described her attempt to circulate between right and left, "it's been a lot like a mirror world. Things seem perfectly symmetrical. Bigots over here, bigots over there. Apathy over here, apathy over there. Gratitude over here, gratitude over there. Sometimes I get frustrated by the pro-lifers because I feel as if I'm handing out leaflets on tooth decay. I have a terrible sense of urgency about the nuclear thing. I want to grab people by the lapels and put them up against the wall and shake them."[38]

• • •

As hyperbolic as all of this may have seemed to those not part of the movement, the creation of this kind of propaganda was a necessary step in their development. The arguments meant that the right-to-lifers, no longer under the discipline of the Catholic Church, had their own dense infrastructure and ideology in place like any functioning movement. It was now for them to venture out into the unfamiliar world beyond their ranks. Almost immediately, they would encounter trouble. The problems would arise not only from without but even from within. It turned out that making a movement succeed in its goals—or at least this movement—would not be as easy as it seemed.

V.

Advise and Dissent

The conclave took place at the Madison Hotel in Washington, D.C., on February 15, 1979. The atmosphere at the opening was tense. How could it be otherwise? Facing each other for the first time after years of personalized mudslinging were the pro-choice and right-to-life forces, the bitterest of enemies.

They had come together to discuss areas of mutual interest like fertility, contraception, sex education, and support services for pregnant women seeking to carry their babies to term. The dialogue was supposed to be cordial, not confrontational, an effort to allay hostilities long enough to see if the participants could possibly work together on something. They had agreed in advance not to talk about abortion—not even to mention the word. Every time it came up, the speaker was to be gaveled into silence.

Some of the biggest names in the abortion controversy were there. On the pro-choice side were Eleanor Smeal, president of the National Organization for Women and the hostess of the affair; Karen Mulhauser, president of the National Abortion Rights Action

League; and Fay Wattleton, president of the Planned Parenthood League of America. On the right-to-life side were Mildred Jefferson and a representative from Marjory Mecklenburg's American Citizens Concerned for Life.

These women had taken a considerable risk to come. The prochoice women were under fire from within the feminist movement for sitting down at the bargaining table at all with people who in the past had been uncompromising. Right-to-lifers felt just as anxious about their archenemies, and had an additional concern. They had been asked to the meeting on January 22, the anniversary of the Supreme Court decision allowing abortion. January 22 was a high holyday for the right-to-life movement. The publicity attendant on the feminists' offer almost obscured the press coverage of the right-to-lifers' annual March for Life on Washington. Some sign of smoldering displeasure came from Nellie Gray, March for Life organizer, who declined her invitation to the meeting by telling the press, "I do not sit down and negotiate with baby killers."

As the hours passed, the women actually began to relax and accomplish some work. They came to the general agreement that more research should be done on male contraception, and on making all birth control safer, and that men should share with women more responsibility for sexual activity. More surprising, they had a frank exchange on sex education, agreeing that there was a need for more of it for people of all ages. Everyone felt a sense of relief that this parley to end all parleys had been such a success. There were even stirrings of warmth and quiet admiration. No one was able to voice it this way, but they were beginning to realize that the overriding condition of being female was a bond among them.

Just as they were stepping up to the microphones to describe what they had shared, it happened. Three young women walked to the center of the room and turned to face the group. The three were members of a group from Cleveland called People Expressing a Concern for Everyone (PEACE). One, Jean Matava, held a blue receiving blanket in her arms. Another, Nancy Hackle, made a simple statement: "Out of respect for NOW we came in good faith and not to disrupt this meeting. However, for those of us who love the unborn and for those who do not know the unborn, here is our sister killed by abortion."

Matava then pulled the receiving blanket aside to reveal a perfectly

formed but terrifyingly tiny black female fetus. Pandemonium broke
loose. The summit abruptly ended.[1]

Members of PEACE who had not been a part of the disruption
wrote a sorrowful letter of apology to Eleanor Smeal. The moderates
noted carefully that they had not known in advance of the three
women's plans, and that they sincerely hoped that the incident would
not "damage the possibility of continuing the dialogue."[2] They stated
as much to the reporters on hand. The newsletter of American
Citizens Concerned for Life made a point of reporting on the event
in a way that downplayed the protest. Even the militant Mildred
Jefferson condemned it with faint praise. "I sympathize with the
anguish which caused them to make such a demonstration," Jefferson told the press. "Different people have to express themselves
in different ways."[3]

Other right-to-lifers, however, capitalized on the press attention
to reiterate their sole demand. As if disciplining the troops, NRLC
president Carolyn Gerster issued a defiant press release clarifying
that organization's stand:

> Those offended by the visible evidence of the violence done to
> children in abortion clinics . . . should re-examine the reasons for
> their objections. . . . Should we be shocked by the appearance of
> the body itself or by the knowledge *that this death is condoned
> by the nation's highest court and has become the law of the land?*[4]

NRLC staff member Judie Brown, who was soon to go on to
bigger things, rebuked any right-to-lifers who may have felt that ties
with the feminists could be productive: "The reality of the issue is
death—the answer is a HUMAN LIFE AMENDMENT. Nothing less will
suffice."[5]

The PEACE members who had caused the disruption had ob-
tained their fetus from an abortion that had occurred a few days
earlier, and another from an abortion that very morning, although
the second was too mangled to show to the cameras. They named
them "Mary Elizabeth" and "Ruth." The next day, the PEACE
members, the NRLC staff and assorted right-to-life onlookers held
a funeral service for "Mary Elizabeth" at Washington's Mount Olive
Cemetery. A priest read from the Book of Jeremiah for the occasion:
"Before I formed you in the womb, I knew you. Before you were
born, I dedicated you." The fetus was then buried beneath a grave-

stone inscribed with the words "Mary Elizabeth Peace: Born Thru Abortion: Died By Abortion: Feb. 12, 1979." "Ruth" was buried in Cleveland.[6]

A constitutional amendment banning abortion was indeed the right-to-lifers' best recourse, as Judie Brown had declared. Marjory Mecklenburg, Mildred Jefferson and Carolyn Gerster, during the collective length of their tenure at the National Right to Life Committee, tried to bring that about. They were able to blunt the effect of the Supreme Court decision with a barrage of local, state and federal legislation, meanwhile putting the pro-choice movement on the defensive. The right-to-life leaders also oversaw the launching of various political initiatives, including the development of a single-issue party with a full-fledged candidate for President, a plank in the platform of the Republican Party and the start of their own major thrust into national politics. What they could not do—and left for the man who would take over—was to establish an effective enough electoral apparatus to pack the Congress with votes for the amendment.

Before the formation of the NRLC, an attempt had been made at establishing fetal personhood without the constitutional amendment. In 1972, Robert Byrn, a Fordham University Law professor, had sought the status of "guardian *ad litem*" for the fetuses being aborted under the liberalized New York law. A state judge did grant a temporary injunction against abortions, but the injunction was stayed and no abortions were stopped. A month after ruling abortions legal, the Supreme Court declined to hear Byrn's case.[7] This avenue of challenge was pretty much closed off.

Right-to-lifers therefore sought other grounds, using the complementary methods of local, state and national legislation. Before long, they had hundreds of bills pending in municipal councils and state legislatures all over the country attempting to limit abortion. The earliest of these simply banned the procedure outright and were immediately judged unconstitutional. Among the other major issues that the laws raised were whether parents and spouses had to give consent for abortions and whether abortions in the second and third trimesters of pregnancy had to be done in hospitals. Additionally, some of the laws required the woman to wait twenty-four hours before giving informed consent for abortion or receiving it; the doctor to personally inform the woman of facts relating to her pregnancy, including the anatomy and perceptual abilities of the fetus and the possible dangers of abortion; the "humane" disposal of fetal remains; a pathological report after each abortion; and a second physician attending during the abortion of a potentially viable fetus. Some of these provisions had the definite potential for giving a woman second thoughts about having an abortion; among them was a statement in a proposed Illinois law that a physician would be required to impart, to the effect that the child the woman was carrying was a living human being whose life should be preserved. Kentucky's law would have required the physician to show the woman photographs approximating the stage of development of her fetus—"in full living color," as James Bopp, the lawyer for NRLC, enthusiastically put it before a convention workshop.[8]

All of these legislative attempts were met with counterchallenges from the pro-choice forces, chiefly the American Civil Liberties Union, Planned Parenthood and the New York–based Center for Constitutional Rights. In some cases, lower federal courts struck down the laws, pending Supreme Court review, but up until after the turn of the decade the Court declined to rule on all but a few issues. The critical one that the Court did address was that of spouse and parental consent.

The first of these cases was decided in July 1976, when the Court ruled by a vote of six to three in *Planned Parenthood of Central Missouri v. Danforth* that the Missouri law giving husbands veto power over their wives' decisions to get abortions was unconstitutional. By a separate vote of five to four, the Court also decided that the parents of an unmarried girl could not have such veto power.[9]

Three years later, the Court's attitude seemed to have changed. Elaborating on the parental-consent portion of *Danforth*, the justices ruled in *Bellotti v. Baird* that states could require a pregnant minor to obtain one or both parents' consent after all, as long as the state law provided other alternatives, such as allowing the minor to seek consent of a judge. Then, in *HL v. Matheson* in 1981, the Court upheld Utah's requirement of parental notification when the girl seeking the abortion was an unemancipated, immature minor.*[10]

---

*At the time of the decision, 4 out of every 10 girls then 14 years of age would become pregnant before their twentieth birthday; and teenagers constituted 18 per-

In the initial Missouri ruling, the Court had also declared unconstitutional a provision barring use of amniocentesis. That and the 1979 dismissal of a Pennsylvania law mandating criminal liability for a doctor who failed to try to save a fetus after an abortion, and of another Missouri law obligating the doctor to tell the prospective abortion patient that her fetus, if born alive, would be made a ward of the state, left hanging a number of important issues. At the time, twenty states and several municipalities had passed laws requiring hospitalization for second-trimester abortions, among them Virginia, Missouri and Akron, Ohio. The Court finally agreed to consider these, as well as provisions requiring the waiting period, the counseling, the disposal of the fetus, the pathological report and the second attending physician, although consideration would not come for some time. [11]

If state action proved slow and unwieldy, the federal Hyde amendment would fare much better. This, a rider to an appropriation bill, was a restriction on the use of Medicaid money for abortion. Its primary sponsor was Henry Hyde, who has made his career on the issue of abortion and little else. A big man standing six feet three inches tall and weighing 260 pounds, Hyde once introduced himself at a National Right to Life convention by saying that he stood before them as "a 626-month-old fetus." Beloved by the movement, he is one of those ever-more-typical anomalies, the white ethnic Catholic Democrat turned Republican. Born in Chicago in 1924, son of a telephone company coin collector, Hyde grew up in an Irish neighborhood where, as he put it, everyone was loyal to "God, the Democratic Party and the White Sox," in that order. He graduated from Georgetown University and Loyola University School of Law and then went into politics, switching parties in 1952 to campaign for Dwight Eisenhower. After serving in the Illinois legislature, Hyde got elected to Congress in 1974. He first offered his abortion rider that same year. If voted in, it was expected to lower by about 250,000 to 300,000, or one third, the number of abortions performed each year. He reintroduced it every year until it finally did pass in 1976. [12]

cent of sexually active women, but had 46 percent of the illegitimate births and 31 percent of all abortions in the country, according to a study by the Alan Guttmacher Institute.

Almost immediately after its passage, Planned Parenthood challenged it. Judge John J. Sirica of the federal district court for the District of Columbia declined to rule on the case, but the next day the late Brooklyn federal district court judge John Dooling, Jr., found the rider unconstitutional. The case had come about when Cora McRae, a twenty-four-year-old woman suffering from varicose veins and blood clots, was denied an abortion at a Planned Parenthood clinic because of the lack of federal Medicaid funds. McRae sued, the case later becoming a "class action."

The Dooling decision prevented implementation of the Hyde amendment for that congressional term, but Hyde filed it again the following year. This time, just as it was being deliberated, the Supreme Court ruled in June in another case, *Maher v. Roe*, that neither the Constitution nor current federal law required the states to pay for "nontherapeutic" abortions. Nine days afterward, the justices set aside Dooling's injunction and advised him to reconsider in light of *Maher*, but about a month later Dooling began to hear evidence in the case.

John Dooling, Jr., according to the account of a lawyer who clerked for him, was responsible, thorough and highly intelligent. He would take thirteen months to hear the evidence, which ultimately amounted to dozens of witnesses and thousands of pages of testimony. Dooling eventually issued a 622-page decision striking down the Hyde Amendment for the second time.

Dooling's careful deliberations would be for naught, however. Barely six months later, in June 1980, the Supreme Court overruled him, and the Medicaid money for abortions was summarily cut off.[13]

This was probably the right-to-lifers' finest hour, to their way of thinking, and a most significant accomplishment. It was one of the few measures that had the support of large numbers of voters, and one of the few areas in which they could command consistent, decisive victories. They would not have nearly so much success from now on, although that would not become apparent for a while.

To all appearances, the movement was making great strides on the political front as well. The Bicentennial, 1976, was particularly a banner year. It was then that the movement finally achieved recognition as a potent political force, fronting its own presidential candidate and, by virtue of her showing in the primaries, making its way into the platform deliberations of both the Democratic and Republican parties.

The candidacy of Ellen McCormack, a housewife from Merrick, Long Island, was initially treated by the media as little more than a joke. The wife of a New York City police inspector and the mother of three grown daughters and a ten-year-old son, McCormack ran her campaign with the help of a handful of friends, most of them also housewives, who were neophytes at the political process. Only two months into the primary campaign, she was conducting a major battle to secure federal matching money, charging officials at the Federal Election Commission with discrimination. Eventually the FEC certified her as eligible to receive $250,000, half of her total campaign chest, under the new matching-funds law. The following month, McCormack got the government to provide her with the Secret Service protection normally afforded a legitimate candidate. Ultimately, running as a Democrat in a very crowded field, McCormack entered or was listed in primaries in nineteen states. As she herself admitted, all she needed was 2 to 3 percent of the vote to worry the other politicians, and in many states she did a good deal better than that.

In March, McCormack won her first big test, tallying up about 25,000 votes, or about 4 percent, in Massachusetts, running just behind Birch Bayh—almost like, as one ecstatic right-to-life publication put it, an "avenging angel." By September, she had won a total of 267,590 votes and rolled up significant percentages in Pennsylvania, Indiana, California, Wisconsin and New Jersey. In Florida she beat Sargent Shriver, Fred Harris and Frank Church.[14]

The only thing that marred all this was the continuing infighting within the movement. During the spring, the official diocesan weekly of Wichita, Kansas, the *Catholic Advance*, attacked Marjory Mecklenburg, then heading her own American Citizens for Life, for a long list of sins, among them that she tried to stop Ellen McCormack from raising enough money in Minnesota to qualify for federal matching money ($5,000) before the primary deadline. The story was picked up by the national Catholic newspaper, *Our Sunday Visitor*. It was an ugly sort of charge, particularly when directed at Mecklenburg, who had been one of the major forces behind the formation of a national movement. Chances were that it was also in error. As the biweekly movement newsletter *Lifeletter* pointed out, Mecklenburg, even if she had done the dirty deed, had been unsuccessful. McCormack did raise enough money, and more, and did it by the deadline.[15]

Despite all the backbiting, the McCormack campaign sparked interest in a whole new approach—a drive for a constitutional convention at which right-to-lifers could introduce a constitutional amendment banning abortion. Using the McCormack "machine," Dan Buckley, former aide to Senator James L. Buckley of New York (but no relation), got the effort under way. Almost immediately, state legislatures began responding. While interesting as a tactic, the so-called Con Con was probably doomed to failure from the start, although this too would not become apparent until later. For one thing, it required getting resolutions out of thirty-four state legislatures, a process that many right-to-lifers considered difficult and probably debilitating. For another, their drive was invariably confused with the similar one for a balanced budget, which didn't always help. Moreover, the opposition lined up shoulder to shoulder against Con Con, fearing that it would open the way to abrogation of controversial parts of the Bill of Rights.

The McCormack primary-campaign victories and the quick shift into Con Con gave the movement visibility, the campaign managing to cut slightly into the margins of the other Democratic candidates. The professionals were suitably impressed.

The Platform Committee of the Democratic Party took under advisement a plank calling for a constitutional amendment to ban abortion. In the interests of party unity, Jimmy Carter's forces were ultimately able to squelch the attempt.

The Republicans, however, were another matter. Interestingly, their internecine battles presaged the kind of trouble the women's movement was going to have a few years hence. Presidential candidates Ronald Reagan and Gerald Ford had both come out in favor of a constitutional amendment. The only force protesting their positions was an unofficial women's caucus cutting across Ford-Reagan lines, the Republican Women's Task Force. The Task Force that year had gone to the convention hoping to come out with strong support for the Equal Rights Amendment but refused to engage in a floor fight on abortion for fear of weakening the other cause. The anti-abortion plank eventually passed a platform subcommittee handily by a thirteen-to-one vote and was confirmed on the convention floor by voice vote in the wee hours of the morning. It wasn't the strongest possible statement, but it definitely made the point. The Republican platform read:

The question of abortion is one of the most difficult and controversial of our time. It is undoubtedly a moral and personal issue, but it also involves complex questions relating to medical science and criminal justice. There are those in our party who favor complete support of the Supreme Court decision, which supports abortion on demand. There are others who share sincere convictions that the Supreme Court decision must be changed by a constitutional amendment prohibiting all abortions. Others have yet to take a position; or they have assumed a stance somewhere in between the polar positions. We protest the Supreme Court's intrusion into the family structure through its denial of the parents' obligation and right to guide their minor children. The Republican Party favors the continuance of the public dialogue on abortion and supports the efforts of those who seek enactment of a constitutional amendment to restore protection of the right of the unborn child.[16]

The next year's annual National Right to Life convention in Chicago was a jubilant affair. The successes with local legislation, the Hyde amendment, McCormack and Con Con as well as the Republican Party support gave the movement a sense of invincibility. NRLC was claiming more than three thousand affiliates around the country. "We're now the biggest movement in America," Mildred Jefferson announced to the press. Jefferson asserted also that, from that point on, the right-to-life movement was going to move full tilt into politics, and that it expected to have enough sympathizers in Congress to pass a constitutional amendment within a matter of years.[17]

Right-to-life momentum alarmed pro-choice forces dormant since legalization of abortion. American Civil Liberties Union executive director Aryeh Neier, worried particularly about the growing number of states passing Con Con resolutions, predicted that "the danger is very real that in 1978, the 25 additional states needed will pass such calls." The ACLU chose abortion as a top priority for the coming year.[18] Not long afterward, the newly appointed president of Planned Parenthood, Faye Wattleton, announced that she was "putting the world on notice" that her organization also was going to mount an aggressive drive. Three areas in particular were going to be the focus: restoring access to abortions for the poor, putting reproductive biology "on the highest level of the nation's research agenda," and formulating and pursuing a national strategy for reducing the incidence of teenage pregnancy.[19]

The organized women's movement was vociferous as well, but here there were some problems. Feminists were on the defensive with respect to abortion at the same time that they were trying to get the Equal Rights Amendment passed. The general consensus was that since the Supreme Court had secured abortion rights for the time being, the priority should be the ERA. Indeed, some feminists could get very angry at those among them who were attempting to concentrate on abortion rights for risking defeat of the ERA. The internal friction was just beginning to hamper the effectiveness of either course of action.[20]

In any event, regardless of any of these pro-choice efforts, the right-to-life movement was generally acknowledged to have racked up some electoral gains in specially selected places. Ellen McCormack's run for the Presidency, for instance, created an organization that eventually had an immense impact on county government and ultimately even on New York State as a whole. McCormack's strength initially was in Suffolk County, at the eastern end of Long Island. This is an area to which largely Roman Catholic city-dwellers had escaped earlier in the century once they had accumulated enough of a nest egg to leave Manhattan. As early as 1976, antiabortion forces had been a major factor in three out of nine county races. By 1978, the county was involved in a major imbroglio between the legislature, which had voted to halt all Medicaid funding of abortion, and the county executive, Republican John Klein, who refused to implement the decision. That same year, McCormack organized a Right to Life Party, under the banner of which she ran for office again, this time for governor. The Right to Life Party did so well that McCormack racked up more votes than not only the failing Liberal Party but also the more viable Conservative Party.[21]

The situation in Minnesota was equally fertile, and gave a hint of what was to come. Minnesota was one of the strongest right-to-life states, with its leadership in the Mecklenburgs, its sizable Catholic population and the extremely active Catholic Church. The ties to the church were so close that for a while the executive director of the state Catholic Conference also served as the head of Minnesota Citizens Concerned for Life. MCCL held regular demonstrations, vigils and fasts and once a birthday party for unborn fetuses. Every election year, the group also conducted a survey of candidates' attitudes on abortion, which was reprinted in the diocesan newspaper, *The Catholic Bulletin*. All of this finally paid off. In 1974, the legislature passed a law making it a felony to perform an abortion after four and a half months of pregnancy, although the courts quickly invalidated it.

By 1978, the hold of right-to-life forces on local offices in the state was so great as to move a pro-choice organizer to complain, "You can't run for dogcatcher in Minnesota without declaring your position on abortion." Six of eight members of the congressional delegation usually voted against abortion funding for poor women. However, this lockstep did not influence Democratic Representative Donald Fraser, who was an outspoken supporter of abortion rights. When Fraser came up for reelection, the movement and the church joined forces against him.

Fraser's primary opponent, the self-made millionaire Robert Short, was able to attack him as a big-spending, big-taxing liberal. Short also pleased the business lobby, according to *The Almanac of American Politics*, by criticizing Fraser for his leadership in setting up a Boundary Waters Canoe Area in the northern part of the state along a waterway that the business interests wanted to develop.

Another factor in the race was the politicking by members of the Reverend Sun Myung Moon's Unification Church. Fraser had conducted investigatory hearings into Moon's immigration and tax status, in retaliation for which Moon had accused him of being a Communist, a charge dutifully passed down through the Moonie ranks. By the time of the primary, Moonies had made it out to Minneapolis in force, and they went to work canvassing the neighborhoods. One organizer reportedly told a retired woman on his beat, "I have to do this because we want to save America from the Communists."

Indeed, it was probably not just the right-to-lifers who defeated Fraser, but rather they in coalition with other conservative interests, among them the business community, the anti-environmentalists and the Moonies. The Fraser election was one of several in 1978 that saw the emergence of this coalition of forces that by 1980 would be recognized as the mark of the New Right.

But the election was even more complicated than that. Voters ultimately defeated Fraser's opponent too and chose instead a liberal

Republican. This suggested that the original vote against Fraser was not conservative after all, but rather a lucky break for conservatives who brought out their numbers in the primary, with its typically small turnout of voters, to defeat a man who, had the vote been more widespread, might possibly have survived.[22]

Whatever the true explanation for Fraser's defeat, right-to-lifers did manage to secure credit for it. To consolidate this and other apparent electoral gains, Carolyn Gerster instituted a three-year plan to elect enough representatives to Congress to enact a constitutional amendment. The plan consisted of a voter identification survey for the purpose of finding and mobilizing right-to-life voters; a National Right to Life Political Action Committee to collect and distribute money to right-to-life candidates; and a citizens' lobby to remind the politicians who did win on the right-to-life vote of their obligations. The plan detailed a target date for moving the Human Life Amendment out to the states, through either congressional action or the Con Con route, by the spring of 1983. Germane to this "blueprint for winning in the '80s," as Gerster called it, was a sensible, pragmatic and nonvindictive approach to the political game. "Being pro-life does not *qualify* a candidate to hold public office," Gerster rallied the troops, "but the failure to support legislation to protect dependent life does *disqualify* a candidate."

Gerster had a few other sage bits of advice for the movement, which she aired in an editorial in *The National Right to Life News*. NRLC was now relatively heterogeneous, a situation which right-to-lifers should continue to encourage, she suggested. "Public statements of hostility," she warned, "should be reserved for our enemies."[23] Gerster's words were particularly prophetic, given that the right and left wings of the movement were inevitably headed for conflict.

Dr. John Willke would now take over the National Right to Life Committee to preside over implementation of the three-year plan. Willke was a different kind of character altogether from Carolyn Gerster. He was much less tolerant than she of differences of opinion within the organization, but also much better at getting his point of view to prevail. He was much more capable, too, of actually getting something done. Paradoxically, it was precisely because of this organizational ability that Willke made a lot more enemies than she did. By now the ultimate populists, the right-to-lifers who didn't agree with him didn't want Willke stepping on their toes.

Willke's first task was to extract some kind of consensus from the membership on the wording of a constitutional amendment. The first suggestion to gain some approval was that proposed several years in succession by New York Senator James Buckley. Buckley's amendment defined personhood much as the original NRLC draft had done, to apply "to all human beings, including their unborn offspring at every stage of their biological development, irrespective of age, health, function, or condition of dependency."[24]

This approach had a number of problems. First, right-to-lifers could not agree when "development" began, whether at "fertilization" or "implantation." The distinction was critically important, since, as their opposition did not hesitate to point out, if the amendment were to read "fertilization," that might serve to outlaw certain forms of birth-control devices like the pill and the IUD. This occasioned more virulent debate, since right-to-lifers who didn't believe in the use of the pill or the IUD anyway, and chose the "fertilization" wording, were accused of allowing the movement to appear too Catholic. If the right-to-lifers began to feel as if they were trying to dance on the head of a pin, the situation could only get more complex.

The polls consistently had shown Americans neither ready nor willing to ban abortion completely. Keenly mindful of public opinion, Congress was thought not to be especially eager to adopt such an amendment, which would require a vote of two thirds. Moreover, the effort to secure passage by the necessary three quarters of the state legislatures might go the same dismal way as the Equal Rights Amendment.

Even if right-to-lifers were able to jam it through Congress and state legislatures, the Buckley amendment would be difficult to implement. There was no guarantee that states would pass laws in accordance with the amendment. In the absence of those laws, it was highly unlikely that state courts would insist that they do. Certainly the Supreme Court would shrink from it. "Assuming good faith implementation of the amendment by the Court," wrote the respected constitutional lawyer John Noonan,

> the task of remedying this situation was left to the Court. Would it, could it, order a legislature to pass a criminal abortion statute

and prosecutors to prosecute under it? Would it simply enjoin
all abortions except those necessary to save the mother's life? The
proposed amendment, if it were to work, required a Court at
least as determined to prevent evasion as the Court had been in
enforcing desegregation.[25]

Impatient souls eager to get some kind of measure through Congress later attempted what was actually the Buckley amendment in
the form of a bill. Republican Senators Jesse Helms of North Carolina and Orrin Hatch of Utah introduced the Human Life Statute.
Its advantage was that it required only a simple majority vote, but
it had the same problems as the amendment, and the additional
drawback of opening itself up to an immediate lawsuit that would
send the whole matter back to the Supreme Court, where it would
probably be judged unconstitutional.

All of this prompted right-to-lifers to attempt other ways of wording
the amendment to obtain the same result. John Noonan proposed
the so-called "states'-rights" approach. This amendment would have
thrown the decision back to the judgment of the legislative bodies
of the various states. As Noonan argued:

> [Abraham] Lincoln believed in the self-government of states
> within the federal system, but, trusting in the moral lights around
> us, he also believed it unnecessary for the national government
> to extirpate the evil of slavery in the states where it was established.
> Committed to the proposition that slavery was an evil, he saw
> that eventually freedom must spread throughout the land. His
> respect for federalism could never be confused with the "don't
> care" philosophy of [liberal Supreme Court Justice William O.]
> Douglas.[26]

Under the influence of right-to-lifers who preferred it, Orrin Hatch
abandoned personhood (Helms did not) and adopted the states'-rights
approach. But Hatch put a new twist on it. He refined the amendment so that it led off with a sentence stating unequivocally that the
Constitution does not allow abortion; this became known as the
Hatch or "federalist" amendment.*[27]

---

*The exact wording of this amendment is: "A right to abortion is not secured by
this Constitution. The Congress and the several States shall have concurrent power
to restrict and prohibit abortions: *provided* that a law of a State which is more
restrictive than a law of Congress shall govern."

Complicating matters still further, an NRLC at-large board member from the Mecklenburgs' Minnesota Citizens Concerned for Life, David O'Steen, suggested an even more Byzantine approach, which he called "the two-step strategy." In a long internal memo, O'Steen reminded the NRLC board that it had taken three amendments over a period of four years to secure true freedom for the slaves after the Civil War. The Thirteenth Amendment, passed in January 1865 and ratified the following December, simply outlawed slavery. The Fourteenth Amendment, which conferred citizenship on the former slaves, was passed in 1866 and ratified two years later. The right to vote was not granted until the passing of the Fifteenth Amendment in 1869 and its ratification the year after that. O'Steen's idea was to pass and ratify an amendment authorizing Congress to protect all human life including the unborn; then to pass federal and state laws protecting the unborn; and finally to pass and ratify a second amendment establishing personhood for the unborn. A number of right-to-lifers provided a variation on this theme by suggesting that the passage of a Human Life Statute would require the eventual passage of an amendment.

The NRLC would finally back the Hatch approach, but only after a power play by Jack Willke, whose continuing strong-arm tactics made many right-to-lifers wonder about this small-town baby doctor. Willke was born in Ohio in 1925. At the age of five, he and his family moved to Kneipp Springs, Indiana, where his father, a doctor, took a post as the director of a sanitorium run by Catholic nuns. For the next six years, Willke and his five siblings received tutoring from the nuns instead of going to a regular school. Later the family moved to Cincinnati, where his father set up a private practice. Willke then went to St. Claire's School and Roger Bacon High School. After graduating from Oberlin and finishing medical school, young Jack was a practicing physician like his father by the early 1950s. Willke and his wife, Barbara, have six children.

Willke was brought into the movement by the eccentric "Father Mucus," Paul Marx.[28] The doctor is his own curious blend of the superannuated and the up-to-date. He talks with the rubber-band twang of his native Ohio and gives off a deceptive naïveté. Actually, Willke is quite acute, as his politicking in the organization was to reveal. He and Barbara, a nurse, started out as sex educators, a course highly unusual for Midwesterners from a small town. Their material, which appears in a number of large-print, simply designed and written books, seems simple-minded to a worldly audience. In *How to Teach Children the Wonders of Sex*, this is their sage advice for parents of boys who play with their penises: "[T]he parent should act in the same manner as though the child was pulling at his ear or poking a pencil into it. You should simply tell your child, . . . 'Your penis is for passing urine, let it alone and don't rub it or it will get sore.'" They instruct parents to tell tiny children who are too young to grasp the complexities of intercourse, fertilization, pregnancy and birth that babies come from God. They caution fathers against displaying their penises to their little girls: "We would disagree with the 'liberal' attitude of certain parents who parade around naked in front of their children, considering it 'part of their education.' This type of blatant 'seductive' exposure is a far cry from the natural, reverent, occasional exposure that occurs at times in families." It almost seems like nonsex education, and, at times, it is. The Willkes recommend no sex, not only before marriage, but also after. Their favored form of birth control is the good old-fashioned Catholic rhythm method.

If this all sounds terribly familiar, for the parochial, repressed and largely Catholic audiences to whom the Willkes brought their message it was quite revolutionary. They dared to mention the words *sex, penis, vagina, masturbation, intercourse* and *contraception*. They gave unblushing counsel on matters formerly left to bathroom-wall consultations. In the same passage in which they proscribe immodesty and "seductiveness," they encourage breast feeding, appropriate displays of affection, and a certain charming naturalness: "For children of any age to see mothers nursing a baby, or to see parents kiss and hug each other is good."[29] In their world, the Willkes are liberals.

Willke was also instrumental in establishing the early face of the movement. Right-to-lifers put out a great volume of propaganda on what abortion did to the fetus. In the beginning, this had been, in fact, virtually their only organizing tool. The ambitious Willke was one of the prime promoters of the approach. Willke was the one who developed the grotesque term "candy apple baby" for the reddish outer tissue of a fetus that had been through saline abortion and had its skin "burned off." Under the imprint of his own Hayes Publishing Company, Willke created a whole line of visual-aid materials. Partly due to his influence, movement books, slides and pamphlets were unnecessarily sensationalistic and designed to appeal to primitive instincts. One widely distributed handout displayed a garbage pail filled with bloody fetal parts.

Willke had another talent which made him beloved by at least some segments of the movement. He knew how to relax and present a folksy kind of visage to the outside world. At one National Right to Life annual convention, he and his wife started off the festivities wearing matching fringed cowboy suits and singing a tremulous version of "Happy Trails to You."

Despite his "liberalism," his pioneering propaganda and his some-time charm, many of the "progressives" within the movement never particularly trusted this would-be cowpoke. It may be because Dr. Jack Willke is in a position with Hayes Publishing Company to make money from the movement. It may be because he is so determined to have his own way. It may be because he does not seem to have as much interest in acting on the rest of the Social Gospel beyond abortion as they do. Most of all, it's probably because, in looking out for number one, Willke, in their opinion, does not adequately look out for right-to-life interests. The feeling apparently is mutual. Willke does not appear to like the "progressives" any better than they like him. Over the coming years, their mutual antagonism would only fester.

If he disliked the left, he apparently really couldn't abide the right, a fact which he didn't bother to disguise. Willke managed with no trouble to alienate Paul and Judie Brown, who were fast becoming two of the most important people in the movement. Already they had been locked out of one major decision. Before Helms had introduced his statute, one of his aides, Carl Anderson, had gotten together a meeting of most of the movement leadership. Among those attending were Ernest Ohlhoff, from the National Committee for a Human Life Amendment, and Jack Willke. Paul Brown was not invited. Brown was so angry that he fired off a telegram to Helms. "I told him that I thought the statute was political suicide" is the way Brown explained his missive in an interview, "and also dumb. Carl took it to mean I was saying the Senator was dumb. So we had somewhat of a heated exchange." Once having been slighted, Brown was particularly sensitive to its happening again.[30] And that is precisely what Jack Willke would end up doing.

Eventually Willke would put together an action faction devoted to him and his principles, and would begin to strong-arm his positions through the National Right to Life Committee. His nimble-footedness, while stifling cantankerous divisiveness, did not amuse those whom he left behind. The split between them would open up the National Right to Life Committee to the possibility of a major coup from the right in the persons of Paul and Judie Brown.

VI.

The Right's Choice

The United States is a profoundly conservative country. Its roots in a revolution fought for religious freedom, its sudden wrenching from a feudal past, its long heritage of protecting individual rights, its geographical isolation and splendid self-sufficiency, its rough-and-tumble rush into capitalist expansion—all of this has militated toward the development of a society that is God-fearing, individualistic, suspicious of too much government, devoted to unfettered free enterprise and jealous of maintaining its prerogatives in the world.

This conservatism is the dominant attitude that most Americans carry around with them, a widely shared consciousness. The vast majority attend regular religious services, quietly raise their families, grumble about paying higher taxes, dream of striking it rich by owning their own business (or do so), and applaud the country's adventures overseas. This is not to say that Americans are incapable of appreciating the importance of reform. Quite the contrary, they are not ideologues; rather, pragmatists. They can rationalize change as long as it does not run up against these basic beliefs.

The modern conservative movement—as distinct from this prevailing conservative consciousness—came about as a reaction to the winds of social change that periodically blow through the country. Protesting the Progressive Era, the New Deal, the New Frontier and the Great Society, the conservative movement came to see itself as the true guardian of the country's economic, political and cultural heritage. At the advent of the civil-rights, antiwar and women's movements, these organized nay-sayers proceeded once again to hitch themselves to the flip side of most of the progressive issues of the day, one of which was abortion.

The conservative who "discovered" abortion was Richard Viguerie. Viguerie's true talent lay in his ability to plumb the depths of the conservative consciousness and come up with ways to appeal to it. Early on, he also recognized the vulnerability of the populist right-to-life movement and its need for firm leadership and a strategy for success. Viguerie and conservative colleagues Paul Weyrich, Howard Phillips and John "Terry" Dolan—along with "Mr. and Mrs. Anti-Abortion America," Paul and Judie Brown—were able to introduce the original right-to-life movement to forces that could produce results and pay their way. It was an offer the right-to-lifers could hardly refuse.

In doing so, Viguerie and the rest created a new kind of conservative. Abortion was not a traditional conservative issue. Indeed, the polls consistently showed massive support for it. Rather, conservatives like Viguerie saw its strategic value in possibly reaching a huge constituency that they hoped to include in a conservative voting majority that in turn would bring to power their kind of leader under the aegis of the Republican Party.

Paradoxically, Viguerie brought the right-to-lifers into the conservative fold by imitating the very forces that had created the abortion issue in the first place, the New Left and the women's movement. Borrowing their ideas, their style and even some of their words— Viguerie likes the sobriquet "New Right"—he transformed conservatism into a movement that seemed to speak to everyday concerns.

With some justification, he could finally boast that the "real revolutionary shift" that had occurred in recent American politics resulted largely from the New Right having "learned to play the single-issue game as well as and sometimes perhaps even better than the liberals," as he once maintained in a speech before a like-minded audience. The New Right had gotten a corner on the majority of the high-visibility issues of the day, such as busing, taxes, government spending and defense, and their success had begun to worry the liberal community. The most important of these issues was abortion. "The ironic thing," Viguerie concluded the speech, "is that [the liberals] virtually created this issue. We never wanted it."[1]

Louisiana has a primordial aura to it, like the fog that periodically gathers off the Gulf. The place is alive with movement, from the crocodiles slithering through the mud off the bayous to the armadillos romping through the countryside. This is the home of Richard Viguerie's people, who still bear the stamp of their heritage. Viguerie's mother spoke only the distinctive French of the Cajuns until she started school, and she retained her accent into adulthood. Viguerie is a practicing Catholic, but also a believer in spiritualism and reincarnation.

Arthur and Elizabeth Viguerie had a hard time during the Depression and were forced to sell off all their land in Louisiana. They moved to Golden Acres, Texas, right outside Houston, in 1933, a short time before their son was born. They were an ambitious, hard-driving couple. Arthur started out as a construction worker with Shell Oil, eventually advancing to a top management position. Until he was securely established, he worked another job hauling dirt in a secondhand truck. During World War II, Elizabeth worked in a paper mill. Viguerie remembers as a child selling the milk of their cows to the neighbors to bring in a little extra money.

Viguerie went to college at Texas Agricultural and Industrial, intending to become an engineer. "Why?" he asks rhetorically in his political autobiography The New Right: We're Ready to Lead. "Well, I had read that engineers were making a lot of money in South America so I figured I would make some quick money down south and come back to Houston—and run for Congress." His ambition did not help him do well in school. His low marks in algebra convinced him to switch from engineering to pre-law. After a poor showing of a semester and a half at the University of Houston Law School, he decided to quit that too.[2]

Always short for his age, Viguerie had as his heroes "the two Macs," General Douglas MacArthur and Senator Joseph McCarthy, for their toughness, conservatism and anti-Communism.[3] Viguerie first got involved in rather less strenuous politics helping with the Eisenhower campaign in 1952 and 1956. He worked his way up through the ranks after the election, to become chairman of the Young Republicans of Harris County, the district that includes Houston. Long before it became a widespread phenomenon, Viguerie was practicing the art of coalition politics, seeing himself as a conservative first and a Republican afterward. After serving as campaign manager for conservative Republican John G. Tower in his 1960 bid for the Senate seat of Lyndon Johnson, Viguerie landed a job in the New York office of the newly created Young Americans for Freedom.[4]

YAF had actually grown out of a rump attempt at the 1960 Republican convention to nominate Barry Goldwater to run for Vice-President. Goldwater was an essential catalyst to the conservative movement of the time. He was the first national postwar politician to articulate the modern conservative platform, embracing rugged individualism, free-market capitalism and limited government in equal measure with fervent anti-Communism, jingoistic nationalism and an almost paranoid militarism. Goldwater was also not wary of joining with any kind of allies who would advance the cause, from disgruntled conservative businessmen to the most reactionary, redneck elements of the Old South. After his defeat, William F. Buckley, Goldwater supporter, *National Review* publisher and the foremost conservative spokesman of the day, arranged for a gathering of the young people who had worked on the campaign to meet that fall at his Great Elm Estate in Sharon, Connecticut, and there YAF was born.

During Viguerie's tenure, YAF engaged in a number of activities that presaged the direction in which he and the conservative movement were heading. In February 1963, two national YAF officers sent a letter to members announcing that they had agreed to serve on the Committee for the Monroe Doctrine, a group formed to agitate against United States "accommodation" with Cuba. In typically urgent style, the YAF mailing stated that "no greater hoax has ever been perpetrated on the American people than this so-called 'settlement' of the Cuban problem." This was just one of several such committees put together by Goldwaterite Marvin Liebman.

Viguerie's association with Liebman proved to be a remarkable bit of good fortune. One of the many ex-Communists active in the conservative camp, Liebman was the inventor of direct mail as a technique for advancing political causes and candidates. He also originated the single-issue campaign and the strategy of combining single-issue groups to forge a coalition of conservative interests that gave the appearance of vibrant activity and broad-based support.* The Liebman complex operated with the implicit sanction of better-known conservatives such as Goldwater and Buckley, who were officers of some of them. Their boards, many with interlocking directorates, represented widely differing tendencies within conservatism, from moderates to members of the John Birch Society. Program proliferation and cooperation was one of the techniques that Viguerie would later use to great advantage.[5]

Significantly, abortion did not show up on the Liebman agenda. This is somewhat surprising, since it was already of concern to the Catholic Church. Indeed, YAF sponsor William F. Buckley, himself a Catholic, had close ties with a number of people within conservative church circles. His brother-in-law and political ally Brent Bozell, for instance, was deeply involved, heading a group from the *National Review* crowd calling themselves the Committee for a Conservative Catholic Magazine. Buckley himself had been on the Advisory Board of the conservative Catholic lay organization Pro Ecclesia, one of the tenets of which, according to a fund-raiser, was the following: "We must do more than pray... We must not fail to *fight back*... to combat the slanders and abuse that are being heaped upon God, religion in general, the Pope in particular, morals, honor and just about everything else that you were taught to give primary consideration in your life."[6] If anything, however, conservatives, particularly those from the South, then actually favored abortion. Assuming blacks to be sexually promiscuous, these Southern conservatives looked at abortion as one way of decreasing an unwanted excess black population and stopping miscegeny. Indeed, George

---

*Others of the organizations in the Liebman complex were the Committee of One Million Against the Admission of Communist China to the United Nations, the American Committee for Aid to Katanga Freedom Fighters, the American Afro-Asian Educational Exchange, the American Jewish League Against Communism, the Emergency Committee for Chinese Refugees and the National Committee Against the [test-ban] Treaty of Moscow, according to exhaustive research done by Wes McCune of the Group Research Center in Washington, D.C.

Wallace's running mate, General Curtis LeMay, would some years later support the legalization of abortion. Viguerie himself never evinced much interest in the subject until later.

Viguerie discovered other useful things at YAF. He claims that when he arrived there the books were in shambles and Liebman suggested he visit various old-time conservative donors, which he did—his first glimpse at the right-wing money tree. His explanation of what happened next is a beguiling account of how he discovered his true vocation. "I'm basically a shy person," Viguerie explains in his book, "and I did not feel comfortable asking for money directly. So I began writing letters instead, and they seemed to work. So I wrote more and more letters, and before many months, direct mail was my whole focus—for fundraising, . . . membership, everything."[7]

Viguerie moved to Washington with YAF in November 1962. These were critical years for the organization, which was chosen by Goldwater advisers to participate in a strategy to bring the Republican Party around to the Senator in time for the next election. The idea was to target vulnerable organizations within the GOP, such as the Young Republicans and the National Federation of Republican Women, and infiltrate them with enough conservatives to pack the party convention.

The leader of the women's putsch was none other than Phyllis Schlafly, then a conservative Republican activist, who some years later would go on to become one of the foremost detractors of the women's-liberation movement. Like Buckley, she was not yet revealing any particular interest in abortion, although she too had numerous ties with the Catholic right wing. Like Viguerie, she used the Goldwater campaign to develop the network that would put her in an excellent position to organize later around the social issues. In anticipation of Goldwater's run, she wrote A Choice Not an Echo, which repeated the old conservative canard about a small European clique that was supposed to be running the United States in conspiracy with its actual leaders. An estimated 750,000 copies of the book were distributed free in California, more on the convention floor and still more within conservative Catholic circles.

For the young people, YAF was to be the wedge, taking over YR with tactics the memory of which rankle for some Republicans even today. In Los Angeles, for instance, a YAF member who was to go

on to take a pivotal position in the Goldwater campaign gained
enough putative support through neighborhood clubs supposedly
pledged to him to assume a leadership role, although his "pledges"
later turned out to be phony. YAF member Donald "Buz" Lukens
rose to the top YR leadership and helped sway the influential California delegation. Well schooled in campaign tactics, Lukens was
later to be of great service to Viguerie and his New Right colleagues.[8]

Conservatives had a cautiously optimistic interpretation of the
outcome of the 1964 election. Goldwater lost every state but Arizona
and the five of the Deep South, Mississippi, Alabama, Georgia,
South Carolina and Louisiana. Regardless, F. Clifton White, campaign manager for Goldwater and later for Ronald Reagan, felt that
the campaign was the start of a long, slow but inevitably victorious
conservative takeover of the country.[9]

For Richard Viguerie, the campaign was positively inspirational.
Believing, like White, that conservatism could only get more powerful, he saw the hours of ward-walking and door-knocking as valuable training for the troops. He also learned how to practice his
trade. After years of floundering, Viguerie discovered his calling.
While retaining his commitment to the cause, Viguerie would make
money from it. He would become a businessman, marketing conservatism to millions. The small man from the small town in Texas
would finally make good.

He started the Richard A. Viguerie Company (RAVCO) in 1965.
Viguerie's first client was YAF, but others followed quickly. That
beginning year, he claims to have made $100,000. In 1968 and
1969 he was boasting of having mailings in excess of 20 million
letters. Only eight years later, by 1977, Viguerie would be said to
have a computerized list of 25 million names and to be sending out
approximately 77 million letters per year. He also would have started
two publications, *Conservative Digest* and *The New Right Report*.
Additionally, he would set up the Diversified Mailing Company to
print the letters, the Mail House to prepare them for mailing, and
Prospect House to publish and distribute books and the two news-
letters. In all, Richard Viguerie would have created a labyrinth of
interdependent business operations making a cool profit of something
like $10 million per year or more.[10]

Viguerie made money in three ways. He got outright contributions
from old-line conservative donors that helped finance his burgeoning

political consulting enterprise. He also picked up new clients, some of them the predictable lot coming out of conservative circles, others a little odd. Finally, he made front-end loans to some of his clients to help them get started, which he then recouped, with interest. Some of his fund-raising techniques were the conventional stuff of political consulting; others were considered by at least some government agencies to be decidedly not kosher.

His first big list came out of the Goldwater campaign. In his book he gives a touching rendition of how that happened. Shortly after the campaign was over, he went directly to the office of the clerk of the House of Representatives, where the donors' names were kept, and painstakingly copied all 12,500 of them. This was the beginning of his formidable computer data bank index.[11]

Viguerie has always been reluctant to name his clients. "The advantage of being a private corporation," he once explained, "is I don't have to let everybody—my competition—know who my clients are. I'll tell you, though, it's not all political. We also work to house and feed orphans and help lepers."[*][12]

As a result, Viguerie became a very successful man. He bought a new $250,000 home in Williamsburg complete with a kidney-shaped pool and decorated with the French period antiques that his wife, Elaine, liked to buy at auctions. He also owned a two-hundred-acre farm in the Virginia countryside, although what time he spent there was usually devoted to working. He learned to appreciate fine foods, bought a black Lincoln Continental and even hired a chauf-

---

*One client among those representing "orphans and lepers" was the Korean Cultural and Freedom Foundation, a front for the Reverend Sun Myung Moon and his Holy Spirit Association for the Unification of World Christianity. The Unification Church has been charged with having politics as its real mission, having gotten its start and continuing financial backing from the KCIA, the Korean secret police. Indeed, Viguerie's association with the church was one of many such direct and indirect ties by conservatives to the South Korean dictatorship. It was in connection with the foundation that the charge that Viguerie was soaking his clients first arose. New York State ultimately denied the foundation the right to solicit funds because of "unconscionably high fees paid to professional fundraisers." In an investigation, according to Alan Crawford in *Thunder on the Right*, the state found that of the $1.5 million raised ostensibly to help feed hungry children, less than $100,000 went to them and more than $900,000 went to Viguerie. The states of Ohio and Connecticut also barred Viguerie from doing mailings after similar discoveries. Viguerie explained such high fees, which came to be a mark of his business, as the equivalent of the initial capital outlays of any growing concern.

feur for a while. He paid his employees well, favored them with company parties, athletic events and special notice in the RAVCO publications, and treated everyone with courtesy and generosity[13]— everyone, that is, except the liberals. Them he accused of a multitude of sins: losing Iran, Afghanistan, Vietnam, Laos and Cambodia; crippling the FBI and the CIA; selling the Russians computers and "other sophisticated equipment which have been used to stamp out freedom"; letting "hardened criminals out on the street to kill, rape and rob again before their victims are buried or out of the hospital"; and failing to "help human beings who are daily being killed and beaten up by Marxist dictators."[14]

It was this kind of style that helped make his business grow. The letters Viguerie created for his clients were simple, personalized, emotional—and effective. As Viguerie explained it to approving colleagues, "Direct mail is like having a water moccasin for a watchdog, silent but deadly."[15]

Conservatives coveting political power vacillated in the post-Goldwater years between trying to capture the Republican Party and trying to supplant it with a third party. At first Viguerie was as irresolute as the others about the question and experimented with various possibilities, in the meantime exercising his considerable entrepreneurial talents. His business empire eventually established enough credibility within the conservative movement for him to become one of its movers and shakers. Abortion—the issue that would ultimately bring him so much gain—was almost an afterthought.

One of Viguerie's early pet projects presaged a clever tactic he would use later with great success. This was the development with Buz Lukens of a group called United Republicans of America. The name gave the appearance of a connection that did not exist to the party, the artful touch drawing in people who otherwise might have had nothing to do with the whole thing. URA's explicitly stated goal was to form a "party within the party"—that is, a fifth column of conservatives in the GOP. At one point, an enterprising reporter found a pirated tape of instructions from a URA higher-up who was also a Republican Party official, explaining how right-wingers could take over a meeting. In 1966 it was disclosed further that a small group of southern-California businessmen—their names were never revealed—paid for the expenses of a full-time URA organizer to travel to Coeur d'Alene, Idaho, ostensibly as a public-relations expert. His real assignment was to infiltrate the Idaho GOP to find and field right-wing candidates. It later came out that seven identically commissioned operatives had been sent out to eleven other states. The following year, the scheme was linked to a recall drive against Idaho Senator Frank Church, who would remain a target of conservatives. URA eventually fielded candidates openly, in 1968 recruiting eighty-six people representing forty-three election campaigns across the country. As usual, Viguerie was able to use the drive not only to feed more information into his computer but also to make a healthy profit. Of a total of $475,453 amassed that year, Viguerie was reportedly collecting $240,000 and passing along to the candidates only $43,035, or about 10 percent. [16]

URA having failed to revive the GOP, Viguerie's next move was the formation of outside organizations in anticipation of another kind of bid for power. This time, the idea was to make a third party. The vanguard for the strategy were Paul Weyrich, Howard Phillips and John "Terry" Dolan and their associates. Each had a background in conservatism, some having come from YAF, some from the conservative wing of the Republican Party, some from the exotic ultraright and even some from Richard Nixon's "dirty tricksters."

Taking advantage of his YAF background, Viguerie created organizations like a proud and lusty papa fish. He had the best of both worlds, making good colleagues out of his clients and good clients out of his colleagues. The way Viguerie did it was to front-end money to help them get started, sometimes even providing office space, in return for which he received not only payment but also access to their growing lists. In this fashion, Paul Weyrich's Committee for the Survival of a Free Congress paid various of Viguerie's corporations $248,807 from January to June 1978, and Viguerie advanced Howard Phillips $100,000 to form the Conservative Caucus as well as a preliminary list of 11,200 names. John "Terry" Dolan's National Conservative Political Action Committee carried a debt of $80,198. [17]

Each of the people in Viguerie's network brought a unique set of skills. Paul Weyrich was the strategist. It was Weyrich who recognized that anti-abortion sentiment could be helpful to conservatives as the key issue in a counterrevolution against the liberals, the left and the women's movement—the personal politics of the 1960s turned right face. Weyrich made abortion into a legitimate conservative issue, providing the justification for conservatives to form a fifth column within the right-to-life movement, and then got the right-to-lifers into what he termed a "winning coalition" designed to help them actually win congressional seats. Under Weyrich's keen gaze, abortion would ultimately become as meaningful for the right as it had been for the left—the right's masterful choice—and the conservatives would ultimately become as important to the right-to-lifers as the Catholic Church had been.

Interestingly, Weyrich, like Viguerie, came from a modest background. His father was a German immigrant who shoveled coal for a living. Weyrich retains the precise orderliness of his Teutonic forebears, but none of their rollicking good humor. His mien is that of a formal, slightly constipated owl. He speaks in the clipped phrases of a man in a hurry.

Weyrich got interested in politics in high school, and he claims to have lost a bid for student office because he failed to ask enough people to vote for him—a lesson he did not forget. His conservatism surfaced in 1968 when he converted to Greek Orthodox because he was so disturbed by the liberal changes in his own Roman Catholic Church. After a stint in radio and TV, he joined the staff of Colorado Republican Senator Gordon Allott.[18]

While other conservatives disdained the issues that the liberals, the left and particularly the women's movement had brought to the fore, Weyrich recognized their crucial nature. "We talk about issues that people care about" was the way he put it in an interview in Viguerie's *Conservative Digest*, "like gun control, abortion, taxes and crime. Yes, they're emotional issues, but that's better than talking about capital formation."[19]

In order to capture the emotion, Weyrich read between the lines of the classic pro-choice argument to perceive that feminists were actually calling for a great deal more government involvement in private life in the form of not only publicly paid abortions for the poor, but also a greater governmental responsibility for the family and child care—what was, of course, anathema to the conservative mind. In this context, Weyrich came up with the public-relations gambit which ostensibly provided the ideological justification for conservatives to enter this battle at all. Weyrich's brilliant innovation was to rename the right-to-lifers. Instead of "pro-life" he called them "pro-family." This allowed conservatives to broaden right-to-life concerns to cover what they saw as the proper role of government with respect to family matters, and its cost. It also gave them the justification for entering the right-to-life movement and assuming immediate leadership—what otherwise might have opened them up to charges of being spoilers.

Weyrich also transformed two other ideas supportive of abortion rights—the need for population control and the racism underlying attempts to ban abortion—into a conservative counterassault. In answer to the liberals' assertion that if abortion were banned population might rise, Weyrich, like Robert Sassone, contends that the country needs *more* people, not fewer, to work its factories and fight its wars. "We don't have a population problem," he asserted in an interview, "we have a population distribution problem. Too many people have been attracted to the metropolitan areas which have a lot of things going for them, higher welfare payments, easier jobs, better entertainment. Why, you can drive for miles and miles and miles and hours and hours in this country and not see a single soul on a freeway. I have driven for four hours on a freeway on a Sunday morning and not run into a single car." As distinct from the more "progressive" arguments of a Robert Sassone or a Randy Engel, Weyrich takes a distinctly supply-side position on population. He would look to the free-market system to correct the problems of resource development, pollution and hunger.

Weyrich also turns around the old redneck conservative complaint that banning abortion would encourage blacks to reproduce. "After all," he says, "it's the white middle-class women who are having all the abortions."

Weyrich's first brush with the conservative movement, by his account of it, came as a surprise. It appeared to him as if conservatives did not have the weapons they needed to fight the battles that came along. Determined to correct the situation, Weyrich created a mini-empire of his own under Viguerie's wing.

In order to do this, Weyrich used techniques he admits proudly to having filched from the liberals and the left. As he tells it, he inadvertently sat in one day on a meeting of liberals planning how to get an open-housing bill enacted. Present at the meeting were a high White House official, a newspaper columnist, representatives of the think-tank Brookings Institute and various black organizations and aides from at least a dozen key senatorial staffs. During the meeting, each member took on a task. The White House official promised to monitor the Administration's plans; the columnist, to write a story; the Brookings man, to get together a research report suitable for use during congressional debate; the representatives of the black groups, to have people demonstrating in the streets; and the congressional aides, to commit their bosses to make specific statements and contact their colleagues. "I saw how easily it could be done with planning and determination," Weyrich concluded, "and decided to try it myself."[20]

In 1973, using money provided by Colorado brewer Joseph Coors, Weyrich created the Heritage Foundation as an ultraconservative information and resource center. It was apparently an idea whose time had come. Heritage quickly acquired quite a following within the crowd that regularly gives to ultraconservative causes—the eccentric multimillionaires, the foundations set up by them and their heirs, and the corporate-related blind trusts. The foundation's head, Edwin Feulner, claimed that in 1980 Heritage got money from eighty-seven corporations listed on the Fortune 500. The fabulously wealthy heir to the Mellon fortune, Richard Scaife, who in a year gave, through a family trust, a reported $955,000 to various conservative causes around the country, was the largest contributor, kicking in several million. According to records in various periodicals covering the world of foundations, Heritage also received huge sums from something called the Texas Education Association; from the Davis Foundation of the family of T. Cullen Davis; from energy construction king and nuclear supplier J. Robert Fluor, the Reagan friend and contributor; from oilman Sam Noble, another backer of Reagan; from still another oilman and Reagan supporter, Henry Salvatori; from the Smith-Richardson Foundation of the wealthy Richardson family, yet another Reagan donor; from the funding vehicle for former Treasury Secretary William Simon, the J.M. Olin Foundation; and from the libertarian Koch Foundation; in addition to Joseph Coors's gifts.[21]

Heritage was plagued at first by dissension, frequent staff changes and a lack of credibility caused by its association with the poorly regarded extremist Coors. Once the foundation began producing its reports—on topics such as welfare, nuclear power, foreign affairs, terrorism, national health insurance, urban policy, SALT II, the Department of Energy and illegal aliens, as well as, of course, abortion—it gained some respect. The material was written from the conservative perspective, but was plausible. Staid observers like the *Foundation News* began to give it good ratings. *The New York Times* started printing its material. Heritage launched into a full program of seminars, training sessions for Capitol Hill interns and maintenance of the communications network that Weyrich had wanted. At a moment's notice, the Heritage Foundation can now send speakers around the country to discuss current affairs.

Heritage would also receive adverse publicity. The Scripps-Howard news chain would print a story in March 1978 about how the foundation had received a $46,000 federal contract for a transportation study in New Hampshire via Governor Meldrim Thomson, a Heritage associate. The U.S. Department of Commerce would investigate and would eventually force Heritage to return part of the grant. By that time, however, the foundation was well enough established to withstand the damage of such a disclosure.[22]

Weyrich next started the Committee for the Survival of a Free Congress—what *Conservative Digest* called "the heart of the operation"—in 1974 with Douglas Caddy, a former YAF director and a bit player in Watergate.[*][23] The Committee for the Survival of a Free Congress was expected to draw its support not just from the new guard of conservatives like Viguerie, Phillips and Weyrich, but also from the Old Right. By 1980, for instance, Weyrich was writing a regular weekly feature in the John Birch Society publication, the *Review of the News*.[24] As well as lobbying, CSFC oversaw election campaigns, cultivated the press and chose the issues over which conservatives should fight. Weyrich was also constantly on the watch for new single-issue groups to add to the growing conservative coalition.

Weyrich's coup de grâce was the organizing of Coalitions for America, three regular meetings of groups designed to map out conservative strategy. The way in which he arranged the conclaves

---

*The night the Watergate burglary was discovered, Caddy, who was working for the same company as E. Howard Hunt, rushed down to the jail at three o'clock in the morning to help the defendants. His appearance was inexplicable, since none of the burglars had yet made calls out of the jail. A Virginia newspaper subsequently disclosed that Caddy received $8,500 in cash from Hunt shortly after the burglary.

was particularly ingenious. Both the attendance and the agenda of the meetings were secret, but their existence was not, giving the outside world a sense of a powerful but unseen conservative presence. The Kingston Group dealt with overall electoral strategy, the Stanton Group with military policy, and the Library Court group—so named for the place where the Committee for the Survival of a Free Congress then had its offices and where the group met—with the "social issues," abortion among them. Altogether, Coalitions for America served as a forum for about 120 conservative groups, and as the vanguard for the "winning-coalition" strategy that the New Right was going to try to implement in the 1980 election.

Once the strategy was in place, the New Right needed to get together the centralized structure to make it work. Howard Phillips was to be the New Right party-builder. Phillips knew where to go to attract the kinds of conservatives he needed, right-to-lifers among them. They were not in the halls of power, in Washington or the principal seats of the professions, business or the media. They did not come from among white-collar voters. Their strength was in the heartland, in the parishes and churches that honeycombed the nation. Once having penetrated their network, Phillips believed, conservatives should capitalize on their presumed alienation from society by "organizing discontent."

Phillips' origins were like Viguerie's and Weyrich's. He grew up in Brighton, Massachusetts, a neglected section of Boston. Like its neighboring Back Bay, Brighton was fashioned from the muddy flats of the Charles River in the nineteenth century, but it never acquired the charm of the more affluent section. It has since been in perpetual transition. Today Brighton is the shifting turf of the students of Boston University on one side and the Jews of Brookline on the other. Phillips' grandfather was a Russian Jewish immigrant who drove a cab. His father lifted himself a bit further to become an insurance broker. Howard was the brainy son who went to Harvard.[25]

Also like Viguerie and Weyrich, Phillips dabbled in Republican politics as a youth. As he tells the story, one day shortly after he graduated from high school he called up the local Republican headquarters and announced, "Hello, I think I'm a Republican."[26] From that inauspicious start, he rose to be head of the Boston GOP—a post, Bostonians joke, that requires an office no bigger than a phone booth. From 1966 to 1968 Phillips worked at the Republican National Committee and then served as campaign manager for Richard

Schweiker's senatorial race. President Richard Nixon brought Phillips into the administration and in 1969 offered him the position of acting director of the Office of Economic Opportunity.

Phillips also had had a great deal of contact with the conservative movement. He had attended the founding convention of YAF at the Buckley estate and formed the first YAF chapter at Harvard. Once he got into the administration, Phillips packed the OEO office with his old YAF buddies, causing Washington wags to refer to his bailiwick as the "YAFia."

Phillips had always been an advocate of limited government. Accordingly, at OEO he hit on the idea that he is still advocating today of defunding the left by cutting back federal money. In an extraordinary show of bureaucratic self-abnegation, Phillips pushed throughout his entire three-year tenure to have his own agency abolished. Nixon was leaning in that direction when Watergate made him think better of it.

Phillips ultimately proved himself to be something of a viper in the nest. When he left OEO in disgust, he turned on Nixon and, with Viguerie, formed the short-lived Conservatives for the Removal of the President, the acronym of which was so devilishly close to that of Nixon's disgraced Committee to Re-elect the President that Phillips and Viguerie could call theirs CREEP II. [27]

In 1974, Phillips started the Conservative Caucus. *[28] Its purpose was to rally grass-roots conservatives all over the country around electoral campaigns and issues. The plan was to have coordinators in every state and a director, a caucus and a newspaper in every congressional district. The Conservative Caucus developed five publications, many of which explored congressional voting records on hot-button issues. It was active in fights against taxpayer financing of congressional campaigns, labor-law reform, the Equal Rights

---

*The first national chairman of the Caucus was Heritage associate Meldrim Thomson, the eccentric Governor of New Hampshire who while in office did such things as recommend that the National Guard be trained in nuclear weapons, proclaim "American Before U.N. Week," go on a goodwill mission to South Africa, suggest that the islands of Nantucket and Martha's Vineyard secede from Massachusetts and join his state, and lower the flags over the State House to half mast to commemorate Good Friday. Additionally, Thomson attempted to obtain the confidential tax records of some of his political opponents. Despite all this, Viguerie's *Conservative Digest* described him as "a remarkable citizen politician." The *Digest* continued: "Underneath beats the heart of a man who is so principled, so genuinely American that even his admirers can scarcely believe he is for real."

Amendment, the Strategic Arms Limitation Talks and the Panama Canal Treaty, as well as abortion. In 1976, Phillips would visit all 435 congressional districts to try to start up the chapters, according to Burton Pines's *Back to Basics*. As Phillips told Pines, "My goal was not to leave any meeting without signing up at least one volunteer to carry on."[29] Because many of his recruits were inexperienced, Phillips developed a "leadership manual" to tell them how to do everything from fund-raising to complying with the law. The manual outlines a twenty-step formula for organizing a district in precisely 153 days, with explicit daily instructions. On Day 1, for instance, the director is to "make a personal commitment to get the job done." By Day 87 the chapter will have a steering committee and the director will be announcing a meeting time and location for it. On Day 153 the director can sit back and accept "the congratulations and gratitude of all concerned."[30]

A great hulk of a man, Phillips always looks as if he could use a trip to the cleaners. With his rumpled clothes and his oily hair hanging limp on his forehead, he seems to have no time for appearances. In a routine mailing of June 1977, Phillips would express just how serious he is about his objective. "Our job," he wrote, "is not merely to slow down socialism, but to fulfill an alternative vision of America's future. Start thinking about what we should be doing when we take power."[31]

With strategy and party, the New Right could presumably go on to grab the country's reins of power. The man who was next to go into high gear in order to accomplish this was John "Terry" Dolan. Dolan was to serve as the New Right's political technician, overseeing and manipulating the elections that were supposed to bring conservative congressmen to the Capitol.

The debonaire Dolan is the youngest in the Viguerie coterie. He has been active in the conservative movement since he went to Georgetown University, graduating in 1972. Dolan's origins were more middle-class than the others. His father was the manager of a Sears, Roebuck store in the genteel New York City bedroom community of Fairfield, Connecticut. Until he joined up with the New Right, Dolan lived in the shadow of his brother, Anthony, a Pulitzer Prize–winning journalist and a speechwriter for Ronald Reagan.

Terry Dolan formed the National Conservative Political Action Committee in 1975 with two other former members of YAF, Charles

Black, onetime aide to North Carolina Senator Jesse Helms, and Roger Stone, another minor Watergate dirty-trickster. *[32] Dolan was executive director until April 1977, when he would replace Black as chairman.[33] Operating with the feisty, pugnacious spirit of its director, NCPAC was to become for a while one of the most feared political-action organizations in the country. Its style was relentlessly brash; one early NCPAC mailing warned conservatives that their tax money was going toward teaching schoolchildren that "CANNI-BALISM, WIFE-SWAPPING and MURDER of infants and the elderly are acceptable behavior." Ever pragmatic, Dolan shrugs off charges of exaggeration and with pride describes NCPAC as a "gut-cutting organization."[34]

Of all the New Right leaders, Dolan exhibits most openly their strong streak of libertarianism. "Ninety nine percent for Defense— keep America strong," he once summed up his philosophy of government, "and one percent on delivering the mail. That's it. Leave us alone."[35]

Weyrich, Phillips and Dolan all work out of modest-looking quarters. Having abandoned Library Court, Weyrich has a complex of buildings opening out onto a tiny, weed-infested courtyard across the tracks from Washington's Union Station and a short walk from Capitol Hill. Phillips is located in Vienna, Virginia, in a single-story fake-wood-front store-and-office development on a stretch of highway bristling with fast-food outlets. Dolan is crammed into a suite of rooms cluttered with unfinished mailings in a nondescript high-rise in Arlington, Virginia. All three have snapshots of each other adorning the walls, and, inevitably, a photograph of Richard Viguerie.

By 1975, the time seemed right for a definite move for all these ready, willing and able conservatives. Watergate had put the Republican Party on the defensive, and the sitting GOP President had resigned in disgrace. *National Review* publisher William Rusher raised the possibility of a third-party candidacy in his barely disguised

---

*Stone implemented the plan to head off the presidential primary challenge of California Republican Congressman Pete McCloskey by giving a contribution to the McCloskey campaign in the name of the Young Socialist Alliance and then informing the right-wing editor of the *Manchester Union-Leader*, William Loeb. Loeb dutifully printed the hoax in one of his famous vituperative front-page columns.

conservative manifesto, *The Making of a New Majority Party*. Rusher asserted that the country now had enough disgruntled conservatives from both parties to win the presidential election or at least make a good stab at it. Rusher based this thesis on two things: the results of recent public-opinion polls and the work of a bright young Nixon administration official, Kevin Phillips (no relation to Howard Phillips).

Rusher claimed, quoting figures from Gallup Poll tallies, that 26 percent of the American people considered themselves liberal and 38 percent conservative. If the remaining undecideds were divided up according to the relative percentages shown by those who did declare themselves, that meant that 59 percent of the American people were conservatives, Rusher reasoned. His methodology may have been a bit suspect, but Rusher argued anyway that such a huge number of conservatives could easily dominate the country.

Rusher also relied heavily on the analysis of Kevin Phillips. Phillips had laboriously studied all the election results since 1928, concluding that traditionally Democratic voters, especially those whites in the suburban South, Southwest and southern California and ethnic whites in the inner cities, were gradually switching to the GOP. If they were not actually changing their registration, Phillips observed, at least they were voting the Republican Party line. Phillips reasoned that by targeting these voters the Republicans could win back the Presidency. Although he denied it, his idea had been the foundation for Richard Nixon's tooled-up version of Goldwater's Southern Strategy, for which Phillips had been subsequently rewarded with employment in the Nixon Justice Department.

Kevin Phillips had put a place and a face to the Silent Majority, which Rusher felt could be diverted from its flirtations with the GOP into a third-party effort. Borrowing a phrase from William Butler Yeats popular at the time, Rusher said of conservatism that "such a movement has been on the very verge of success in this country for at least fifteen years—slouching around Bethlehem, as it were, trying to be born."[36]

The imagery indicated just how strongly conservatives felt about the man whom Rusher's book goes on to promote as the perfect conservative candidate for a third-party run for President, Ronald Reagan. Reagan had been the secret savior of the conservatives since the night of October 27, 1964, when he had delivered a half-hour

speech on national television to boost Goldwater's bid in the primaries. The Speech, as it came to be called, was the standard stuff
of right-wing rhetoric, but it was given in a manner so appealing
that conservatives were profoundly touched. Reagan had made the
Speech apocalyptic in tone. "You and I have a rendezvous with
destiny," he told the television audience in conclusion. "We'll preserve for our children this, the last best hope of man on earth, or
we'll sentence them to take the last step in a thousand years of
darkness." Richard Viguerie many years later claimed he was "elec-
trified" by it.

Early in 1975, Rusher began making regular trips to Los Angeles
to discuss with Reagan the possibility of his running as a third-party
candidate in 1976. Rusher suggested Clifton White as manager of
the campaign. Reagan seemed hesitant about the offer, using what
appeared to be an excuse that White had too many enemies. In-
tensifying his effort, Rusher sent Reagan a copy of his book in galley
form. Reagan shied away from making any commitment.

Rusher was not alone in his hopes. Richard Viguerie, Howard
Phillips and Kevin Phillips were having similar thoughts. In the
summer of the same year, they rented a suite at the Madison Hotel
in Washington and asked Reagan to join them for a conservative
summit conference. Their pitch, adapted from Kevin Phillips' analysis, was that Reagan as an independent could hope to receive as
much as 30 to 35 percent of the vote and possibly could even win
the election. They pointed out that, no matter what happened, it
was a no-lose situation. If he wasn't elected, Reagan would give
such credibility to the conservative movement that either he or
another conservative could try again in 1980.

Apparently Reagan did not believe them. Acting the Republican
rather than the conservative, Reagan was more interested in building
what was then being called a new second party, a post-Watergate
GOP revitalized around conservative concerns. The California Governor gave Viguerie and his colleagues a blunt no.[37]

His refusal sent Viguerie into the eager, awaiting arms of Alabama
Governor George Wallace. Wallace, of course, in addition to his
support among Southern segregationists, was becoming by default
the heir apparent to a significant portion of the Silent Majority. For
his presidential run, Wallace wanted Richard Viguerie for the names
in his computer, but Viguerie just as fervently wanted Wallace for

the names in *his* computer. Altogether, Viguerie claims he raised about $7 million for Wallace between 1973 and 1976.[38] Of more significance, Viguerie began to tap into the diehard segregationist sentiment and incorporate its believers into his regular mailings. Many observers noticed that Wallace softened up the South again for conservative Republicanism. Few realized that, with the help of Wallace, Viguerie was systematically bringing into the conservative network the governor's fundamentalist following.

This tendency accelerated when Viguerie picked up another Old South client, the astute Jesse Helms. This ultraconservative North Carolina Republican had first gotten into politics in 1951, when he enlisted in the congressional-election drive of Willis Smith—what has been called the meanest campaign in the state's history. Smith was chairman of Duke University's trustees, and his opponent, Frank Graham, was the president of the University of North Carolina. At the eleventh hour, the state was flooded with pamphlets entitled "White People Wake Up" suggesting that Graham was pro-black. Helms claimed later that he didn't have much to do with the Smith campaign, but others said he had a major part in developing the strategy. Smith did win, and he hired Helms as his administrative assistant. When Helms left that post he returned to North Carolina to head up the state's bankers' association, and then became the editorial voice for the Raleigh television station WRAL.

Helms ran successfully for the Senate in 1972, accumulating a $150,000 debt. He decided to retire it by creating what amounted to a full-time conservative banking operation, the Congressional Club[39] run by his former campaign manager, Tom Ellis.[*40] Viguerie and Ellis joined forces to raise $7.5 million for Helms' reelection. Helms was subsequently to put together a number of organizations, operating out of his office, that would later help right-to-life forces, among them the American Family Institute, funded, interestingly, by money again from brewers.[†41]

It was nearing the end of the decade. Reagan and Wallace having

---

*Ellis was a onetime director of the Pioneer Fund, a research outfit that justified its existence by exploring the dubious proposition that blacks are genetically inferior to whites.

†According to foundation records, AFI specifically got donations from the DeRance Foundation, the same Miller Beer fortune that capitalizes Father Paul Marx, and the Adolph Coors Foundation.

failed them for the time, conservatives returned to the gentler waters of the GOP, now more clear than ever on what they had to do. By this time, Viguerie and his colleagues had a bewilderingly complex network of associations that they could use even more effectively than he had used the old URA to bully the GOP into line. Viguerie's own massive multimillion-dollar operation was the constituent data bank; Weyrich's Committee for the Survival of a Free Congress was the information and strategy center; Phillips' Conservative Caucus was the proto-party; and Dolan's National Conservative Political Action Committee was the electoral apparatus. It all came to look curiously like a national political machine. The feminists had even provided them with an issue, abortion, upon which Viguerie was more than ready to seize. All that were missing were the people. That's where Mr. and Mrs. Anti-Abortion America came in. Enter Paul and Judie Brown.

The story of the putsch in which Richard Viguerie and the others gained influence over the right-to-life movement began with Paul and Judie Brown. The Browns were ideally suited to the role. Both were Catholic and committed to stopping abortion. Both were politically sophisticated enough to pursue appropriate tactics and leave the inappropriate alone. Perhaps most important, they were both affable, easygoing types who could without too much trouble relate to the grass roots. Judie especially could rouse the troops, and Paul on occasion could tell a good joke. Their only shortcoming was that at times both of them could be just a little too eager.

Paul Brown grew up in Greenfield, Massachusetts, a small town in the western part of the state. Paul jokes of his political background, "I wasn't allowed to say the word 'Republican' until I was thirty-six years old."

Judie Brown comes from California and has always been a self-described conservative. As a girl, she worked in Los Angeles in the Goldwater campaign, and she joined the Young Republicans about the time that YAF was making a bid for its control. Judie says that her right-to-life tendencies come equally from her conservatism and her Catholicism.[42]

The Browns met while he was an employee in a Kresge department store when she, the company auditor, told him to punch a time

card. He told her to go to hell. It is characteristic of both of them.
Judie is clearly a manager, and he brags about being a male chau-
vinist. She brushes his hair, shines his shoes and fetches his coffee.
She is proud to proclaim him the dominant one of the relationship.
His response: "When I have permission."

Paul and Judie came into the movement together and early, and
outlasted many of the more fair-weather couples, their persistence
eventually earning them their title of Mr. and Mrs. Anti-Abortion
America.[43] They first got involved when they were living in Seattle.
They had been married barely a year and a half, and Judie was
pregnant with their first child. In 1968 the city had an abortion-
law-repeal movement. Inspired by a sermon at their church about
the law, the Browns passed out literature and worked with other
right-to-lifers to defeat the initiative, but they lost.

Paul was working at the time as a store manager and was transferred
from place to place. When they eventually moved to Ohio, Judie
joined the state right-to-life group. In 1976, the Ohio Right to Life
decided to send one person from each congressional district to Washington for the annual March for Life. Judie was chosen to go. The
visit convinced her that the action in the right-to-life movement was
in the capital, and she decided she'd like to move to Washington.
Paul was not excited by the idea, but fortuitously he got offered a
position there, and they moved.

Judie moved up through the ranks of the National Right to Life
Committee to become indispensable. Her management experience
with Kresge had given her skills that the organization badly lacked.
She had joined NRLC just in time for the 1976 elections, and she
realized then the organization's weakness. "Calls were coming into
our office every day about politics," she recalled in a joint interview
with her husband in 1981. "The National Right to Life at that time
had no involvement in politics whatsoever, and so we had to say,
'We can't tell you who to vote for. All we can tell you is their
positions.' It was just terrible."

After years of toying with the idea, Paul decided to get involved,
too. He was among the first within the right-to-life movement to
contend that they would never get anywhere until they started in-
fluencing elections. With Robert Sassone, the population analyst,
Paul formed the Life Amendment Political Action Committee
(LAPAC). Paul has high regard for Sassone, calling him "a walking

genius." Indeed, before the 1978 election Sassone did put together a prospectus that laid out an analysis of the political situation and a strategy for changing Congress that, although roughly drafted, made some sense. Sassone elaborated on the basic thesis: a small number of militant organizers could shift about 5 percent of the vote in a carefully chosen congressional district, largely by catalyzing nonvoters, and win what otherwise would have been a close election. "[Y]ou may feel that our chance of changing Congress," Sassone wrote in his inimitable style,

> is about the same as that of an insect defeating the human in a fair fight. Let's not forget that more humans who have died during human history have died probably as a result of the bite of just one (1) insect, than from any other cause. We have a substantial chance of winning... What we have to do is examine the adversary and determine what his weaknesses are and then apply our strength against his weakness. This is the type of tactic that has made the leading cause of human deaths during practically all of history to be malaria, which is spread by the bite of a single mosquito.

Sassone's imputation of intellectual prowess to the mosquito notwithstanding, he went on with some accuracy to describe the kinds of races right-to-lifers should target. Ignore races where the prochoice candidate was likely to win by a landslide, he advised, and those where right-to-lifers had no competition. Instead adopt an incumbent congressman elsewhere and raise money to help his constituents defeat him. Soften up an unbeatable candidate for a later campaign by harassment. "Anything you can do to give him bad publicity would be helpful," Sassone counseled. Most important of all, concentrate on those races in which victory was possible.[44]

Despite all the good advice, LAPAC did not get off to a good start. In an effort to raise money, Brown tried to use a $1,000 seed grant to put on a benefit concert at the Kennedy Center in Washington. He had lined up Joe Fraser, José Feliciano and the three "Charlie's Angels" to appear. Shortly before the event was supposed to take place, Brown got a call from the producer of *Charlie's Angels*, who was furious. The producer apparently didn't know anything about his three beauties showing up at any right-to-life concert. "It turned out that the Charlie's Angels we had were three bimbos who had nothing to do with the show," Brown, wincing, described the error later. LAPAC had to send out retractions of all its advance publicity. Rona Barrett quickly picked up the story and embarrassed the new organization before it even got off the ground. "I learned one thing very fast," Brown concluded. "Stay out of show business. Stick with politics."

Along with its initial fumblings, LAPAC began developing an intense rivalry with the National Right to Life Committee, a conflict exacerbated by NRLC's internal problems and the Browns' part in them. Judie had come in under the presidency of Mildred Jefferson, and remained loyal to her even after she left under a cloud; Paul had been Jefferson's second in the battle with the board.

It was during the tenure of Mildred Jefferson at the National Right to Life Committee that Paul Weyrich at the Committee for the Survival of a Free Congress invited the Browns to start attending some of the regular weekly meetings of the Library Court, the group that discussed strategies concerning the "social issues." Among those also coming to the meetings, according to Judie Brown, were representatives of the Heritage Foundation, the Viguerie Company, Young Americans for Freedom, and several congressmen. Altogether, there were about 50 groups. They exchanged information, coordinated lobbying efforts and planned out campaigns. From Library Court, Judie Brown learned her first New Right lesson. "It was very important to build coalitions with other organizations," she explained in the interview. "You become much more effective when you share information and become involved legislatively with other organizations that agree with you in principle, even if they are not involved in the same issue. For example, the National Rifle Association is not involved in abortion, but if something comes up like the lobby-disclosure bill, it could have actually destroyed us both."

Jefferson may have also realized at the time that the New Right had access to a great deal more money than the perpetually wanting National Right to Life Committee. Whatever her motivation, she and Judie Brown saw eye to eye on the necessity for continuing the connection. Mildred Jefferson, a good deal smarter than most people gave her credit for being, had set up Judie Brown so that she could be a conservative fifth column within the right-to-life movement.

Once Jefferson was gone, Judie's remaining time at the NRLC was unhappy. She became increasingly disturbed about NRLC's method of operation and its policies. Along with its petty jealousies, the fifty-member board was so large as to be unwieldy, taking months and sometimes years to make decisions. NRLC also refused to take positions on anything other than abortion. Judie wanted to examine the possibility of starting a campaign against Planned Parenthood, taking a position against what she calls abortifacient contraceptives like the pill and the IUD, engaging in the debate about sex education and exploring religious questions. Worse still, the NRLC's financial troubles were becoming legion. To help out, Judie offered to cut her salary in half. Instead of graciously accepting, the board drew up an order demanding the cut, without her even being present. It got so bad that Judie came home every night in tears.

About this time, Paul got a call from a prominent conservative—he won't say which one—who was interested in starting a conservative right-to-life organization. Paul and Judie decided that she would be a natural to help him out. They moved LAPAC into the two-story frame house just vacated by Paul Weyrich's Committee for the Survival of a Free Congress in the alleyway called Library Court, a short walk from the Capitol. In time, Judie started American Life Lobby (ALL). Paul Weyrich advised them both on targeting electoral campaigns and planning strategy; Richard Viguerie gave the help of his now massive computer list. By the spring of 1981 Judie would be claiming 68,000 subscribers to her newsletter and liaison with four thousand groups.

Both Paul and Judie recognized their debt to the New Right. "I credit a lot of the success of our operation," Paul Brown admitted readily, "to Richard Viguerie and Paul Weyrich." The New Right may not always have been so happy, however, with the Browns.

Paul Brown had always had the distinct drawback as a public spokesman of speaking and acting quickly and often without thinking. One of his more injudicious comments involved Karen Mulhauser, the former head of the pro-choice National Abortion Rights Action League, LAPAC's archrival. During a hearing on Capitol Hill, Mulhauser mentioned that she had been raped, an admission that stunned the congressmen present and figured prominently in media accounts of the testimony. Not to be outdone, Paul Brown countered by proposing that Mulhauser had made the story up. As he explained his preposterous assertion in an interview, "Karen Mulhauser said she had been raped. We are skeptical of that claim to start with. It strikes me as a personal-convenience-type rape. It happened while she was testifying on the Hill on the issue of rape. She proudly tells the story on national television. And we can document time after time when all abortionists have been caught in lie after lie. So we feel we had a legitimate reason to doubt the veracity of her story."[45] Brown couldn't even stop there. He gratuitously told a *New York* magazine reporter, "Well, let me tell you, Karen is not the most beautiful creature in the world, so when I hear her say she was raped, my response is, 'You wish!'"[46] *Time* magazine reprinted the story, to the shock of the right-to-life movement.

This was only a first sign of what would become a habit of making serious and damaging mistakes.

Abortion suddenly became the right's issue, and what an issue it was. As the bottom-line demand of the women's movement, it was a quick and easy symbol for sexual permissiveness and feminism, and opposition to it signaled uneasiness about the whole feminist agenda. It was a Catholic issue, theoretically capable of mobilizing those millions of voters. It was a moral issue, giving conservatives that human dimension they so often seemed to lack. It had a fanatic following who had already demonstrated their capacity to work tirelessly. It was definitely the kind of issue that people could rally around.

Richard Viguerie also recognized its potential for being for conservatives what opposition to the war in Vietnam had been for liberals, a hook to acquaint them with a whole new world view. At a workshop in political organizing put on by Paul and Judie Brown for conservative right-to-lifers, Viguerie presented the hypothetical case of an imaginary man who had never before been involved in any kind of political activity. Suddenly, his life changes. As Viguerie described it, larding the account with his own interpretation of the facts, the Supreme Court abortion decision, permitting "deformed infants" to be "put to sleep with their parents' consent," disturbs the imaginary man. After hoping that his concern would go away, he realizes that he feels the compulsion to do something about it. For the first time in his life, he joins a political group. With other political neophytes like himself, he tries to change the law. Gradually his group's purview enlarges until the imaginary man and his fellow anti-abortion activists become interested in a wider variety of issues. "They discovered," Viguerie explained to his audience, "that abortion was only one front in a bigger war against family, religions and many traditions they hold valuable and dear."[47] Epiphanies like that of the imaginary man and his group, Viguerie maintained, were the stuff of the New Right's ascendancy.

One measure of Viguerie's organizing skill was the speed with which the Old Right—or at least some of them—accepted the new line. William F. Buckley, for instance, came around fast. Buckley's position was that the Supreme Court had overstepped its bounds as the highest court in the land by becoming an arbiter of moral authority, with its abortion decision being a particularly egregious example. Buckley may have been influenced by his brother James, an original sponsor of the Human Life Amendment, and by his colleague *National Review* co-publisher James McFadden, who had become quite an activist on the issue. McFadden had organized a right-to-life lobbying outfit on Capitol Hill, the Ad Hoc Committee in Defense of Life; a scholarly quarterly, *The Human Life Review*; and a biweekly newsletter, *Lifeletter*. Equally compelling may have been the rising chorus of voices condemning government payment for abortion. Some other old-guard conservatives like Barry Goldwater, continuing to believe that the Supreme Court's word was sacrosanct, never did accept the anti-abortion line. William Buckley, however, became a frequent contributor to the debate.

Another measure of the success of Viguerie and his cohorts was the facility with which they began to influence the original right-to-life organizations—or at least some of them. It was as if they had been waiting for someone like Richard Viguerie to happen along.

This did not occur immediately, however. Some members of the National Right to Life Committee accused the Browns of stealing their membership lists. Judie hotly denies it. "Richard would have loved it," she asserted in the interview. "At least it could have given us something to start with. As it was, we had nothing." If anything, the Browns claim, Jack Willke tried to take them over. Paul Brown tells the story of how at one point LAPAC needed to raise some money quickly and approached NRLC for its lists. Willke agreed, on the condition that NRLC be allowed to put enough members on LAPAC's board of directors to give the NRLC contingent a decisive vote. "Well," explained Paul, "Judie and Mildred don't fight back. I do. I try to stay a step ahead of people." What he did was change the bylaws to require a larger majority to win a vote. He got the list, and NRLC got nothing.[48]

The skirmishes continued, but a funny thing began to happen. As Willke and the others at the National Right to Life Committee watched the New Right pile up victories, they started realizing that Viguerie and his political operatives might have something going for them. While fiercely guarding their own organizational base, Willke and the rest began to copy the New Right analysis and tactics, eventually adopting the political methodology wholesale. New Right and right-to-life became less distinguishable, with the consequence that the one began to be able to speak for the other. That was all Viguerie needed.

The putsch having succeeded, Richard Viguerie and his colleagues went on to their next challenge: tapping into the growing fundamentalist movement. These were people naturally even more inclined toward conservatism than the Catholics, and they provided an ever larger potential constituent base. The only difficulty with them was that they were not accustomed to participating in the political process. The New Right had to get them to spread the word while they were spreading the Word. Central to this was introducing the fundamentalists to the issue of abortion.

VII.

The Unborn and
the Born Again

"Do you really have to go?" Ed McAteer's wife asked anxiously. It was bitter cold outside. Snow was falling all over the Middle Atlantic States, even as far south as the capital, and farther. The freak storm might make the flight dangerous. Besides, she pleaded, business could always wait.

McAteer didn't like to alarm his wife, but he had no choice on this one. He hadn't spent the better part of his adult life peddling Bibles for nothing. He just couldn't miss the fateful first encounter of New Right political operatives Paul Weyrich and Howard Phillips and up-and-coming preacher the Reverend Jerry Falwell, particularly since he, McAteer, had arranged it,

"I've got to go," McAteer announced with finality.

As it turned out, his wife had been right. The snow was so bad that McAteer's plane couldn't make it all the way to Lynchburg, Virginia, Falwell's home, and McAteer had to rent a car to drive the rest of the way. Even after a night of howling winds, the storm still had not let up. At five o'clock the next morning, he got a call from Howard Phillips, who was also reconsidering.

"Ed, do you think it's necessary that I come?" Phillips asked.

McAteer and Phillips were old friends, so McAteer felt he could be frank. "Howard," McAteer replied gravely, "I think it's absolutely essential." He then repeated the ground rules of the meeting. Falwell, he reminded Phillips, was a very busy man. He didn't have time for chitchat. "Howard, you've got just one hour. You have to have your barrels loaded. You make sure that you fire right."

They were scheduled to talk over lunch. When the time came, Phillips was so concerned about getting his message across that he wolfed down his salad and then apologetically started the pitch. Before he had gotten more than a few words out, Falwell interrupted him. "Wait a minute," the preacher told the nervous Phillips. "This is the most important thing I'll do today." Falwell apparently meant it. The meeting lasted until nine o'clock that evening. Out of it came the idea for the Moral Majority, the single most crucial entity since the Catholic Church to making the right-to-life movement a dangerous force on the right. It was at that meeting that the New Right, through go-between Ed McAteer, introduced to future Moral Majority leader Jerry Falwell the issue of abortion.[1]

It was January 1979. The country had been experiencing for about a decade a revival of fundamentalist Protestantism. Independent preachers like Falwell were springing up all over the nation, attracting huge followings. As had happened a hundred years earlier, these ultrareligious Christians, at the instigation of the preachers, were suddenly becoming interested in politics for the first time in their lives. Fundamentalism was, moreover, catching the attention of right-wing ideologues with a lot of money, some of whom were bankrolling their own personalized preachers and using the occasion of the religious awakening to try to institute their own brand of politics. It was their understanding that the United States was actually meant to be a Christian Republic, and the born-again bankrollers, some of them among the richest men in the world, wanted to do everything possible to make that come about.

The New Right political operatives had perceived in the revival a way to help bring about the conservative voting majority they were seeking. By combining the right-to-life movement and all its committed Catholics with the growing legions of fundamentalist believers, the New Right politicos believed that they could form the most potent voting block since the creation of the New Deal coalition.

To that end, Richard Viguerie and his ilk essentially wrote the book by which the preachers and their evangelical followers entered the political scene. New Right leaders encouraged the preacher politicians to enter politics and drew them into over-arching organizations with a religious name but an explicitly political focus. New Right leaders met with the preachers on a regular basis, joined the boards of directors of their ministries and invited them onto their own lay boards. New Right leaders gave the preachers advice and a workable plan to win elections. However heartfelt, opposition to abortion was simply part of the plan.

Similarly, the large and growing evangelical constituency was appealing to the right-to-life movement. For the largely Catholic following, fundamentalists were another breed altogether, but they offered a couple of very important things. They had access to phenomenal resources, the kind of ready cash that the typical right-to-life activist had never even imagined. They had media exposure over their multimillion-dollar cable network. Moreover, they offered release from the still-insistent criticism that the Catholic Church controlled the movement. As time went on, however, the movement to bring about a Christian Republic would acquire greater and greater importance and visibility until the original goals of the right-to-lifers involved in it would almost be subsumed by the idea.

The modern-day movement for the Christian Republic actually began in 1974, the year before the Catholic bishops got involved in the politics of abortion. That was also the year that Rus Walton, an ultraconservative syndicated columnist and a participant in the presidential campaigns of Barry Goldwater and Ronald Reagan, published a book called *One Nation Under God*. Walton's thesis was much like that of the nineteenth-century National Reform Association, but slightly updated. Walton claimed that the most important historical event since the appearance of Jesus Christ was "the founding of this Republic under the Constitution, because it provided the standard form of right for government." Walton further asserted that the "Constitution was designed to perpetuate a Christian order" and that the country's free-enterprise system was just as surely a "Christian Idea," being part and parcel of the Christian notion of "stewardship." The current crisis in the United States Walton attributed to the fact that "this nation is now more of a democracy than it is a republic." According to Walton, the solution was the adoption of an entire prefabricated program, essentially the classic conservative line: less government, lower taxes, a balanced budget, increased military spending, renewed anti-Communism, and withdrawal from the United Nations. In order to bring about a new order, fundamentalist Christians would have to elect other fundamentalist Christians to office.[2]

In June of that year, a group calling itself Third Century Publishers convened a secret meeting in Washington, D.C., to help elect "the right kind of Christians" to public office. Third Century Publishers was a new outfit that put out evangelical Christian books, most prominent among them *One Nation Under God*. Attending the meeting were Walton, Richard DeVos, president of the Amway Corporation, Arizona Republican Congressman John Conlan and about twenty or so other wealthy conservative lawyers and businessmen, as well as some evangelical Protestant activists. In addition to airing the idea of creating the Christian Republic by getting out the vote, the organizers were asking for money. Ten of those present agreed to give $25,000 apiece toward the Third Century Fund.

Interestingly, in these early days, abortion was not on the roster. When Third Century published one of its first lists of issues for fundamentalists to consider, busing and coed gymnasiums did appear, but abortion did not.

Barely a year later, Third Century held an organizing seminar to train those who were being recruited as regional directors for the effort. According to the account of a former FBI agent and theological-seminary director, Dick Laine, who was there, the meeting gave extremely specific instructions on how to go about doing the work. First, the regional directors were supposed to recruit and manage a team of representatives from each congressional district who would develop home study programs. The home study approach was a natural for evangelical Protestants, who participated in this kind of thing as part of their worship all the time. The purpose of the study was to teach them the basics of political organizing and imbue them with the political philosophy necessary to proselytize for "Christian candidates." One of the tools the regional directors was to use was a home study kit complete with Rus Walton's *One Nation Under God*.

Laine's report revealed that the meeting also included specific instructions on how to evaluate who were the appropriate Christians to organize. One of the participants suggested that the regional directors screen potential recruits by asking two questions. The first was "Do you feel Christians should get involved in politics and government?" The follow-up was "How do you feel about Nelson Rockefeller or Ronald Reagan as presidential candidates?" If the person leaned toward Rockefeller, the attempt at recruitment was terminated with some vague reference to getting together at some later date. Those who favored Reagan were signed up immediately.

At the time, Richard DeVos was one of the principal bankrollers of the new organization, and a likely leadership figure at that. His company, Amway, markets household products in much the same way as is done with the better-known Avon cosmetics or Tupperware. Amway, which stands for the American Way, has assumed a place in the nation even larger than its substantial sales warrant. This is on account of the outside activities of DeVos, president, and his high-school buddy Jay Van Andel, chairman of the board. The historian of the two, DeVos has narrated a twenty-seven-minute film, available through the Amway Free Enterprise Institute, on the virtues of capitalism. Called "Man's Material Welfare," the film explores DeVos's own theorem, $MMW = NR + HE \times T$, or man's material welfare equals natural resources plus human energy multiplied by tools. According to the promotional literature describing it, the film goes on to feature DeVos himself discussing another of his original ideas. DeVos sees all civilizations progressing through an immutable cycle: "Bondage—to Spiritual Faith—to Courage—to Liberty—to Abundance—to Selfishness—to Complacency—to Apathy—to Dependency—to Bondage." The challenge for the United States, he asserts, is to break the cycle. Obviously, the theorem and the theory would be laughable if DeVos weren't deadly serious about the whole thing. This and other similar Amway films are available to schools or corporations for a modest fee.[3]

It is Jay Van Andel, however, chairman of the board and chief executive officer, who has given a name to what these entrepreneurs see as in their best personal and professional interests: the establishment of the Christian Republic. Van Andel travels widely and lectures to audiences all over the country, expanding on the DeVos thesis. In a typical speech given in 1981 as part of the Ludwig von Mises Lecture Series at the conservative Hillsdale College, of which he is a trustee, the white-maned Van Andel extolled individual initiative, free enterprise and the American way in general, and then expounded upon the ethical system under which he thought they had to exist. "A free society," Van Andel asserted, "is competitive, because human beings are not born with equal abilities and do not develop equal motivation." By contrast, an "egalitarian society" reduces its people to their "lowest level of achievement" and takes wealth from the producers and transfers it to "those who've not earned it." The free society can coexist with neither Communism nor Socialism, but only Christianity, Van Andel continued. The lesson, therefore, is that American economic strength will falter in an apocalyptic "day of judgment," Van Andel warned, unless society returns to what he calls the "Christian Consensus."[4]

Van Andel's personal worth was estimated by *Fortune* at about $300–500 million,[5] and DeVos, judging by his beneficence, is not far behind. With their growing wealth, both DeVos and Van Andel have assumed prominence within the American business and political community. In 1978, Van Andel started the Citizens Choice program of the United States Chamber of Commerce, designed to cultivate pro-business candidates; his partner Richard DeVos was active in both the National Association of Manufacturers and the closely related Business-Industry Political Action Committee (BI-PAC). Van Andel subsequently became the Chamber's chairman of the board, and DeVos the head of the Republican Party Finance Committee.

If DeVos was the link with the business world, Third Century's contact with politics was two-term Congressman John Conlan. Son of major-league umpire Jocko Conlan, John Conlan represented the Four Corners area of Arizona, embracing everything from the Navajo Indian reservations in the northeast to the posh suburbs of Phoenix farther south. He first won the seat in 1972 in a fierce contest in which, according to *The Almanac of American Politics*, the two contenders spent $500,000, the most expensive congressional race up until that time. In his reelection campaign, Conlan received the support of Billy Graham, but gained the ire of another old-time conservative in a conflict that presaged later similar scuffles. When Barry Goldwater endorsed his opponent, Conlan remarked of the senior Senator from Arizona, "Maybe it's the pain, maybe it's the drinking he's been doing."[6]

Conlan had been involved in fundamentalist affairs for years, doing speaking engagements all over the country and drawing together wealthy businessmen to give donations. Conlan's contribution to the evangelical debate was the notion that the official religion of the country was coming to be "humanism" or "secularism" rather than Christianity. This pernicious philosophy, Conlan contended, was slowly encroaching on many aspects of American life, but especially the media and the schools. The most extreme form of secular humanism was found in big government and Communism. The world was now engaged in a Manichean struggle between Christianity and secular humanism, Conlan concluded, a conflict that was reflected in the United States Congress.

"The House of Representatives," Conlan told an audience in 1975 in a typically hyperbolic speech reprinted in the Campus Crusade for Christ newsletter, *Worldwide Challenge,* "which is composed of 435 members, is controlled by a single majority of 218. Those 218 people can determine who sits on what committee and who is chairman—in other words, the direction of all legislation. At this time, there are at least 218 people in the House who follow in some degree the secular humanist philosophy which is so dangerous to our future. Similar conditions are true among the 100 members of the Senate."[7]

At the meeting described by the former FBI agent Laine, Conlan apparently elaborated to the fledgling converts on some further qualifications for political office beyond being a good Christian. The names of former Iowa Senator Harold Hughes and Oregon Senator Mark Hatfield, both devout evangelicals, had come up because of their prominence in national affairs. Conlan reportedly informed the recruits in no uncertain terms, "No, these are not the kind of people we want in government. We don't even want them to know what's going on."

The chief organizer of Third Century was Bill Bright, head of Campus Crusade for Christ International and a friend of Conlan's for fifteen years. The Campus Crusade had been around since 1951, started by Bright and his wife, Vonette, as a student ministry on the campus of the University of California at Los Angeles. Bright stressed the concept of "aggressive evangelism," which means putting into action "Four Spiritual Laws." The "Laws" emphasize God's love and plan for His people; the sinfulness of men and women; the possibility of reconciliation through Jesus Christ; and the need for personal faith to achieve salvation. The Campus Crusade, in addition to the classic evangelical ministry, included the Agape movement, a sort of overseas Christian peace corps, and Athletes in Action, a fellowship of athletes committed to aggressive evangelism.[8] In the mid-1960s, a message hit Bright with a terrible urgency. He felt that the nation was facing a grave crisis and that unless there were "a miracle of God" by the end of 1976 "we will have reached the point of no return and in a few years we will lose our freedom." He expected that if, on the contrary, the gospel did get spread throughout the United States, the country's full salvation would be realized by 1980.

The mission through which he intended to fulfill the plan was Here's Life, America!, a massive evangelistic campaign for the country and eventually the world. The goal was to train five million Christians from fifty thousand local churches to carry out three-week saturation campaigns in every major city. The slogan of the campaign was "I found it! You can find it too!" which would go on billboards, radio and TV followed by a telephone number to call. Individuals who contacted Here's Life, America! would be trained from the various cooperating churches and given the appropriate religious materials. The pilot program for Here's Life, America! was launched in Atlanta in 1975. Similar campaigns followed in eighteen cities the following year, with plans for the strategy to be implemented all over the country. Bright's original goal was to raise $100 million, $35 million of which was targeted directly for Here's Life, America! and raised locally, and the rest of which was supposed to go toward similar efforts overseas.

Bright has always played a low-key role. He refused early on to acknowledge to curious reporters that his was really a political movement. In 1976 he told the liberal Protestant evangelical magazine *Sojourners*, "Campus Crusade is not political—in twenty-five years it never has been." With prodding he admitted, "I am involved in getting Christians involved in good government." He was a little more candid with his own Campus Crusade publication *Worldwide Challenge* that same year, setting forth an agenda of sorts that echoed Conlan's line:

> Part of the great spiritual awakening is a plan to help bring Christ back into government. There are 435 congressional districts, and I think Christians can capture many of them by next November.

> The reason that we have not done it in the past is that Christians
> have never gotten together, though Christians represent the ma-
> jority of our population. Every group is organized, and I'm un-
> ashamedly saying to Christians, "Let's get involved."

Bright also set up a mission in Washington called the Christian
Embassy that was thought to be a central office for the plan to back
and assist candidates.

About the same time that Bright went into action, Richard DeVos
was becoming involved with the Christian Freedom Foundation,
also an old-time group. This had been founded in 1950 as a forum
for right-wing economics with a Christian flair. By the midseventies
the foundation was floundering philosophically and was almost bank-
rupt. DeVos proposed a reorganization, new board members and
hefty financial support if he and the other backers could change the
purpose of the organization. What they really had in mind was an
administrative and tax-exempt fund-raising vehicle for the Third
Century political campaign. The regional directors of Third Century
by fiat became regional directors of the Christian Freedom Foundation; later their title was changed to "consultant," and they were
also encouraged to do consulting work for the various businesses
fronting money for the organizing.

The men involved in Third Century, Campus Crusade for Christ
and its Here's Life, America! program, and the Christian Freedom
Foundation maintained that there were no organizational links between them. However, the boards of the four shared interlocking
directors. Philadelphia's National Liberty Insurance head Art De
Moss, one of the directors of both Campus Crusade and the Christian
Freedom Foundation, admitted that the ties among them were all
so knotted that he couldn't always remember under which auspices
he had attended meetings and participated in evangelical politicking.
"There is so much mutual interest and overlap between people, in
Campus Crusade for Christ, the Christian Embassy, Third Century
Publishers and the Christian Freedom Foundation," De Moss ob-
served, "that it is very hard for me to keep it all straight."[9]

By May 1977, Bright claimed to have reached at least 60 percent
of the American population with Here's Life, America! by having
had his missionaries visit 165 cities. Altogether, some seven million
personal contacts were supposed to have been made, with 550,000

people expressing an interest in accepting Jesus Christ as their personal savior. Not all of this was quite as effective as the numbers suggested, however. A study by Win Arn of the Institute of American Church Growth, in Arcadia, California, showed that in the two cities of Indianapolis and Fresno, of 29,000 phone calls made for Here's Life, America, 1,665 people received Christ, but only 101 ble study course and subse- 2 percent success rate.[10]

t have made many converts, Campus Crusade, the Christian Embassy did have some ed elect Dr. Ron Paul in a wenty-second Congressional side of Houston, prime Sun r and physician, Republican ian in Congress and one of the gold standard. So con- ted in and out of office, his 1978, for example, of about was he that his 1980 rating olitical Education would be of Businessmen rating 100

Reverend Robert Thoburn, compasses Alexandria, Virashington, D.C. Also archentalist Christian school to ie both send their children. not only was he born again Unlike Paul, Thoburn never

supported was Frank Wolf, the Interior and lobbyist. A d of Rus Walton's and was He aspired to represent the and its surrounding suburbs. Wolf would run three times before he finally succeeded in 1980.

A fourth was the Reverend Robert Billings, then the president of Hyles-Anderson College, an evangelical school in Hammond, Indiana, prime Bible Belt country. Billings started out as a missionary in the Bahamas. After being approached by the Third Century group, he attempted a run for Congress from his Indiana district. Although he didn't make it, Billings went on to have a successful career on the religious right, acting as treasurer of the Free Congress Research and Education Foundation, an offshoot of Paul Weyrich's Committee for the Survival of a Free Congress; helping Terry Dolan start the National Conservative Political Action Committee; and giving the Moral Majority its first office space in a brownstone on Capitol Hill.[13] Eventually, Billings would make it to the White House as special liaison with the evangelical community for Ronald Reagan.

The issues then becoming commonplace for fundamentalists figured to a greater or lesser degree, depending on the candidate, in these campaigns. However, Paul, Thoburn, Wolf and Billings did not show any particular interest in abortion. That would come later.

When the progressive evangelical magazine *Sojourners* exposed Third Century in 1976, the conventional wisdom was that the Protestant right-wingers would recede from the political arena. DeVos was more than happy to encourage the misconception. He told the same magazine in November 1977 that the plan to save America was dead, and that the Third Century operation was laid alongside it in its grave.[14]

It didn't quite happen that way. Revivalism was sweeping the country. Everyone from Charles Colson and Anita Bryant to Eldridge Cleaver and Bob Dylan had been born again, and it was becoming quite the thing to do. According to a Gallup poll of 1976, one out of every three people in the country, 34 percent of the adult population, nearly fifty million Americans, were born again. Forty-eight percent, or almost half of the Protestants and a remarkable 18 percent of the Catholics interviewed considered themselves thus saved. Not only that, but they were attempting to increase their numbers, 47 percent of them (58 percent of the Protestants, 38 percent of the Catholics) reporting that they had tried their hand at least once at converting someone to their faith. Moreover, religion in general was apparently growing in popularity. Church attendance was rising for the first time in two decades, with 42 percent of Americans reportedly going to church or synagogue in a typical week, and six out of ten people claiming that religion was a "very important" part of their lives. George Gallup, himself born again, called 1976 the "Year of the Evangelicals."[15]

This development offered the ideal opportunity for an ambitious, energetic political technician to make a move. Ed McAteer was uniquely qualified to become the link between the political operatives in Washington and the preacher politicians all over the country, with his background in sales and the religious right. By trade, McAteer is a traveling salesman, one of the professional nonpreachers who often join up with Christian causes. One of his favorite expressions, which aptly describes him, is, "I'm a marketing man." That is precisely what he subsequently did for fundamentalism: marketed it.

McAteer started his career in 1948 working for the Colgate-Palmolive Company in the toilet articles division. In those days salesmen learned the business from the ground up, so he was responsible for building displays in windows, working in the warehouse and traveling around to sell his products. His first sales territory was Kansas, then Colorado, Oklahoma, Illinois. With his winsome smile and gift of gab, McAteer had no trouble moving up. In 1958 he was promoted into the management end of the company and was transferred to Memphis as sales supervisor. Five years later he was made sales manager for the whole Southeast.

McAteer had first realized that he was dissatisfied with the thrust of modern society in 1974, when he began to apprehend the changes in curriculum of the Memphis public schools, which his two sons attended. "They were bringing in the 'sensitivity training program,'" McAteer elaborated in an interview. "That was where teachers and students sit around and feel all over each other and excite the basic instincts of people. My soul alive! When a man starts fondling a woman, and the girls and boys, what do you think happens? 'Are you crazy?' I said. 'Boy, trying to promote that stuff, closing your eyes, feel of each other.' I said, 'I'm not some prude, but I'm not a donkey neither.' I said, 'That's not what kids go to school for. They go to school to learn how to read and write and do arithmetic.' Well, the local papers started promoting it, but the majority of the people in the city was against it. So I went down to the school board with a group of people, and I said, 'How did these monkeys get elected to the school board in the first place?' So, naturally, that's what brought it into focus." At the time, McAteer did not mention abortion, but it would become important to him later, too, just as to all the others.

McAteer volunteered his services part time with a California-based group called Weekly Bible Translators. The two positions allowed him to make contacts all over the country and the world. That year he was one of the few laymen invited to be a delegate to the Congress in World Evangelism, part of the Billy Graham organization, in Lausanne, Switzerland. The background in sales and Bible peddling made him an irresistible find. The Christian Freedom Foundation offered him a job organizing members, and he quit Colgate after twenty-eight years and signed on. At first he functioned as the Southeast regional director, working only part time. The rest of the time he worked for a company called CRS Industries in Tampa, Florida, as a "consultant"—a not unusual arrangement for the religious group that allowed them to operate at less cost. Eventually McAteer was asked to head up the foundation. So far, his was a fairly typical career for a member of the professional elite of the evangelical movement. It was only a matter of time before those skills would be recognized by the New Right.

McAteer had been working only about a year when the directors decided to disband the operation. He returned briefly to business, but it wasn't long before he got a request from Howard Phillips to help set up a new organization, the New Right's Conservative Caucus. Phillips asked McAteer to come on as director. McAteer felt that his talents would be better put to use as field director, and he became that instead. He served in the position for a short period of time, but missed having the religious base. As an alternative, Phillips suggested the salesman start a branch of the Conservative Caucus to deal exclusively with the religious right. "So what I did," McAteer relates, "was I got on my pony and started out to see these high-powered preachers."

McAteer traveled the country back and forth setting up meetings between the New Right leadership and prominent evangelical preachers. His peregrinations accomplished two goals: he was the catalyst that brought almost all the major fundamentalist missions under the wing of his new organization, the Religious Roundtable; and he introduced Howard Phillips and Paul Weyrich to scores of preachers all over the country, including Jerry Falwell.

At that eventful meeting in Lynchburg in January 1979, Paul Weyrich was the one who articulated exactly what it was that they all were trying to accomplish. They were discussing whether it would be possible to somehow put together a political group espousing religious values without disturbing the IRS. "One thing is for sure,"

Weyrich observed sometime during the conversation. "There is in our country a moral majority out there."[16] The Christian Republic had found a new name. From there it was only a short step to the formation of the organizational vehicle for fundamentalists.

Jerry Falwell is probably the best known of the new breed of fundamentalist preacher-politicians and, although a relative newcomer to the field, an excellent ally for the New Right. Falwell's rise to revivalist stardom occurred soon after graduation from college. He first went public in a big way in 1976, when he started his I Love America rallies. The following year he joined up with both Phyllis Schlafly and Anita Bryant.

With dedicated application—what he called "saturation evangelism"—he created an entire empire complete with foundation, lobbying organization and political-action committee, as well as the church, the college and the treatment center for alcoholics, in addition to the four clubs associated with his TV program, *The Old-Time Gospel Hour*. As of 1981, Falwell reportedly had become very successful. His various operations employed 1,200 people, and weekly donations totaled one million dollars.[17]

Falwell's world view is very much like that of Richard DeVos. Falwell gives credence, for instance, to the idea of a Christian Republic and the importance of its values to bolstering the economy. He also believes that the source of legitimacy for any political authority comes from God, and he sees a "vacuum of leadership" in America.[18]

The Moral Majority was thus a direct-line descendant of the Third Century complex. On its board were two of the aspiring politicians whom Third Century had supported, Reverend Robert Thoburn and Reverend Robert Billings.[19]

Once the New Right interested him in abortion, Falwell spoke out against it with the same fervor he brought to all the rest of his preachments. "From the days of Hammurabi" was the way he once put it in his book *Listen America!*,

civilized people have always looked upon abortion as one of the vilest of crimes. Now, in our society, we are losing respect for the sanctity of human life. America has allowed more lives to be killed through abortion than in all our wars and traffic accidents. Only a perverted society would make laws protecting wolves

and eagles' eggs, and yet have no protection for precious unborn
human life.

He referred to abortion clinics as "butcher shops," and predicted,
"If we expect God to honor and bless our nation, we must take a
stand against abortion."[20]

Falwell was a master communicator. Unlike the Catholics before
him, he did not have to worry about too great an identification with
a single religion. His argument on that score was that he was trying
not to launch a theocracy or have any particular church take over
the state, but merely to get "moral" Americans into power. His
message, with the anti-abortion kicker, probably reached more people in a few months than the right-to-lifers had in years.

If Falwell served as the public figure who explained the interre-
lationship of biblical morality, abortion and politics, Paul and Judie
Brown were the ones who actually organized the fundamentalists
into their version of the right-to-life movement. The Browns made
the links in a couple of ways. For one, they invited the religious
fundamentalist leadership to their New Right/right-to-life gatherings.
For another, the Browns offered to do the fundamentalists' mailings—in the process getting a percentage of the take, keeping an
eye on what was being sent and acquiring a whole new list of names
themselves.

One of those whom the Browns thus brought in was Murray
Norris, a former newspaperman who, by his account, on election
day 1972 "made a deal with the Lord" to dedicate his life to stopping
pornography and abortion. A devout fundamentalist, Norris runs an
organization he calls Christian Family Renewal in conjunction with
a school he calls Valley Christian University in the small town of
Imperial, California. He has also put out numerous pulp publications full of his views about the immorality of abortion, which he
has had printed up in a number of foreign languages and sent overseas. Through his various activities, Norris reaches a community
remote from Washington and the world of the Browns. With them,
he cooperates on sending out their material to all those potentially
conservative voters.[21]

Another connection probably even more significant is that with
the Mormon community. The Church of Jesus Christ of Latter Day
Saints had come out strongly against abortion in 1975, when church

patriarch and former U.S. Agriculture Secretary Ezra Taft Benson proclaimed that abortion jeopardized future membership in the Kingdom of God. With its authoritarian metaphysic, its tightly knit community structure and its emphasis on welfare and service work, the Mormon Church, like the Catholic, was ideally suited to disciplining its numbers and signing them up for right-to-life activities. With its upwards of 4.7 million believers scattered throughout the country, and particularly in the Southwest, Mountain and Plains States, the church was a valuable ally, although one not accustomed to joining coalitions.[22]

The Browns dealt with this by teaming up with individual Mormons, some of whom had their own possibly competing agendas. One of their best ties to the community is Jaynann Payne, who fortuitously affords the New Right yet another link as well.[23] Payne is the staff person for the Center for Family Studies of the Freeman Institute, a lay organization with strong ties especially to Mormons who happen also to be politically conservative. The Freeman Institute is a Utah-based ultraright organization founded and run by W. Cleon Skousen, a Mormon educator, John Birch Society member, former FBI official and onetime police chief of Salt Lake City. The city's Mayor, also a Bircher, fired Skousen in 1960, alleging at the time that the law-enforcement officer was "an incipient Hitler."[24] Associated Press stories in 1980 described the institute as "building a political organization that may be eclipsing the John Birch Society on that end of the ideological spectrum." Skousen told *The New York Times* in the same year that forty thousand people had taken the institute's eighteen-hour seminars around the country. The institute's political arm is the Informed Voters League, the goal of which reportedly is "to consolidate all the right-wing factions and single-issue groups—like the Pro-Family Coalition, pro-life and stop ERA groups—into one potent national political force."*[25] Jaynann Payne is essentially the Mormons' fifth column into the New Right. Payne regularly attends conferences that the Browns and their Viguerie associates put on in Washington, distributes her literature there and takes home theirs.

---

*Skousen was a longtime activist on the right. He was an old associate of Phyllis Schlafly, with whom he cooperated as far back as 1968 on setting up an organization called Americans for Law and Order.

The expanding network of the renewed Christian Republic provided seemingly substantial political support, but the New Right still needed money to keep it going. The man who was most responsible for finding sources for it was yet another fundamentalist preacher-activist, the Reverend Tim LaHaye. A San Diego pastor for thirty years, LaHaye founded the San Diego Christian Unified School System and the Christian Heritage College, as well as Californians for Biblical Morality, and started the Washington, D.C.–based fundamentalist lobby Family America. He was also on the original board of directors of the Moral Majority. Among West Coast evangelicals, he and his wife, Beverly, eventually developed the same sort of reputation as Jack and Barbara Willke. The LaHayes created a series of what they called "family life seminars," actually sex education courses. In 1976, with the publication of a book, *The Act of Marriage*, the LaHayes did for fundamentalists what Alex Comfort had long ago done for everyone else: they sanctioned sexuality. *Act* even discusses the advantages of oral sex.

Outside his own world, however, Tim LaHaye was not renowned so much for his gifts as a sex educator as for carrying on in the tradition of John Conlan the war against secular humanism, with his arguments laid out in another book, *The Battle for the Mind*. LaHaye maintains that the five basic tenets of humanism are atheism, evolution, amorality, autonomous man and socialist one-world view. He has put together a list of some of the more heinous humanist organizations, which include the Ethical Culture Society, the National Association for the Advancement of Colored People, Americans for Democratic Action, the American Civil Liberties Union, the Sex Information and Education Council of the United States, and the National Organization of Women. In true conspiratorial style, LaHaye posits that these organizations "show an interlocking of the same founders who, along with their disciples, were the originators and directors of UNESCO, UNICEF, and the United Nations World Health Organization."

LaHaye, too, defends the Christian Republic, and with a rather more sophisticated argument than most of the others:

> Our forefathers never intended government to be isolated from God or the recognition of His existence. The separation of church and state does not mean that Christian citizens are prohibited

from taking an active part in the electoral process. Our forefathers were simply preventing the establishment of a state religion, which Europe had endured for centuries.

LaHaye then turns the argument on its head, insisting that it is the humanists, and not the evangelicals, who are threatening unconstitutional establishment of religion. Among many others, he quotes Sir Julian Huxley as having predicted that the next great religion of the world would be some form of humanism. LaHaye also contends that the Supreme Court allowed as much in its 1965 *Seeger* decision granting Daniel Andrew Seeger conscientious-objector deferment from military service on the basis of his ethical rather than his religious views.

LaHaye then goes on the offensive:

> Is it conceivable that America could institute a state-controlled religion? The foundation is already being laid. Until 1979, we did not have a tax-supported religion in America. Instead, all religions were free to operate within the framework of minimal legal guidelines. But that changed in 1979, [when] under the guidance of a well-publicized born-again president, the federal government established a Department of Education with a $40 billion budget. Since the educational system has been taken over by humanism, and since humanism is an officially declared religion, we find the government establishing a religion and giving the high priest a position in the president's cabinet. [26]

LaHaye introduced into the Christian political nexus two fabulously wealthy newly born-again Southern businessmen, T. Cullen Davis and Nelson Bunker Hunt, [27] both of them with recently acquired dubious reputations. Davis had committed himself to Christ four months after he was acquitted of murdering his wife and stepdaughter and, in a separate series of charges, of hiring assassins to kill a judge and several witnesses involved in the original murder case. His allegiance was to James Robison, the fiery young Fort Worth preacher, one of the founding members of the Religious Roundtable. [28] Hunt had laid his otherworldly future in the hands of Bill Bright shortly after cornering, and then losing, the world silver market. Eventually both Hunt and Davis were put on the board of the Religious Roundtable, and Hunt backed the Freeman

Institute.[29] Donations from people like Hunt and Davis allowed the ministries to operate on the grand scale, providing the capital for seed money, special projects, a construction drive or a fund-raising campaign.

Determining exactly how much Davis, Hunt and the other large donors give to these causes is not easy. Unless a benefactor wants to advertise the extent of his support, the amount remains essentially his or her business. Often the wealthy prefer to keep their dealings confidential. Public records reveal only the sums contributed through family or corporate foundations, not individual donations.

What is known about the born-again bankrollers is that at least three of the big donors own companies which are among the largest privately held companies in the country. T. Cullen Davis' family's company, Ken Davis Industries, as of 1979 was the eighth largest in the nation, with estimated sales that year of $2 billion. Hunt Oil was the thirty-ninth largest, with estimated sales the same year of $745 million. The Amway Corporation, owned by fundamentalist donor Richard DeVos, was the fiftieth largest, with estimated sales that year of $600 million.[30]

The exact amount that Davis has given to fundamentalist causes is not on public record. Nelson Bunker Hunt gave $5.5 million in 1979 and $10 million in 1980 to the Campus Crusade. Richard DeVos, through a foundation that bears his and his wife's name, gave $12,000 in 1977 and $2,500 in 1978 to various Christian causes, $25,000 in 1974 to the Christian Freedom Foundation, and $50,000 in 1978 to the Garden Grove Community Church of Crystal Cathedral evangelist Robert Schuller.[31]

A glimpse into this world of religious high finance came in July 1980 when some of the richest men in the world gathered at the Houstonian Inn in Houston at the invitation of Nelson Bunker Hunt. This was another of Bill Bright's meetings around the country, but this time the participants were special. Advance ads in the Houston and Dallas newspapers explained their mission this way: "We Are Not Failures. We Are Not Going to Let the World Fail Either." Those individuals who pledged by faith to give or to commit themselves to raise one million dollars or more would, according to the event's organizer, become part of a select group called History's Handful.

The attendance list for the cause, called Here's Life World, was secret, but word of some of the names leaked out. Among them were the redoubtable Hunt, who had already pledged $10 million three years earlier and was chairman of the Here's Life International executive committee, and the flamboyant Davis. Others who had endorsed the effort were an elite bunch including former President Gerald Ford, Watergate special prosecutor Leon Jaworski, John Connally and two other former governors of Texas, astronaut James Irwin, cowboy star Roy Rogers, football quarterbacks Roger Staubach and Terry Bradshaw, Nixon donor and insurance man W. Clement Stone, and Dallas Cowboys owner Clint Murchison.

Unquestionably, they considered themselves the elect. The brochure handed out at the gathering confirmed their collective identity: "By every measure of man, the goal we undertake is impossible, even preposterous... [but] it can be done. But it won't be by mass action. It will come to pass because of the strategic—even sacrificial—contributions of a comparatively small handful who care enough to take their place among the movers of history." Purple prose notwithstanding, these men had no illusions about why they were the chosen ones. "We're here to raise money for all the little people," Anne Murchison, wife of the Cowboys owner, explained to a reporter in Houston. "It's not that this is exclusive. It's just that we're the ones with the bucks."[32]

No matter what they had in the way of money, organization or strategy, however, the fundamentalists could not have carried off a revival unless they had the people to fill the pews and flock to the polls. The reasons why the fundamentalist followers were attracted to the new preacher activists, and to their right-to-life propaganda, were many and varied, and probably more complex than simply a belief in the cause.

Part of their motivation may have come, paradoxically, from an increasing need to feel accepted into modern society. Much like the Catholics who joined the right-to-life movement, the fundamentalists had been for a long time out of the mainstream of American life. They may have found comfort in the knowledge that their resurgence was becoming a national phenomenon—if not appreciated by everyone, at least noticed far and wide. As the knowledgeable if partisan Richard Quebedeaux puts it in his book *The Worldly Evangelicals:*

> The evangelical right and center is getting hard to distinguish
> from the wider society physically, socially and politically. Right

and center evangelicals are richer, better educated, better dressed, and better fed than they used to be. . . . *Success* is a very important word in their vocabulary because, by the world's standards, they *have* become successful. Most important of all, these evangelicals are now respectable.[33]

Jaynann Payne has another analysis that gives some insight into why abortion was important to fundamentalists. She feels that the right-to-life movement provided the social glue that put together a formerly estranged but morally compatible community. "I will say this about the pro-life movement," Payne explained in an interview. "I have been born and raised in Utah, and sometimes groups tend to be a little provincial. I don't mean I'm a provincial kind of person. I've traveled to Europe several times and to Israel, and last year my husband and I went all the way around the world. But it's been excellent for me to get out there and see what other people are doing. I think that's one of the most important things about this movement. The Catholic Church, for instance, has tended to keep sort of to themselves, and the Baptists and the Methodists. So to the extent that churches in the past have been isolated, we have discovered a lot of things that have happened lately, especially these moral issues. The moral issues are the things that united many, many people."[34]

The fundamentalists who joined the right-to-life movement share many characteristics with the already active Catholics. The fundamentalists, too, are politically diverse. The women, although many have large families—Jaynann Payne, for instance, has thirteen children—also seem to have that same wanderlust that takes them out of the home and into this family-oriented outside activity. One woman interviewed at a right-to-life conference was not atypical in her strong aversion to the classic feminine role. "I worked from the time both of my children were six weeks old," she explained. "I took a leave and then went right back to work. If you stay home all the time and you're miserable, that reflects on your children." These women are just as fearful and guilt-ridden about sexuality outside marriage.

What distinguishes them from the Catholics, not surprisingly, is a stronger missionary streak. Except for the extremists, Catholic right-to-lifers tend to stick pretty much with the abortion-related issues. Fundamentalists, by contrast, appear to want their whole message to be accepted by the world. They have unquestioningly embraced the idea of a Christian Republic. Most of them cannot phrase it as eloquently as Bright or Falwell, but they do have an overriding sense of God as Lord and Master of everything, including the political system. Indeed, the idea of the Christian Republic is second nature.

"The enemies of God have always wanted abortion" is the way Murray Norris describes his right-to-life commitment, "even in Roman days when the Romans would abandon their babies under bridges, and Christians would dash down and snatch them and make them part of our family. So we've been fighting abortions since the beginning of Christianity. Because now we have an organization, the Christians have just kind of slacked off, so the enemies of God have picked up the ball and they're carrying it. I really think abortion is just another thing the Lord has allowed to happen to try to bring people back to God. Really, he wants all of us to come to a knowledge of Christ and be saved."[35]

The grass-roots right-to-life fundamentalists seem a great deal more naïve than the Catholics, making them easy game for the sophisticated conservative political operatives who have drawn them in. The interest of the grass-roots fundamentalists in abortion has very little to do with the rough and tumble of politics and almost nothing to do with the politics of the New Right. Many of them are concerned about fulfilling the service function of their religion and helping people.

Ann and Jim Pierson, for instance, are a friendly couple from Pennsylvania who run homes for unwed mothers. Born-again Christians, Ann, forty, and Jim, forty-four, have been doing this kind of work since about a decade ago when they suddenly and dramatically uprooted themselves from their home in Washington, D.C., and devoted themselves to their Christian "ministry." One of the striking things about them is their modesty. Apparently, the Piersons have had the opportunity to expand their operations, but have kept them at only two homes in an effort at avoiding self-aggrandization. "You know how some people, they do something that no one else could ever do," Ann explained in an interview. "That's not what we wanted.

"I feel it's a call that God has put on our lives" is the way she described what they are doing. "There's no question about that. I think one of the things that really affected me, I read a little pamphlet by Norman Vincent Peale once, and he said that we all should ask ourselves what we want our lives to say when it's all over. And then he gave a little exercise at the end. He said, 'Write down on a piece of paper what you would like your life to say, and tuck that into your wallet. And whenever you get discouraged and you don't think your life is going anywhere, take the piece of paper out and renew your commitment to that dream.' I did that. I put on the piece of paper that I wanted to have a major impact on changing something that had gone against what God wanted, but I wanted to do it in love. I didn't want it to be a real fanatical kind of thing. I wanted it to be gentle. At the time, I wasn't quite sure what it was going to be, but of course now I know. That's really what I want my life to say. I want people to say, 'She really cared about something. She really believed in it. God was her resource for her strength and she put that into reality, and she made it so that others could do it, too.'"[36]

However much the grass-roots loyalists like Payne, Norris and the Piersons consider abortion a moral issue, the fundamentalist political operatives in Washington talk openly—and in terms explicitly political—about why it is useful to them. One such is Gary Jarmin,* staff person for Christian Voice, the outfit that would at election time mobilize fundamentalist voters. "The right-to-life movement provided some expertise to the Christian political movement," Jarmin offered in the interview in 1981, "because they had been involved in many of these political fights for a long time."[37]

William Billings was even more candid about it. Billings, who started his political career working in the Stop ERA campaign of

---

*Gary Jarmin came to the right-wing Christian fold through a slightly circuitous route. Like Richard Viguerie, Jarmin had ties with the Unification Church of the Reverend Sun Myung Moon, where he served as staff director until 1973. Jarmin finally left the church, he explained in an interview, for a couple of reasons. "First of all, I began to have some doubts about some of the teachings, and I was questioning the lifestyle. I began to feel it was too confining. It is a rather rigid and disciplined environment." In 1975 he teamed up for a very short time with the conservative Leadership Foundation to work on the issue of school prayer and then joined the American Conservative Union, one of the vanguard New Right organizations, to conduct its campaign against the federal Occupational Safety and Health Administration (OSHA). The following year, he worked on Ronald Reagan's presidential-primary campaign, and the year after that for a California group called American Christian Cause, which eventually turned into Christian Voice. Interestingly, some ex-cultists who keep track of the Moonies believe he has never really left them, even though he professes to have had a born-again experience.

Phyllis Schlafly in Florida, heads up the National Christian Action
Coalition, a group that gravitates around the special private schools
set up to avoid the "secular humanist" education of the public
system. Son of the more famous Reverend Robert Billings who set
up NCAC, the younger Billings has taken on abortion as one of
several issues around which to organize. "Abortion is one of the key
issues because it's a yes or no question. On some other issues, say
arms control, there's a lot of areas for shades of involvement and
commitment. In abortion, it's an up or down question. As we judge
people in Congress, who are the good guys and who are the bad
guys, you have to look at their votes on the issues. If you rate most
people on defense, there are so many votes that everyone comes out
around forty or fifty percent. With abortion, it's very clear. How
have they voted on the Human Life Amendment?"[38]

In the same way, the millions of evangelicals were important to
the original right-to-lifers. In 1980, a rogue group of conservatives
took over the Southern Baptist Convention, the largest of all the
Baptists' conventions, representing 13.4 million members. Up until
that time, on the strength of a resolution adopted in 1971 even
before the Supreme Court decision on abortion, the Southern Baptists had deplored abortion—except in cases involving rape, incest
or a threat to the life of the mother—but avoided advocating any
restrictive laws, on the grounds that such laws would violate the
principle of separation of church and state. At the 1980 conclave
the conservatives, led by Reverend Bailey Smith, rammed through
a number of resolutions, one of them concerning the convention's
abortion policy.

"There's an awakening on the abortion issue going on among
evangelical Protestants," former National Right to Life Committee
president Carolyn Gerster commented to reporters after the Southern
Baptists' vote. "I'm a Protestant and have always felt the support for
the right to life was there among Protestants but has not been articulated. The Southern Baptists' decision will have a very profound
impact." Reverend Edward Bryce of the Catholic Conference heartily seconded her opinion. "I thank God for the Southern Baptist
decision and await the other major Christian bodies. I see many
Protestant people in agreement with the Catholic Church that abortion on demand is immoral and not a sound basis for public policy."[39]

Paul Weyrich's Coalitions for America was now complete. Once having formed a network with the right-to-life movement, the New Right and the evangelicals got to work readying themselves for the upcoming 1980 election.

The plan to save America had taken a new guise: this host of independent preachers and their flocks, loosely held together by a common background, belief and set of goals. These preachers were about to go public again in the context of democratic elections— all perfectly legal, aboveboard and American. The actual genesis of their electoral aims, however, was not widely fathomed. That this current version of the Christian Republic was inspired by the New Right political operatives and their wealthy friends would not come out until much later.

Meanwhile, the right-to-life movement had joined with forces that looked as if they might help bring electoral success, but also yet another—and unfamiliar—political perspective. If the New Right introduced anti-Communism, pro—free enterprise and pro-militarism to the right-to-life agenda, the fundamentalists were bringing the Christian Republic, a notion that had very little to do with— and might easily prove hostile to—the Social Gospel out of which right-to-life sentiment had emerged.

For now, it didn't matter. They were fast approaching their time in the sun. All the rest had been preliminaries. This was where they were hoping to win.

VIII.

Ballots for Babies

The year 1980 was an apparent turning point in American history. The salad days were gone. The economy was on a fearful slip-slide of stagflation. Global politics were reflecting the economic shifts of a country that could no longer play international cop. More and more nations had the bomb. The mood of the American people was correspondingly demanding. They were suddenly aware that they were not going to be able to fulfill their childhood dreams. Concern about poverty, drugs and unemployment, the elderly, the sick and the lame gave way to insecurity. Instead of hope, people felt resentment, anger and a loss of control. They wanted a return to normalcy, and especially a stable financial life.

The cure for these unprecedented times was elusive. Politicians seized on the cynical, easy response. Instead of proposing real solutions to economic turbulence, they fixed on flashy, simplistic formulas. Instead of acknowledging the shift in world politics, they retrieved the tired truisms of the past. The campaign rhetoric of 1980 actually was no more than an update of the classic conservative credo supporting free enterprise and limited government. The politicians added to that an endorsement of the so-called social issues as a way of promising stability.

The election seemed to confirm the politicians' instincts that this was what the people wanted. The winning President campaigned on the explicit platform of reversing the course of public policy of the last fifty years. The incoming Congress for the most part appeared eager to do his bidding. The commonly accepted analysis of the returns was that the American people had turned conservative. Certainly that was the message of the conservative columnists, and eventually much of the press. The Silent Majority, it seemed, had finally spoken; the Republican majority had finally emerged; the Moral Majority was about to have its day. And the New Right leadership was right there to take credit for it.

A closer look at the election told quite another story. Because such a relatively small number of Americans were registered to vote, and so few of those went to the polls, Ronald Reagan won by getting the endorsement of only 26 percent of the adult American population—almost the same percentage that determined Jimmy Carter's squeaker of a win in 1976. Furthermore, in fifteen of the states that Reagan carried, a majority of the voters actually chose a combination of candidates other than him.[1] It was an election really determined by the nonvoters, whose reticence could have meant a lot of things. One possible interpretation was that they didn't feel they needed to register an opinion at the polls because they were simply doing fine. Another was that, whatever their condition, they considered politics irrelevant. Or, alternatively, they could have been engaging in a silent protest against the candidates for not having articulated any intelligent understanding of the nonvoters' dreams, desires and needs, or any workable solutions to their problems.

The outcome of the congressional elections was just as ambiguous. This fact was not lost on the New Right leadership, who were frank about it when speaking among themselves. During an address in front of a right-to-life audience about a year later, Paul Weyrich was careful to pat himself on the back, not for having swayed large numbers of people at the polls, but for having concentrated on those who would make the critical difference. Weyrich candidly explained how he had helped activate his "winning coalition" to bring out that small percentage of the electorate—from 5 to 15 percent—who could determine the election, either by voting when they otherwise wouldn't have voted or by switching parties. By Weyrich's reasoning, the New Right counted most on three elements in the "winning coalition": the grass roots, with anti-abortion activists chief among them and the fundamentalists not far behind; the Republican Party; and the business community.[2]

Weyrich's analysis notwithstanding, the "winning coalition" was not always victorious, and many of the campaigns for which they took credit were not really theirs to claim. Moreover, abortion was only an incidental part of the agenda of the coalition as a whole. The election was the first time, in fact, when it finally became apparent for anyone choosing to observe it that the New Right was using abortion to accomplish its real objective—seizing power; and that its power, once ostensibly seized, was not quite what it seemed. In short, the New Right's electoral claims—and, by association, those of the right-to-lifers—were an elaborate smoke-and-mirrors game.

The right-to-life movement, born of religious conviction, did not take a political direction for a long time. The bulk of its activities corresponded to the kind of moral witness that the country had seen in past populist campaigns, its people being much more comfortable in ceremony or education than in outright campaigning. The initial ventures into politics were so amateurish as to be widely dismissed as the work of fanatics. This was one of the reasons, in fact, that the movement took so long, first, to distinguish itself from the Roman Catholic Church, and then to fashion itself into a credible political vehicle.

Right-to-life activists did not immediately comprehend the importance of electoral involvement, or the necessity of making strategic coalitions in order to win. These were by and large not political people, and they had no experience in wielding power. Their assumption was that their cause was so just that any thinking person seeing their pictures or hearing their arguments could not resist them; those who did must have sinister motivations. As Carolyn Gerster described the tendency, "Although we gave political activity lip service, we had no really good plans how to accomplish it. Most pro-lifers are people who believe we should put our faith in education, prayer and good works. While I certainly don't fault that, that's no way to get a constitutional amendment. They were not facing reality." What changed their minds was the New Right.

While the right-to-lifers had flailed around, the New Right recognized them as a potentially valuable ally in a six-year strategy of the "winning coalition" to capture as many congressional seats as possible for conservatives. The idea was to count on the right-to-lifers, as Robert Sassone had detailed in his plan for the Life Amendment Political Action Committee, to swing a couple of percentage points of the vote in certain strategically chosen areas. The plan had gone into effect in 1978 and was to last until 1982. Those were the years when so many liberal senators who had been elected in the wake of Watergate were up for reelection, the bulk of them in the crucial year of 1980.

Ed McAteer, in an interview after the election, described the New Right as the "leaders" and the right-to-lifers and the fundamentalists as the "troops" in this strategy.[3] Indeed, this was exactly the relationship between them. The heads of the Committee for the Survival of a Free Congress, NCPAC and assorted smaller outfits spent the better part of the time during the crucial summer leading up to the election manning command centers in Washington from which they advised the local leadership and directed the flow of money. Among those at the helm were Paul and Judie Brown, who, having publicly thrown their lot in with Richard Viguerie, cooperated with gusto.

The original right-to-lifers remaining at the National Right to Life Committee and its cooperating state organizations watched Viguerie and his associates prepare for the elections. Slowly, painfully, with all the false starts of a large and diverse organization, these right-to-lifers began to copy the New Right, occasionally working right alongside them.

Carolyn Gerster's three-year plan was swallowed up by the New Right's six-year plan. The odd thing about this alliance was that the right-to-lifers often didn't realize what they were doing, and when they did, they tried to cover it up. The NRLC, in fact, never acknowledged—either to themselves or to the outside world—how completely they were buying into the New Right strategy.

There is almost nothing on the record about any coordination between the right-to-life movement and the rest of the "winning coalition"—a coordination that, if open, could have been illegal. What is known is that virtually all the members of the "winning coalition" produced target lists, and that they all had ongoing ties with one another. The Committee for the Survival of a Free Congress, NCPAC and LAPAC all targeted almost exactly the same set of senators and congressmen as the right-to-life movement, the fundamentalists, the Republican Party and a surprisingly high number of business- and trade-association political-action committees. For instance, CSFC, NCPAC and LAPAC all went after Senators George McGovern, Frank Church, Birch Bayh and John Culver; so did the National Right to Life PAC; so did the Moral Majority and Christian Voice; so did the Republican Party; and so did the United States Chamber of Commerce and the National Association of Manufacturers' Business-Industry Political Action Committee (BIPAC).

If this was mere chance, it was only because they failed to take advantage of the many opportunities on which they were together to talk about it. A little bit of New Right memorabilia is the rare announcement of the membership of one of Paul Weyrich's secret groups formed to coordinate political strategy, which proves that many of the members of the "winning coalition" met regularly. Published in early 1979, the announcement was actually to welcome Christian Voice into the fold. Named as other members were the Senate Steering Committee for the Survival of a Free Congress; the Conservative Caucus; the American Conservative Union; the Conservative Victory Fund (ACU's PAC); and NCPAC. In addition to these more or less predictable members there were some surprises: the Republican Study Committee, a group of eighty conservative Republican members of Congress; Senator Orrin Hatch; Citizens for the Republic (Ronald Reagan's campaign vehicle); and the National Association of Manufacturers.[4]

The interlocking directorates among some of the members of the "winning coalition," and the long and close association among some of their leaders, made their planning for the 1980 elections look like the work of a small group of old friends who had been looking forward to this moment for quite some time.

Although the National Right to Life Committee never formally became part of the "winning coalition," by close observation of their activities the group in time developed its own fairly sophisticated mechanism, with a contact person in every state to organize an electoral drive, a voter-identification project and a get-out-the-vote canvassing and phone-bank drive, as well as a political-action committee to give financial assistance. The operation was run by Sandra Faucher, a former housewife from Maine who had come up through the ranks of her local and state right-to-life organizations. Faucher's technique was to make contact with state right-to-life organizers at the annual conventions and then give them explicit printed material on how to conduct a campaign, with periodic advice over the year on how to use it.

A primer on voter identification not only is full of the usual exhortations—"WHEN WE ORGANIZE PROPERLY, TRAIN WELL AND WORK DILIGENTLY, WE WILL BECOME THE FIRST CITIZEN LOBBYING GROUP IN HISTORY TO COMPLETE A TASK OF THIS MAGNITUDE"— but contains also good, sound advice. Campaign workers are to be divided into teams with captains, organized along congressional-district lines. They are directed to call all the households in the district during certain specified hours on particular days ("Fridays," the booklet warns, "are usually unproductive"). Once having reached a potential voter, they are to ask a set series of questions in the proper order, jotting down the responses on a pre-printed form. "DO NOT ARGUE," the booklet advises judiciously in several places.

Another primer explains how to set up precinct organizations and, with the voter-ID information in hand, solicit help from volunteers. Among suggested projects are the following: "Place pro-life materials in libraries"; "Monitor radio and TV stations regarding pro-life issues"; "Write letters to the editor"; "Be active in either Republican or Democratic party"; "Help provide maternity/baby clothes for needy girls."

NRLC also put out a glossy eight-by-ten-inch flyer that could be reprinted with the appropriate candidate rundown. The flyer shows a winning photograph of an infant with the message "This Little Guy Wants YOU to Vote in the ——Primary!" These were the handouts that were to be slipped under car windshield wipers during church services. As Sandy Faucher explained at one National Right to Life convention to an appreciative audience, "Do not distribute these at any old shopping centers. That will lower the percentage of people who will be influenced. Try church parking lots—but not the Episcopal or the United Church of Christ. Try the Catholic, the Mormon, the Southern Baptist. You can get rid of a lot very quickly. What I used to do was take a couple of my children out on a Sunday morning, and we could distribute forty to fifty thousand easily."

Faucher, in conjunction with other national leaders, made the decision as to whether to give the National Right to Life Committee's

Political Action Committee money to a candidate based on five
criteria: (1) the inclination of the right-to-life leader in the state; (2)
the candidate's answers to a right-to-life survey; (3) electability; (4)
incumbency ("Always support the incumbent!"); and (5) past involvement in and leadership of right-to-life activities.

Supplemental to all this NRLC literature was a 388-page tome
called *Bayonets and Roses* with minute details right down to the
direction in which to walk down the block so as to effectively canvass
a neighborhood.[5]

The evangelical fundamentalists also tried to rally the troops,
although they were essentially playing catch-up, since they started
so late. By September 1979, Moral Majority spokesmen claimed to
have contacted 72,000 preachers to acquaint them with the political
process. The approach was much more thorough than the simple-
minded appeals that came over the Sunday-morning airwaves. Falwell suggested that fundamentalists, using Scriptural principles as
their guide, evaluate politicians on the issues of, among others, a
balanced budget, lower taxes, a tax-exempt status for private schools,
restoration of capital punishment, an end to busing, renewal of
prayer in the schools, strong laws against drugs, continued crimin-
alization of prostitution and, of course, the outlawing of abortion.
Like the original right-to-lifers, Moral Majority also produced a
booklet to help preachers motivate their flocks. It detailed how to
identify churchgoers who were not yet registered to vote, assist them
in registering and help them get to the polls to vote. The plan went
so far as to pinpoint solutions to that stickiest problem of all, changing
fundamentalist consciousness about the importance of political action. It predicted that fewer than one out of three people in fundamentalist churches who were not registered to vote would admit
it directly, even if asked. An "easy and unembarrassing" way for
pastors to identify them, the plan advised, would be to have the
entire congregation stand after a service, or any other church-related
event, and ask those who were registered to sit down. The unregis-
tered miscreants would stand out—literally—quite plainly.[6]

The Religious Roundtable, the National Christian Action Coalition and Tim LaHaye's network proposed similar programs for the
elections. Additionally, NCAC worked up a quick-check voting index to show how various congressmen and senators had voted on
the issues.

Christian Voice was another very active group, although its efforts were more hortatory than organizational. One Christian Voice mailing typically informed voters: "This Letter Will Make you Angry! But I'm going to tell you the truth about militant gays, liberal educators, cruel atheists and Godless politicians." Christian Voice also mounted a media campaign by referring conservative lawmakers to broadcast preachers across the country and distributing a videotaped version of a half-hour political documentary, "The Doomsday Report," starring Senator Orrin Hatch. As Christian Voice staffer Gary Jarmin explained to a reporter, "The beauty of it is that we don't have to organize these voters. They already have their own television networks, publications, schools, meeting places and respected leaders who are sympathetic to our goals."[7]

The fundamentalists relied a great deal on large events to rally followers and command attention from the press. On April 29, 1980, about 200,000 evangelicals marched and prayed through downtown Washington, finally ending up at the Washington Mall for a "Washington for Jesus" rally, organized by Ed McAteer's Religious Roundtable, among others. There the Reverend Pat Robertson, the most successful of the electronic evangelists, founder of the Christian Broadcasting Network and host of the 700 Club, told the gathering, "There is one ruler over the affairs of man, God Almighty. Every leader in this city holds his tenure only so long as God wills it, and they have no authority except as God gives it to them." Bill Bright of the Campus Crusade for Christ spoke of the deterioration of the moral and military might of the United States, a condition that could thrust the country into "a world aflame."[8]

In August, again under the sponsorship of the Religious Roundtable, the fundamentalists gathered again, this time in Dallas, for a rally and a series of seminars designed to teach the faithful how to get involved in politics. The crowd ranged from about seven thousand to fifteen thousand for the closing speech, which was delivered by presidential candidate Ronald Reagan. One of the most electrifying speakers at this event was the fiery Reverend James Robison. The Dallas rally was paid for in part by Robison patron and participant T. Cullen Davis. H. L. Hunt was also there, although, as the *Dallas Times Herald* noted, he slipped out for a soft drink when the preachers took up a collection.[9]

The last day of October, just three days before the election, Christian Voice held a news conference to display what staffer Gary Jarmin called a morality report card on congressmen. The "morality rating" was based on their voting record on bills that had come before Congress, covering, in addition to the usual items, such unlikely subjects as Taiwan security, sanctions for Rhodesia, unionization of teachers, the Department of Education, sexual and racial quotas, the nomination of a particular judge to the U. S. Court of Appeals for the District of Columbia, and federal budget controls. Not surprisingly, federal funding for abortion was on his list, too.*[10]

Through its Moral Government Fund, Christian Voice was spending huge sums of money on the election. Gary Jarmin originally announced that his 1980 war chest would amount to one million dollars—later withdrawing the estimate by saying it was "just a figure I pulled out of the air." Actually Christian Voice had about $200,000 as of the beginning of October, and expected half a million by the end of the month.[11]

If the right-to-lifers and the fundamentalists bore witness to their convictions by neighborhood organizing and public meetings, the input of the Republican Party on both the national and state levels was much less direct about its goals. The political operatives at the GOP who were sympathetic to conservative goals could not be entirely open about it unless they constituted a critical mass within the party. Before the 1980 election they were a minority, and therefore circumspect. Their tacit alliance with the New Right was thus an odd kind of relationship, akin to a very public extramarital romance: everybody knew about it, but they weren't supposed to utter a word. By and large they didn't.

One of those extending a hand to conservatives was former U.S. Senator William Brock, then chairman of the Republican National Committee. The dalliance presumably was not difficult, since he had come from a right-wing background himself. Brock is from the Third Congressional District of Tennessee, the site of the Scopes evolution trial. His particular base is Chattanooga, a city that tra-

---

*The descriptions of some of the bills were clearly inflammatory, for instance that on the sanctions for Rhodesia, which Congress had originally imposed to exert pressure on the white minority regime. This is the way Christian Voice couched the problem:

Ending economic sanctions would lift an enormous and unwarranted burden from this Christian, pro-American nation under attack by atheistic Marxist forces seeking to destroy Christianity and Rhodesian democratically elected racially integrated government.

ditionally has voted Democratic but that lately has been switching
to the GOP ticket. Brock is very much representative of the New
South trend toward young conservative Republicans, except that his
conservatism has a long history to it. As a youth, he was a member
of Young Americans for Freedom. When he first ran for the Senate,
in 1970, he campaigned as an opponent of busing and a proponent
of school prayer. In 1972, he headed Young Americans for the
President (Nixon). Brock might have won his 1976 reelection drive
but for an embarrassing tactic on the part of his opponent. The
Democrat demanded full disclosure of his income-tax returns. Brock,
heir to a candy fortune, refused. The voters apparently thought he
had something to hide, and Democrats capitalized on it by discov-
ering that Brock had (legally) paid no income tax; they forthwith
distributed bumper stickers reading, "I paid more taxes than Brock."
He lost by 6 percent of the vote. [12]

Brock's appointments at the RNC revealed his allegiances. For
one, he brought into the official Republican fold Charles Black. A
lawyer who graduated from the University of Florida, Black too had
been active in Young Americans for Freedom. He was Florida state
chairman and then went on to join the national organization as
head of its chapter services, a position from which he came to know
YAFers all over the country, and to understand political organizing.
In 1972 he left YAF to work on the senatorial campaign of Jesse
Helms, for whom he became a top assistant. Black was active in the
promotion of conservative Republicanism among young people,
through both the Young Republican National Federation and the
independent conservative Committee for Responsible Youth Politics. In 1975 he was elected to the board of the American Conservative Union as part of the new blood that took it over. The same
year, Black became the first chairman of the National Conservative
Political Action Committee (NCPAC). In 1976, he took a leave of
absence from Helms's staff to work briefly for Ronald Reagan's presidential race. For his party-related efforts over the years, Black—
only twenty-eight years old—was finally rewarded with the position
of campaign director at the RNC in April 1977. [13]

Working with him at NCPAC had been Treasurer Roger Stone,
who later was to be lauded during a successful drive for the chair-
manship of the Young Republican National Federation. The reason
for the plaudits: Stone had been deeply involved in the dirty tricks
of the 1972 Nixon campaign; he had helped spy on Democratic

campaign headquarters. Apparently true to character, he had allegedly spent $35,000 on the Young Republican victory—paid campaigns of any kind being unprecedented for the organization. Black brought Stone with him to the Republican headquarters. Another colleague Black took along was former Reagan campaign aide Paul Russo, who was to serve as the GOP liaison with the far right.[14]

The parties were facing a singularly important moment anticipating the coming census of 1980. It was expected to show a major population migration from the Northeast and the Great Lakes industrial states to the Sun Belt, a demographic shift likely to produce a change both in the allotment of congressional representation and in voter registration, from which the Republicans could benefit. That required electing Republicans at the state level, where the redistricting decisions would be made.

Brock announced in February 1978 that the Republican National Committee was budgeting $1.75 million to elect state legislators around the country. The extraordinary effort was part of a six-year plan—extending, interestingly, over the exact same time span as the plan of the New Right—to strengthen the GOP. About $1 million of the total would go directly into Republican candidates' campaigns. In charge of the campaigns was Charles Black. Black explained to the press that the money and advice would flow most heavily to states, small or large, where "we have a real chance of taking over the Legislature by 1981." That was not all that Brock and Black had in mind. As they explained at the time, the massive Republican effort would go toward developing candidates not only for the short range but also for the more distant future.[15] This meant that the New Right, in the person of Charles Black, was having an inordinate amount of influence over the kinds of candidates that were going to be running for office under the Republican banner.

Black was only encouraging a process that was already under way. One way in which this was happening was the infiltration of YAFers, of workers from Reagan's 1976 campaign and of other conservatives into the state and local party structures. In California, of course, the process began as soon as Ronald Reagan became governor and continued on up through his presidency, and after Black went to the GOP the same started to occur in the populous states of Texas and New York.

The relationship during this period between Black and his old colleagues at NCPAC as well as the other New Right groups has never been fully established. Certainly, both the Republicans and the New Right were working to help elect the conservatives. Any cooperation between them would have been a violation of the federal election laws. They maintained the appearance of strict independence but their separate activities resulted in a mutually advantageous one-two punch. First, the New Right, and particularly NCPAC, would "soften up" the Democrat in the primary, making him vulnerable to a challenge. Then the party would step in with the kind of massive funding that can afford even the most obscure, miserable and mean-spirited candidate—as yet virginal and untouched by the press—instant visibility and the media image of a nice, clean, honest guy. Alternatively, sometimes the New Right did all the work.

The 1978 elections in Iowa and New Hampshire had been two early instances in which the Republican Party and the New Right had compatible interests. The races were notable for the part the established party declined to play until the New Right had destabilized the Democrats. Iowa was one of those states in which the right-to-life movement had claimed the credit that was really due to the New Right. Iowa's Dick Clark was one of several of the state's Democrats who in the sixties had broken the ages-old Republican hammerlock on politics. Clark was an outspoken liberal, active particularly in African affairs, the author of an amendment prohibiting United States involvement in Angola and an advocate of U.S. support for a peaceful settlement in Zimbabwe-Rhodesia. He was also unabashedly pro-choice. His opponent was the state's four-term Lieutenant Governor, Roger Jepsen, who, according to *The Almanac of American Politics*, was generally considered such a "lightweight" that the sitting Governor, Robert Ray, refused to support him when Jepsen decided to run for the Senate. Jepsen got the nomination reportedly because no other Republican wanted to take the risk of running against Clark. Jepsen won by staying out of the spotlight and viciously attacking Clark. After the election, however, there were charges that Jepsen had received money from pro-apartheid interests in South Africa, presumably because of Clark's strong stand against that country's racist policies.[16] Jepsen also got a great deal of assistance from the Committee for the Survival of a Free Congress, the National Conservative Political Action Committee, the Committee for Responsible Youth Politics, Viguerie's empire and national right-to-work groups.*[17] Jepsen won the Senate election with only 52 percent.

New Hampshire was the location of another upset when former Allegheny Airlines pilot Gordon Humphrey mounted a vigorous campaign against moderate Democratic Senator Thomas McIntyre. The most interesting aspect of the campaign was the initial hands-off attitude not only of the Republicans but also of the conservatives. Humphrey was such an unknown that nobody wanted to back him. It took Terry Dolan, in one of the many New Right strategy meetings, pounding his fist on the table and declaring, "I tell you, if Gordon Humphrey does it right, he can win!" to convince his colleagues. What Dolan did for the first time in New Hampshire history was to use Boston television advertising, which nobody had dared do before because of its expense.[18] The Republican Party later stepped in with moderate support. Humphrey won with a slim 51 percent.

In races like this in which the New Right played a part equal to or greater than the Republicans, the result was to force the state and national parties over to the right. Another way in which this was accomplished was through issues and lobbying campaigns. The idea was to target a controversial issue, simplify its content, blow it up with some radical rhetoric, force a vote in Congress and use the results against a previously targeted congressman in the next election. Not only were individual congressmen tested that way, but the New Right also started setting the agenda for what would be discussed in Washington. The issues were designed to split the Republicans right down the middle, the objective being for the conservative faction to come out on top—a basic divide-and-conquer strategy.

Such was the case with the fight over the Panama Canal Treaty, a battle so intense, so extremist and so divisive that even in defeat the New Right could claim victory. Although it lost the vote, the

---

*Conservative Caucus chairman Meldrim Thomson, then still Governor of New Hampshire, had his name in the Iowa papers almost as frequently as the candidates. In May Thomson sent out a letter asking for money for Jepsen and heavy with imprecations about Big Labor and liberals. The letter included a major and potentially quite embarrassing error. Thomson stated that Jepsen had won reelection to his lieutenant governorship by "the highest plurality of any Republican in Iowa's history"—which was simply not true. Tracing the mistake back through the maze of people who had created the letter in the first place, an Iowa reporter found that it had originated with the Viguerie organization.

New Right was able to use the issue to wrench the GOP more to the right—"proof," maintains Richard Viguerie, "of the reduced importance of political parties. And of the New Right's ability to engage in and finance important political activity outside a major political party."

The American Conservative Union, for instance, sent out two million fund-raising letters urging defeat of the treaties and put out a film which it claims to have shown in forty-eight states on 193 television stations. The Conservative Caucus mailed over three million fund-raising letters and held, by Viguerie's reckoning, rallies or campaigns in all fifty states, organized by what they called a Truth Squad. Viguerie himself went into high gear and raised a bundle of money. He claims that he accumulated $110,000 and that the Conservative Caucus, the CSFC, NCPAC, ACU and RAVCO, as well as Citizens for the Republic, a Reagan campaign vehicle, contributed an additional $5,000 apiece. Altogether, Viguerie asserts, the conservatives spent about $3 million on the Panama effort. And, as he gloats in his book, "We almost pulled it off."[19]

The attendance at a meeting at Richard Viguerie's house in the summer of 1978 gives a sense of just how many interests were involved. An official emissary from the Republican National Committee was there, as well as two others from the National Republican Congressional Committee and two more from the Republican Study Committee, the caucus of conservatives in the Congress. Representatives came from the vanguard anti-treaty groups like the ACU, the Conservative Caucus and Reagan's Citizens for the Republic, as well as YAF. A great many of the small circle of friends who ran the conservative movement were there. Paul Weyrich came from the Committee for the Survival of a Free Congress. Howard Phillips came from the Conservative Caucus' national committee. Roger Stone came from the Young Republicans. Former Anita Bryant publicist Mike Thompson was there from something called the National Defense PAC. Even right-to-life was represented: Lee Edwards, an old YAFer who had coined the term New Right, had come for his public-relations firm and brought a colleague, Joe Barrett, who was the chief staffer for a short-lived right-to-life group called Life PAC that Edwards had formed.

The participation of none of these was unusual. What was extraordinary was the representation from business associations and Big Business itself. According to a confidential memo, joining all the rest were Fred Radewagen from the national Chamber of Commerce; Bernadette Budde, the chief staff person for the Business-Industry Political Action Committee (BIPAC), the election-minded organization associated with the National Association of Manufacturers (NAM); Wayne Valis from the American Enterprise Institute, a think tank highly prestigious among business leaders; Maiselle Shortley, who happens to be the sister of Terry Dolan, from the National Agents Political Action Committee, a PAC related to the insurance industry; and Don Annett, from the Texaco Political Action Committee.[20]

The business connection was not so surprising, however, to anyone who had kept up with the fast pace of New Right coalition-building. By a year before the critical 1980 election, the alliance between conservatives and business had assumed that same intricate Boolian algebra of overlapping sets already affecting all the other interests on the right. In this context, the Panama Canal campaign was really a dry run for the coming election, which would indicate whether the conservative majority was really emerging. As Richard Viguerie put it, "That November, the New Right really came of age."[21]

Right-to-lifers were among the principal beneficiaries of this emerging New Right "winning coalition" because of the big bucks they got out of it. Perpetually needy on their own, the right-to-lifers could piggyback on the financial leviathan that the New Right, the fundamentalists and the business political-action committees constituted. Indeed, without the indirect access to cash that the "winning coalition" afforded them, the right-to-lifers would probably never have performed the electoral magic the media was soon to make so much of.

One of the developments that made the coalition so fruitful was post-Watergate changes in the campaign-financing laws*[22] intended

---

*Corporate contributions to candidates had been restricted during the early part of the century by the Tillman Act of 1907, enacted during a period of progressive reform. Legislation appeared periodically after that, but the really significant change came only in the 1970s. In 1971 Congress had passed the Federal Election Campaign Act requiring disclosure of contributions and establishing limits on media advertising. In 1972, the disclosure of 153 individuals illegally contributing $20 million to Richard Nixon's campaign prompted further reform. Post-Watergate amendments to the law imposed contribution limits of $1,000 from an individual to a candidate in a single election and $5,000 to a political-action committee, up to a limit of $25,000 in a single calendar year.

to cut down on excessive individual or corporate donations. The so-called reforms had two significant loopholes, however; first, in failing to prohibit groups independent of a candidate from setting up their own political-action committees and acting in that candidate's interests or against his opponent's, and second, in allowing corporations to set up political-action committees to solicit stockholders, officers and middle-level and professional employees for donations. Because of these loopholes, ironically, the new law had exactly the opposite effect to that intended. The conservatives quickly set up independent PACs that free-lanced in any campaigns they set their minds to, and the corporations quickly set up stockholder and employee PACs to do the same.*[23]

NCPAC's Terry Dolan, who would have so much influence on the right-to-life front, was one who appeared particularly to enjoy flouting the intent of the law by taking advantage of the loophole. When the South Dakota Democratic Party filed suit challenging Dolan's "independent" status, charging that he had openly and illegally encouraged the candidacy of Jim Abdnor against George McGovern, Dolan told Morton Mintz of the *Washington Post,* "I know we did it. We *admit* it. *He* [Abdnor] admits it. We just led him up to the nomination. We got an advisory from the FEC that we could do it."†[24]

Altogether, the 1980 election cost $127.3 million. Trade and corporate PACs spent $61.6 million. New Right PACs raised a combined $19 million, a good deal of it for avowedly anti-abortion

---

*In addition to the unprecedented growth of the independents, corporate political-action committees mushroomed. Whereas in 1974 there were only 89, by 1976 the number had jumped to 450, by 1978 had more than doubled to 821 and by 1980 had increased still more to 1,106. During the same period, contributions made a quantum leap.

†At the time, columnist Mark Shields suggested that in a situation like this the candidate had some responsibility. "The candidate has not yet been born in or out of wedlock," Shields wrote, "who cannot tell you everything good or bad, written or spoken, and by whom, about his opponent in the last 36 months. That's the nature of the beast. Any candidate who is unaware that his opponent is being trashed in half a million dollars' worth of television spots by NCPAC and its allied attack dogs isn't a good bet to have in public office." Shields recommended that to avoid even the appearance of wrongdoing, such a candidate should notify the independent PAC that he was aware of its existence, thereby making it no longer independent and all its future activities blatantly unlawful.

candidates. One-fifth of all contributions to Senate candidates came from PACs, as compared to 13 percent in 1978. In four of the critical targeted Senate races, McGovern received $1,885,443, Church $1,900,220, Bayh $2,042,216, and Culver $1,762,794. Their respective challengers got the following: Abdnor, $1,766,737; Symms, $1,771,349; Quayle, $2,134,580; and Grassley, $1,870,028. While in all four of these races but one the incumbent outdid his opponent in raising money, the sums were astronomical for a single race and do not reflect the fact that the conservative challengers were given disproportionately far more by corporate and right-wing sources. [25]

The most perplexing aspect of all this was the change in the nature of corporate giving—the phenomenon that threw the Democratic candidates off balance even more than did the astonishingly large amounts. Never before had oil companies, savings-and-loan associations, defense contractors, the real-estate and insurance industries, builders, truckers, auto manufacturers and dealers, and the utility, chemical and dairy industries directed their resources in such vast quantities toward so many political unknowns of the same ideological stripe.*[26] The 1980 election truly reflected Mark Twain's immortal observation: "I think I can say, and say with pride, that we have legislatures that bring higher prices than any in the world."

Many factors may have motivated business PAC leaders to climb aboard the conservative bandwagon. Undoubtedly among them were

---

*A comprehensive study done by the Free Congress Research and Education Foundation found that corporate PACs were giving a great deal more to conservative, mostly Republican challengers than to incumbents, a definitive change from past practice. In order to examine exactly how the corporate PACs had contributed, the researcher selected 15 independent conservative PACs and analyzed their contributions, labeling as "selected races" those that the conservative PACs had most favored. Using this index, the study found additionally that of the 25 top corporate PACs, or those giving the most money, 9 gave at least 70 percent of their contributions to the "selected races" and, of that money, gave almost overwhelmingly to conservatives; and another 7 gave at least 50 percent of their contributions to the "selected races" and, of that, most to conservatives. The top 25 corporate PACs accounted for 17 percent of the total PAC giving—a huge amount. Not all of them gave to the "selected races" or to conservatives within those races, but the ones that did gave heartily. Of a total of 269 corporate PACs studied, over 60 percent gave "ideologically." The Hunt Energy Corporation of Nelson Bunker Hunt fame, for instance, gave 91.17 percent to the "selected races" and 96.77 percent of that to conservatives.

the specific and elaborate efforts to get them to do so. Both the Republican Party and the New Right introduced the unknown candidates to the PAC leaders in an effort to get them to contribute to the candidates' campaigns. Once having heard the conservatives' pro-business rap, the PAC leaders may simply have acted in what they thought were their own best interests.

The GOP held at least one hundred official campaign training schools, for exactly this purpose. Sometimes these took place in Washington, sometimes elsewhere in the country. A Detroit public-relations expert took advantage of the Republican national convention to put together an all-day seminar July 15 for almost thirty Republican candidates, none of them incumbents, so that they could spend about ten minutes apiece in front of the PAC executives strutting their stuff.[27]

The Committee for the Survival of a Free Congress and NCPAC did political consulting as well. By its own reckoning, CSFC by 1980 had trained one thousand activists and been involved in two hundred campaigns. NCPAC too put on candidates' training schools.[28] As well as helping conservatives organize and developing electoral strategies for them, the New Right groups also advised the campaigns as to which corporate PACs were most likely to give money to them. The Conservative Caucus improved on this by sending out mailings exposing those PACs that were *not* contributing to the right (that is, both correct and conservative, from their point of view) candidates.

Influential individuals also persuaded the PACs to put their money on conservatives. According to an account published in *National Journal*, United Technologies vice-president Clark MacGregor, Richard Nixon's 1972 campaign coordinator, sent a memo around to various PACs in 1978 urging them to support pro-business candidates. In an interview with *National Journal*, MacGregor revealed that he had advised companies on how to set up the PACs and to seek help from business associations like the U.S. Chamber of Commerce and the National Association of Manufacturers' Business-Industry Political Action Committee (BIPAC).[29]

Probably the most effective lobbying for the ideological shift came from the Chamber of Commerce, with its staff of 1,200 and its annual budget of $30 million, and the smaller but still potent BI-PAC. These groups had come under right-wing control long before the election under the leadership of, among others, Richard DeVos and Jay Van Andel. By 1980 the Chamber was sending its 175,000-member businesses a list of its choices of House and Senate "opportunity races"—those in which a candidate favorable to business stood a good chance of winning and needed help. BIPAC, considered the more experienced of the two, had fewer members, about 1,500, but was much more activist in its approach. Every month, BIPAC distributed reports on national political trends affecting business and summaries of campaign developments. BIPAC's list of candidates to support read like a Who's Who of the American political right wing.[30]

However the change came about, it was clear that certain businessmen were delighted with it, among them, for instance, Justin Dart. The chairman of Dart Industries (since merged with the Kraft Corporation), and a member of Ronald Reagan's Kitchen Cabinet, Dart contributed a total of a quarter-million dollars to the 1980 campaign of Reagan and other conservatives. Dialogue between business and politicians "is a fine thing," he remarked to the *Wall Street Journal* about the trend in giving, "but with a little money, they hear you better."[31]

All of this raises an interesting point. Election law prohibits cooperation of candidates and their parties with special-interest groups or business associations or any combination thereof. Weyrich, Phillips and the other New Right leaders have always insisted that they have worked independently of everyone else. Charges of the Democratic Party to the contrary notwithstanding, the Federal Election Commission, which administers the laws, has yet to prove any New Right violation of them. Still the sour aftertaste of the appearance of wrongdoing remains.

For the cocky Terry Dolan, this has become a joke that makes a mockery of the election law. Dolan predicted in March 1980 regarding his New Right colleagues that they could elect Mickey Mouse to the House or the Senate in the right circumstances.[32] This cavalier attitude toward the system of voting—one of the principal foundations of American democracy—may have come about at least in part because many of these New Right leaders were making careers for themselves in this game of politics and, in the process, becoming very, very rich men.*[33]

---

* Charles Black, for instance, the architect of the Republican element of the "winning coalition," eventually left the GOP to form his own consulting firm, the

After the dust had settled, the "winning coalition" appeared to have won—and won big—in the 1980 election, and along with it, riding on its coattails, the right-to-lifers. As in many matters political, however, things were not exactly as they seemed.

The real accomplishment of the "winning coalition"—even more than making the unknown challengers victorious—appeared to be in defeating famous, relatively popular, longtime incumbents who happened also to be pro-choice. The tactic for pulling this off was to mount vicious, wild-swinging negative campaigns the likes of which American politics has rarely seen. These campaigns caught the incumbents by surprise, putting them on the defensive.

The New Right began preparing for the 1980 elections well in advance. The right-to-lifers who had openly teamed up with them were included in the planning from the beginning. In May 1979, Paul Weyrich convened what was called a Pro-Life Political Action

---

New Republican Victory Fund—a name familiarly close to that of a party organization—and another organization set up specifically to facilitate the reelection of Congressman Jack Kemp. Black made $60,000 in fees—20 percent of the gross receipts—in a few short months of operation. "The good thing about PACs," Black candidly told a reporter from the *Miami Herald*, "is, they're year-round work. They're more reliable about paying than candidates are."

NCPAC raised $5.3 million, spent $1,282,000 on the election—about one third of the total—and, of that, gave only $182,000 to the candidates. The figures for the Committee for the Survival of a Free Congress are similar: $1.1 million raised; $172,000 spent; $122,000 of that going to candidates. Terry Dolan and Paul Weyrich apparently learned well at the feet of master Viguerie how to clone their operations for an even better cash flow. In 1978, another new group appeared, called—again in imitation of the party organizations—the National Republican Candidates Committee. That committee is a spin-off of something named MediAmerica, which in turn is a direct creation of NCPAC. The head of MediAmerica is Richard Geske, the former college roommate of Terry Dolan, who advanced Geske $2,000 to set it up. Dolan was a director of MediAmerica, but was replaced by his sister, Maiselle Shortley. The National Republican Candidates Committee did $16,905 in business in 1980, but owed $20,000 to MediAmerica; likewise, MediAmerica's business was almost exclusively with NCPAC, which owed it $836,784 in 1981.

Jesse Helms's Congressional Club—the third best-endowed independent political-action committee after NCPAC and CSFC—likewise raised $7.1 million, spent $766,000, or about one ninth, on elections and gave only $66,000 away to candidates. LAPAC raised $344,000, spent $77,400 and gave away $11,400. Americans for Life, a key right-to-life PAC, raised $67,000, spent $38,000 and gave away exactly 0.

Conference in Chicago. Attending the meeting, among others, were Donald "Buz" Lukens, the Viguerie associate who had helped put together United Republicans of America, and a representative from Paul Brown's Life Amendment Political Action Committee. This was where they put together the pieces of their strategy.

Shortly after the conference, a newly formed organization called Americans for Life appeared in Washington, D.C. As it turned out, Americans for Life was essentially a dummy organization with no program and no membership. Its sole reason for being was as a conduit for money. The money was specifically designated for a project with the sinister sobriquet "Stop the Babykillers." The purpose of Stop the Babykillers was to kick off the New Right's six-year plan to capture as many congressional seats as possible for conservatives by defeating Senators George McGovern, Frank Church, Birch Bayh and John Culver as well as other big-name liberals. [34]

McGovern, Church, Bayh and Culver were excellent choices. Not only were they well known, but they also had serious weaknesses going into the election to which the average person was not privy. This meant that any victories the New Right political operatives racked up would seem even more consequential than they were.

All four of them, for instance, had flirted with a presidential nomination, not necessarily a plus in the eyes of the voters back home. Their states, once very Republican, were turning that way again. Between 1936 and 1970, for instance, the voters of South Dakota had elected only one governor and one congressman who were Democrats; that congressman was George McGovern. Reagan was to sweep Church's Idaho by forty-one points; Bayh's Indiana has always been dominated by a Republican machine; as for Culver's Iowa, no Democratic senator ever in its history has been able to win reelection. [35]

Moreover, they had all distinguished themselves in one way or another that was bound to bring closer scrutiny than to the more typically inactive senator. They often seemed more national leaders than doting servants of their constituents. Their very attention to their jobs gave them a particular vulnerability to right-to-life, New Right, fundamentalist, Republican, and corporate ire. McGovern had run on a platform almost exclusively devoted to stopping the war in Vietnam. Church had headed the investigation into illegal and questionable CIA activities at home and abroad, and was chairman of a committee overseeing the activities of multinational corporations. Bayh had called for the breaking up of the oil companies, and, as chairman of the Senate subcommittee on the Constitution, had been in the uncomfortable spot of having to block constitutional amendments allowing prayer in the schools and banning busing and abortion. Culver, a determined advocate of arms control, was the subject of *New Yorker* columnist Elizabeth Drew's book *Senator*.

Stop the Babykillers consisted of a grab bag of people most of whom had never distinguished themselves beyond their own immediate callings. The honorary chairman of the inventively titled group was George Hansen, a little-known Republican congressman from the Second District of Idaho. First elected to the House in 1964, he lost his seat when he ran for the Senate against Frank Church in 1968, but won it back by running against a relatively moderate Republican in 1974. His congressional career had been lackluster, except that in 1975 he pleaded guilty to campaign-law violations and was sentenced to two months in jail—a sentence later reduced to a $42,000 fine. *The Almanac of American Politics* has called him "one of the authentic zanies in Congress." After the American hostages were taken in Iran in 1979, Hansen made two trips to that country to try to negotiate their release. It might have been a fine and brave act, except that he was hardly the one to do it. He had formerly advocated the setting up of a committee of inquiry to examine past American actions in Iran that had undermined the Shah, a position unlikely to endear him to the zealots who had replaced the dictator. Some observers felt that Hansen's trips may have helped prolong the captives' internment.[36] Hansen had also been active in the John Birch Society and the Liberty Lobby, an explicitly anti-Semitic group, and he was one of those involved in the Panama Canal fight. At the time of Stop the Babykillers, he was on the board of the Moral Majority, an adviser to Weyrich's Committee for the Survival of a Free Congress and head of the American Conservative Union's Stop OSHA project.[37] Interestingly, Hansen, although conservative, had never before appeared to take such an intense interest in matters like this.

Others involved in Stop the Babykillers were the chairman, Buz Lukens; treasurer Michael Patrick, who had held the same position for Third Century–backed candidate Reverend Robert Thoburn; and

J. Curtis Herge, a lawyer who was once campaign assistant to Richard Nixon and then a secretary of NCPAC. Herge was the NCPAC connection, although Terry Dolan—while never hesitating to speak on behalf of the group or to defend its activities—always denied he himself had anything to do with it.[38]

Stop the Babykillers and its associates proceeded to go after the four senators with fangs bared, and there were some especially ugly moments. One letter, over Lukens' signature, read as follows:

> If you think I'm too harsh when I refer to these Members of Congress as Baby Killers, stop and think a minute.
>
> Recall during the Vietnam War when hypocrites like Mc-Govern and these others piously wrung their hands and denounced the brutal slaying of Vietnamese children.
>
> We all hate wars and killings but hypocrites like these need to be reminded that a little baby in its mother's womb has a beating heart, just like you and I, as early as six weeks after conception.
>
> That's a full 7½ months before actual birth. If a little baby boy or little baby girl has a real, live beating heart and is developed enough to have toes and fingers and eyes and ears, can't these holier-than-thou politicians give them the right to life, too?[39]

When asked about the meanness of their slogan, "Stop the Baby-killers," Buz Lukens told a reporter, "Frankly, that was brutal. But we had to get contributors' attention or we would have lost our money."[40]

The defeat of George McGovern was seemingly a textbook case illustrating the way they went about their campaign. The New Right started early, built up momentum, came at the wavering Senator with everything in their arsenal, waged a war in the primary on both the Democratic and Republican sides, used the entire "winning coalition" to great advantage, spent lots of money, and won big— really big. In all, the New Right mounted a truly impressive effort.

Regardless, many people think George McGovern would have lost anyway. One of them is George Cunningham, McGovern's aide, manager and friend, who has been with him since more than a quarter-century ago when they first drove around the state in an old rattletrap during the candidate's stint as executive secretary of the state party. Cunningham feels that McGovern started faltering way back after his 1972 presidential run, before NCPAC even existed. "You can feel the inferiority complex throughout the state," Cunningham explains. "The people of South Dakota think they are not as good as other people. When one of their own becomes too big for his britches, he becomes suspect. After he lost the presidential election, McGovern ran for the Senate again in 1974. We did in-depth polling which showed that what he had to do was go around the state and let everybody figuratively kick him in the pants. He had to say, 'I wanted to run for President in the worst way—and I sure did.' People could laugh with him over the ridiculous idea of somebody from South Dakota wanting to run for President."[41] McGovern won that one, but just barely, by 53 percent. By the time of the 1980 election, he was virtually a sitting duck.

The campaign against him began, as nearly as can be judged, on November 1, 1977, when a nationwide mailing went out over the signature of former Third Century candidate Dr. Ron Paul, as a fund-raising appeal on behalf of Dale Bell, another political nonentity and former NCPAC employee. In this first letter, Paul did not explain precisely what Bell was doing, except to say that he was trying to "bring together conservative elements" to "turn McGovern and his cronies out of office." Paul described other groups participating in the effort as the South Dakota branches of the Conservative Caucus, the Young Republicans, the Gun Owners, the Young Americans for Freedom, the Libertarians and the Society on Political Education (free-market advocates), as well as "young Reaganites." The envelope for sending in contributions was addressed to Dr. Ron Paul in care of the Target McGovern Committee at a post-office box in Spearfish, South Dakota. This was the opening salvo of the "Target 80" campaign, which was to surface a little later. The first solicitation did not mention abortion.

About a year later, in early 1979, Paul sent out another nationwide appeal, this time introducing Bell in a little more detail. The second letter praised "Dale" as having been the Dallas–Fort Worth coordinator of the 1976 Reagan campaign, the Mountain States director of the Conservative Caucus, the state chairman of the Gun Owners of South Dakota and the state director of the "Save Our Canal" media blitz, as well as the director of Paul's first successful congressional campaign in Texas. Paul went on to criticize McGovern for his position on the cruise missile, Cuba, the ERA, homosexual rights and the Panama Canal, and for "his friendship with Jane Fonda." This time, abortion did come up, but again the letter did not make clear exactly what Bell wanted for himself.

In the meantime, on December 1, 1978, and again on January 1, 1979, Bell was sending out his own double whammy of an appeal. With these two letters, he finally revealed the purpose behind the mailings. He explained that he was declaring his candidacy for McGovern's Senate seat in order to qualify under FEC regulations to receive national campaign contributions. Describing himself as a "stalking horse," Bell acknowledged that his expectation was not really to win, but rather to have the opportunity to mount a negative public-relations campaign against McGovern. "Keep in mind," Bell wrote, "our primary goal is to expose George McGovern." Indeed, except for the letters, he never did much in the way of campaigning for office.

The first letter was very blunt, with a hardly noticeable little white lie. It explained that the 680,000 people who comprised the small state of South Dakota were "middle-of-the-road conservative" but were represented in Congress by ultraliberals who could be defeated by the efforts of "trained political managers (who are movement conservatives) who have moved back into the state after receiving much valuable experience working nationally." The erroneous implication that Bell and his colleagues were natives of South Dakota was strategically left hanging. The letter went on to explain that a conservative drive in South Dakota would be easy and relatively inexpensive:

> TV time in South Dakota is CHEAP; i.e. I purchased a 30-second spot for our "Save Our Canal" committee during the Super Bowl game early last year with an estimated viewing audience of 300,000 in the Sioux Falls area, this spot cost $220.00. This same spot in the Houston market, when I was working with Congressman Ron Paul, would have cost $8,000.00–$12,000.00. Yet, both Texas and South Dakota have EQUAL votes in the U.S. Senate.

The second letter was equally frank, revealing Bell's plan to set up a political-action committee to be called "Target McGovern." The committee was going to begin a series of television documentaries to expose "the *real George McGovern*."[42]

Two organizations that ended up giving critical financial support to Bell were the Conservative Victory Fund and the Dart Industries PAC. The Fund was the PAC of the American Conservative Union, which had been so active in the Panama Canal fight; Justin Dart is the member of Ronald Reagan's Kitchen Cabinet whose company gave generously at the office to New Right candidates.

On July 27, 1980, NCPAC officially entered the campaign with a mailing sent out over the signature of New Hampshire Senator Gordon Humphrey, the man Terry Dolan once took credit for having catapulted into office. The letter announced the Target 80 campaign against "five top liberal senators"—McGovern, of course, along with Frank Church, Birch Bayh, John Culver and Alan Cranston. The letter was candid about exactly what NCPAC intended to do. The strategy came in five parts. Step One was a voter survey. Step Two was the hiring and activating of field representatives for all the targeted states. The field representative (always referred to as "he") would marshal all the forces opposed to the incumbent, "such as the pro-life groups, taxpayers organizations, gun owners organizations, and a host of others." Step Three was a massive mailing campaign to all the registered voters of the state, geared to the computerized voter survey. The idea was to alert voters to the Senators' "record of radicalism" and to seek their involvement by asking them not only to contribute money but also to participate in writing letters, walking a precinct, sending postcards to their friends, or putting their names on newspaper ads. Step Four was an advertising campaign. Step Five was "final candidate recruitment." The letter enclosed sample advertisements, among them one entitled "McGovern Sells Out Taiwan and the U.S." The mailing made no mention of Dale Bell's Target McGovern "stalking-horse" campaign, or of the nasty drive that was to follow.

The letter went on to reveal that Stop the Babykillers was going to have its own four-part strategy, one remarkably compatible with NCPAC's. Step One was to give direct campaign contributions to the opponents of the "babykillers"; Step Two was to sponsor free campaign seminars for activists to teach them how to organize a political precinct, recruit volunteers, use political advertising and get out the vote; Step Three was to help the opposing candidates hire "the best political pollsters available"; and Step Four was to fly "campaign experts" into the targeted states to provide "on-the-spot, up to the minute advice for the unique problems that each Pro-Life campaign faces." The letter cautioned that the campaign had to start immediately. It concluded with a plea for donations to raise a projected total of $275,000.*[43]

This classic New Right effort was accentuated by Paul Brown's Life Amendment Political Action Committee, which came to life during the primary. LAPAC had undergone an interesting transformation. The Browns had created a second organization which they called the Let's All Protect a Child Fund, with an acronym conveniently the same as that of the political-action committee. The second LAPAC, however, was a division of Christian Family Renewal, the California-based right-wing fundamentalist outfit of Murray Norris. Having the two sets of identical initials allowed the Browns to receive funds they couldn't otherwise have legally funneled through to a political organization. Whether any money came through the second LAPAC route is unclear.

At any rate, the New Right right-to-life effort in South Dakota was a one-two punch from the Mecklenburgs' Minnesota Citizens Concerned for Life and the original LAPAC. McGovern's opponent in the Democratic primary, Larry Schumaker, like Dale Bell, came from Texas, apparently just for the race. MCCL gave Schumaker much of his financial support. LAPAC didn't contribute much money, but provided the advice for those who were doing the legwork. Paul Brown was also able to win away from the National Right to Life Committee the allegiance of a native South Dakotan, Ellen Dempsey, who was responsible for organizing the Catholic vote. What Brown and Dempsey counted on were the Catholic Democrats.

Only 18 percent of the registered voters in South Dakota are Catholics, but 38 percent of those are Democrats. If they switched parties, the thinking was, they could provide the decisive margin to help a Republican win. Catalyzing the Catholic network in such a small state was exceptionally easy. As Dempsey, before then a stranger to electoral politics, revealed in an interview, all she had to do was mobilize three or four of the state's population centers—Sioux Falls, Aberdeen, Pierre and Rapid City—and she could broker the elec-

*Americans for Life ultimately raised $119,115.25.

tion. After the primary, that is precisely what the plain-talking house-wife did, traveling around the state like a circuit rider, trying to get the priests in the parishes and the leadership of the Catholic fraternal organizations excited about the race.*[44]

The institutional church was active on its own during the campaign. Early on, McGovern was able to secure a three-hour audience with the Catholic bishop of South Dakota, and won from him the dubious praise that all of the Senator's program was to the bishop's liking—except the stand on abortion. According to George Cunningham, the bishop was quite candid in admitting that because of abortion he had no choice but to oppose McGovern. Individual priests apparently followed his lead. At one point, when McGovern was scheduled to give a speech in a parochial school, the bishop instructed the presiding priest beforehand to read a statement first. In order to avoid controversy, the principal of the school decided not to allow the McGovern appearance. The principal stood at the schoolhouse door barring the Senator from entering, an act absurdly reminiscent of other sorts of resistance in the South. The last Sunday before the election the priest in one of the larger Catholic churches in Aberdeen came down from the pulpit, took a small child from its mother's arms, held the babe over his head and advised the congregation to "vote for life." Outside, they were handed the usual right-to-life pamphlets.[45]

McGovern's challenger in the general election, James Abdnor, farmer and schoolteacher and, lately, politician, came from an immigrant Lebanese family, poor and illiterate. Abdnor's political hero was President Dwight Eisenhower, and it was during his administration that the young Abdnor got involved in politics. Abdnor was in the South Dakota Senate from 1956 to 1968, in the last year serving as president pro tem. He was elected as lieutenant governor the following year and afterward spent from 1972 to 1980 in Congress. There he had an undistinguished career, perhaps due in part to his poor communications skills. As *The Almanac of American*

---

*Dempsey turned out to be something of a heroine within the right-to-life movement. Midway through the campaign, her daughter developed cancer—ironically, the same kind that had afflicted Senator Edward M. Kennedy's son—and her leg had to be amputated. Despite the personal tragedy, Dempsey went on working. Eventually, the daughter died of the disease.

Politics put it, Abdnor "regularly mangles the English language."[46] Even *The National Right to Life News* felt compelled to introduce a preelection interview with candidate Abdnor with the disclaimer: "His style is not a soap-box orator; rather, he prefers open discussion." In that interview, Abdnor gave some peculiar answers. When the questioner asked whether the high rate of abortions in the country was due to the sexual revolution or to a general increase in violence and crime, Abdnor replied disingenuously, "To be perfectly honest, I never thought about it." Then he went on to recall the old days when pregnant girls would slip away to have their babies. In mid-interview, he suddenly realized that maybe the old system cost less than the new, since by his reckoning all the "illegitimate children" collected welfare. After stumbling on for several phrases of contra-diction, Abdnor apparently remembered his audience and salvaged the interview by reasserting his moral repugnance for abortion. Not long afterwards, however, he worked his way into a verbal *cul de sac:*

> I had my first experience of campaigning in a girl's dorm. I was up on the second floor of the dorm at the university knocking on doors. This was a new part of life to me.
> They finally asked me to leave; I guess they don't allow politics on the second floor. What else they would allow I don't know. It was sort of fun.[47]

Interestingly, neither Abdnor, a bachelor, nor his supporters ap-parently ever felt any qualms about labeling McGovern, father of five, grandfather of four, a "babykiller."

The national Republican Party as such was not overly visible during the Abdnor campaign. That was exactly as expected, ac-cording to the game plan laid out by party chairman William Brock when he hired Charles Black as GOP political director. Black's job was to ensure that the local parties would begin to take over some of the control of the elections. Thus, much more than the party chiefs in the capital, the Republicans of South Dakota carried on the fight. Just as with the New Right, right-to-life, independent and fundamentalist organizations, however, the party did not have to depend on funding solely from within the tiny state of South Dakota. The national party sent ample money for that purpose, raised on the national level.

In June 1979, for instance, Senator Jesse Helms sent a fund-raising letter to prospective conservative donors with an analysis by the National Republican Senatorial Committee of the weaknesses of the ten most "vulnerable" Democrats up for election, McGovern included. A group calling itself the South Dakota Senatorial Research Committee made a similar appeal not long afterward; among its members were GOP luminaries including Governor William Janklow, Lieutenant Governor Lowell Hansen and a host of other state, county and municipal officials. Another letter from the state GOP chairman had an endorsement from none other than as-yet-unannounced candidate James Abdnor.

Before Abdnor officially entered the race, NCPAC appeared to join forces with the Republicans in promoting him. The candidate met at least twice with NCPAC officials. On the first occasion, in August 1979, Abdnor discussed with a representative of People for an Alternative to McGovern (PAM), a state NCPAC affiliate, the chances of beating McGovern. Around December, NCPAC pollster Arthur Finkelstein contacted Abdnor about a poll that showed he had an edge of "50 to 33 percent." Abdnor also spoke with Terry Dolan about the findings and admitted that they influenced him to run. The week of Abdnor's declaration of his candidacy, March 17–24, 1980, PAM announced it would coordinate a "media blitz" against McGovern. Altogether, from June 1979 to April 1980, NCPAC spent $120,529.62 against McGovern, with the second highest monthly outlay ($16,768.99) in March, "media blitz" month.

The South Dakota Democratic Party filed suit with the Federal Election Commission on May 2, 1980, charging that NCPAC had violated the law in that its "independent expenditures" were really contributions to Abdnor, coordinated with his campaign, the alleged collusion allowing NCPAC to contribute over the maximum allowed limit. The FEC, however, ultimately ruled in NCPAC's and Abdnor's favor.[48]

McGovern lost by a huge nineteen-point margin. His upbringing as the son of a Methodist minister couldn't help him; nor his reputation as a family man; nor his dogged attention to constituent services; and certainly not a nationwide campaign on his behalf by feminist Gloria Steinem and pro-choice and liberal forces. Longtime adviser George Cunningham feels that the New Right did soften

McGovern up and that of all the single issues, abortion hurt him the most. "If it had not been for the New Right and the single issues, the race could have been a lot closer," concedes Cunningham. But he will not say definitively that they were the final cause of the defeat. Cunningham claims that a poll taken by McGovern's people in December 1978 showed him with a favorability rating of 76 percent, but that only a year later, in January 1980, the figure had plummeted to 54 percent. Cunningham points out that South Dakota has only 202,000 registered Democrats to 206,000 registered Republicans. Out-take polls indicated that McGovern did not lose any more than the usual number of the Democrats to Abdnor— the famous crossover vote that the New Right prides itself on getting—but that instead they simply didn't go to the polls at all. "That's what did us in," claims Cunningham. "Our own party went against us."

The campaigns against Church, Bayh and Culver were just as heated as that against McGovern. NCPAC's attacks on the relatively moderate Church, for instance, consisted of lies, innuendos and distortions of the record. A well-financed group calling itself Anybody But Church (ABC) started off the campaign. ABC was much like Stop the Babykillers; supposedly independent, it was really run by New Right hand Don Todd, later to become chief of staff of the American Conservative Union. Todd's early literature, mailed to thirty thousand people, portrayed Church as "one of the architects of the era of appeasement," blaming him for the Iran hostage crisis, the Soviet invasion of Afghanistan, and the presence of Soviet troops in Cuba and of Cuban troops in Africa. Significantly, the ABC letter was signed by Terry Dolan. Later in the campaign, Todd became an overt NCPAC organizer on the NCPAC payroll.[49]

NCPAC's ad campaign starting the June before the election was even more devastating. NCPAC concentrated on what it called "Frank Church's record of shame." One television commercial showed a gaping missile silo and stated that because missile silos were empty "they won't be of much help in defense of your family or mine. You see, Senator Church has almost always opposed a strong national defense..." The obvious implication was that Church was responsible for emptying the silos. In reality, the silo was part of the Titan missile system, which had been superseded by the Minuteman and was no longer needed. Another ad accused Church of having

voted to increase his Senate salary, when in fact the opposite was
true. A third made him out as having pandered to what the spot
called "Zionism," and as being a chum of Castro. Church, with
some reason, labeled the attacks "scummy."[50]

A controversial member of the anti-Church coalition was Nelson
Bunker Hunt, who served on the campaign finance committee of
Church's opponent, Congressman Steven Symms. During the drive,
columnist Jack Anderson disclosed the connection, which was later
expanded upon by the *Chicago Sun-Times*. Apparently Symms, along
with Georgia Representative Larry McDonald and Senator Jesse
Helms, had blocked for three years a government plan to sell surplus
silver—the sale of which could have slowed or halted the rise of
silver profits that brought huge amounts into the personal vaults of
the Hunt family. The surplus was part of a strategic stockpile for
use by critical industries in times of war. In 1978 the government
decided to unload 67 million ounces and use the profits to buy other
commodities that might be even more needed in wartime. The
proposed sale was reportedly stopped by repeated pressure from silver
interests, and was finally blocked altogether by Symms, McDonald
and Helms. The Hunts had given McDonald a total of $13,000
during his 1978 and 1980 campaigns, and had given Helms $5,500.
They had not contributed to Symms in 1980, but the then Congressman had received $2,500 from them in 1978 and also reportedly
had silver holdings of his own.[51]

The "winning coalition" was especially visible in the anti-Bayh
campaign. Indiana—the heart of the Bible Belt—was the home of
longtime National Right to Life Committee bookkeeper Mary Hunt
(Hunt lived next door to Bayh's campaign coordinator in South
Bend), who was cooperating with Paul Brown's LAPAC as well as
with Moral Majority executive director Reverend Robert Billings.
Paul Brown, Hunt and the popular local television preacher Greg
Dixon, Moral Majority board member and Indiana contact, appeared together on TV one week before the election. Bayh was one
of the incumbents who were victims of the famous NCPAC "baloney" ad. In the ad, a large bologna appears on the screen. A cleaver
slices it while a voice in the background intones, "One very big
piece of baloney is Birch Bayh telling us he's fighting inflation." A
price appears on the bologna—$46 billion—with the voice contin-
uing, "That's how much deficit spending Bayh voted for last year

alone." The ad concludes with the voice predicting, "So, to stop inflation, you'll have to stop Bayh first. Because if Bayh wins, you lose."

The combined strength of Catholics, fundamentalists and the New Right was helped by the particular calling of Bayh's opponent, Dan Quayle. Quayle's grandfather is publisher of *Indiana Star-News*, one of the state's most influential newspapers. The *Star* reporters covered the campaign fairly, but the paper's curmudgeonly editor obliged the grandson with a series of vitriolic editorials attacking Bayh—erroneously charging, for example, that Bayh voted against Social Security refinancing. When the paper finally responded to Bayh's request for an apology, the damage may have already been done. The retraction came the morning of election day.[52]

As for Iowa, the right-to-life forces had a dry run there two years earlier during the successful campaign to procure the other short-lived Democratic senatorial seat, held by Dick Clark. Right-to-lifers had received massive national publicity, making them all the more confident and raring to go. And the Republicans in this state, unlike many of the others, nominated a man who had been in politics for a long time, Charles Grassley (Iowa legislature sixteen years; congressman from Iowa since 1974, the only Republican to win in that momentarily Democratic year).[53]

In all three of the contests—against Church, Bayh and Culver—the incumbents lost by relatively small margins. In Church's case, it was only one percent; in the case of Grassley and Quayle, only 6 and 8 percent respectively. The campaign managers of all three races insist that their candidates lost because of the native conservative proclivities of their states, the failure of the voters to come to the polls, the mistakes of Democratic President Jimmy Carter and the abysmal state of the economy, and only to a much lesser extent because of sentiment about abortion and the other "social issues." If anything, these managers feel that their candidates may even have been helped by the New Right, faring better than they otherwise might have because of a backlash against the meanness. Church coordinator Cleve Corbett, a former newspaper reporter, is particularly insistent about this. Corbett pointed out in an interview that Church came out nine points ahead of Steven Symms in a poll published by the *Idaho Statesman* the Sunday before the election, and four points ahead in their own campaign poll. "Church won the race," Corbett asserted, "but lost the election."[54]

Terry Dolan rejects out of hand this notion of a backlash. In an interview, Dolan insisted that "polling data showed that that is not true." When asked for documentary confirmation, he refused. "It shows things I don't care to discuss with the general public," he explained testily.

Dolan also denied strenuously that the New Right operatives like himself were using the abortion issue during the 1980 election. "I wouldn't call it opportunistic. It's certainly taking advantage of an issue on which we agree. I suppose you could reverse that," he bantered, "and say the pro-abortion people were taking advantage of abortion to get rid of John Culver."[55]

Significantly, however, abortion was used only in those races in which the New Right apparently thought it would do some good. One other heavily targeted election gives some insight into this phenomenon. This was the race between the three-term Democratic incumbent from northern Virginia, Congressman Joseph Fisher, and two-time also-ran Third Century–associated fundamentalist Frank Wolf. Wolf had served as an executive of the National Canners Association and as a lobbyist on Capitol Hill for a number of clients. He had a particularly good in with the right-to-lifers, since he had once represented Gerbers Baby Foods, a member of the owning family of which had been on the board of Marjory Mecklenburg's American Citizens Concerned for Life. Wolf certainly could have pushed the abortion issue. He chose not to and ran instead on the state of the economy. His friends and associates played it that way, too. In July, a group calling itself Friends of Frank Wolf circulated a letter soliciting support, signed by representatives of the National Association of Manufacturers, the General Dynamics Corporation PAC, the Standard Oil Company of Ohio PAC, the Libbey-Owens-Ford Company PAC and a host of trade associations. The race was also targeted by the Chamber of Commerce and BIPAC. Paul Weyrich wrote a glowing commendation of the candidate in the New Right leader's weekly feature in The John Birch Society News. Fisher's campaign manager, Lucy Denney, believes that the reason all these groups went after Fisher had to do with the fact that he had been a strong and effective voice in favor of business regulation on the House Ways and Means Committee.[56]

Unlike most other things, it is easier to prove that the abortion issue did not have an impact than that it did. Many of the legislators targeted by the "winning coalition" won, among them Congressman Morris Udall of Arizona and Senators Christopher Dodd of Connecticut and Patrick Leahy of Vermont. Moreover, these were races that could have easily gone the other way.

Morris Udall, the long-jawed chairman of the House Committee on the Interior, was another also-ran for President in prior years. He represents a district that is changing rapidly from an influx of Sun Belt seekers and Hispanics, the first of whom have no particular fondness for an incumbent and the latter of whom are Catholic and extremely devout about it. Moral Majority is strong in his district, particularly among the Mormons. His opponent, Richard Huff, was a developer, which brought out the powerful real-estate industry. Independent oilman Eddie Chiles, head of the Western Oil Corporation, bombarded the Congressman with an expensive series of ads, their theme taken from the popular movie *Network:* "I'm mad as hell."* Chiles's campaign prompted some wits on Udall's staff to counteract with bumper stickers reading, "I'm mad, too, Eddie Chiles," and a radio spot saying, "Texas already has twenty-four congressman. Now they want their twenty-fifth." The last two weeks before the election, NCPAC ran anti-abortion spots on the Spanish-speaking radio stations every half hour, calling Udall a baby killer.[57]

In the Connecticut race, both candidates probably got some mileage out of their family connections, Christopher Dodd's father having been a U.S. senator himself and James Buckley's brother William F. providing the candidate instant name recognition. Buckley waged the classic New Right right-to-life campaign, complete with the "baloney" ads. He had six local bishops give a press conference urging Catholics—who comprise more than half the population of the state—to participate in the political process. His NCPAC-inspired radio ads were so extremist that eventually he had to pull them off the air. He got money from everybody from the oil companies to Joseph Coors.[58] Up until the election, his unfavorability rating just

---

*The world of the conservatives sometimes seems very small indeed. Chiles's ads were done up by Arthur J. Finkelstein, NCPAC's campaign adviser. Altogether, Chiles fielded these quirky commercials on 650 radio stations in 13 states. The PAC of Chiles's company, Western Oil of North America, contributed to 26 conservative candidates in 14 states.

kept going up no matter what he did.

Patrick Leahy is the only Democrat the small, conservative state of Vermont has ever sent to the Senate. On the national level, he outraged New Right operatives by his leadership on the Senate Committee on the District of Columbia—a particular obsession of theirs. Leahy was known in his home state much more for his unrelenting pro-environmentalism: he had once served as the state prosecutor who sued the oil companies for price-fixing. Not surprisingly, the oil companies lavished money on his opponent during the Senate reelection race. As a Catholic, Leahy's moderate position on abortion was anathema to conservative Catholic voters. Shortly before the election, when his elderly parents were on their way out of church, Leahy says, they were accosted by right-to-lifers yelling at them, "How can you hold your head up?" More than in other races, however, the hypocrisy of New Right manipulation of the abortion issue stood right out on the record. Leahy was dogged by an opponent in the primary whose stand on abortion was exactly the same as the Senator's. Still, LAPAC targeted Leahy. As one pro-life activist tried to explain this anomaly to the Senator, "You have a track record, but this guy's new, so his mind might be changed."[59]

Morris Udall won by an eighteen-point margin; his campaign coordinator is convinced it was because the Congressman was ready for NCPAC and, instead of reacting defensively, mounted his own offensive early in the campaign. Christopher Dodd won by thirteen points; his legislative aide is convinced it was because the voters were disgusted by the NCPAC assault. Patrick Leahy won only by a slim single point, but the Senator is convinced that was because of local issues rather than those the New Right brought to the election. In all these races, the New Right had a neutral or negative impact, according to the winners. Abortion, while controversial, did not provide a decisive 5 percent vote for the right-to-life losers and, if anything, may have turned the voters off.

The religious right claims to have had its own special impact on the elections separate from that of the New Right and the right-to-lifers. Christian Voice was unarguably at its most forceful in the South, where a majority of fundamentalists reside. Gary Jarmin contended that Christian Voice's drive to portray Jimmy Carter as a friend of homosexuals was particularly devastating.[60] Indeed, a Gallup poll before the election indicated that fundamentalists favored Carter, but an Associated Press–NBC survey of eleven thousand voters as they were leaving the voting booth showed that 56 percent of the born-again voters went for Reagan, and only 40 percent for Carter. Other out-take polls, however, prove that the fundamentalists were reacting just like everyone else—that is, their shift was based much more on Carter's poor performance and the economy than on any moral persuasion by Christian Voice.

The religious right took credit for congressional elections as well, but any examination of their targeting shows many holes. In their supposed stronghold of Mississippi, for instance, they failed to beat Democratic Representatives David Bowen and Jamie Whitten, the latter the once conservative chairman of the House Appropriations Committee who, since assuming that post, has become steadily more liberal. Moral Majority ally Barry Billington of Georgia also couldn't down Elliott Levitas, a liberal Democrat who supports the ERA, opposes a constitutional amendment to allow prayer in schools and favors limited federal funding for abortions for the poor. On the local level, Moral Majority endorsed nineteen candidates in south Florida, only four of whom won.[61]

This is not to suggest that the religious right had no influence at all, but only that, as with NCPAC, some voters may have been just as turned off by their tactics as others were turned on.

A passing mention must also be made of the race of the unfortunate Robert Bauman. The handsome bespectacled Bauman, a Republican, was first elected to the House in 1973 from the First District of Maryland. Bauman had long been a familiar figure on the right as one of the first heads of YAF and part of the youngblood takeover of the American Conservative Union. He voted conservative in Congress, following the party line on social issues like abortion. He was also one of the Congress's best parliamentarians. With adroit maneuvering, he was able to win, place or draw in most floor fights, including delaying for a whole month the hearings of the House committee investigating assassinations. His one drawback was that his aggressive, stern-faced nature earned him the reputation of having little sense of humor. Still, he was mentioned as a possible contender for the Senate seat of liberal Republican Senator Charles "Mac" Mathias or for the position of House minority leader occupied then by John Rhodes.

Then, on October 3, his aspirations crashed around him. On that day he entered a plea of not guilty to a charge of solicitation of sex from a sixteen-year-old boy. He agreed at the same time to six months of court-supervised counseling. Bauman went into seclusion for five days. He and his family did not even show up at the eighth annual campaign event, the Bob Bauman Trail Ride in Fair Hill, Maryland, where more than six hundred of his staunch supporters had braved the chilly October weather to indicate they were still with him. Bauman finally emerged to describe himself as suffering from the "twin compulsions" of alcoholism and "homosexual tendencies" (although he had never been much of a drinker).

While assiduously avoiding the press for the rest of the campaign, Bauman tried hard to win back the approval of the electorate. His wife, Carol, stayed constantly by his side. Her name was mentioned winsomely in an appeal to voters describing the "hell" he had been through and asking for forgiveness and prayers. "Carol sends her very best," Bauman wrote, "and joins me in wishing you well."

The most interesting part of the Bauman affair was the reaction of his conservative colleagues. Bauman had been one of their best and brightest hopes, and his public disgrace put them in an awkward position. They looked disloyal if they did repudiate him, and hypocritical if they didn't. The head of the Maryland Right to Life group, Gerald Meyer, embraced him. "You're talking here about a personal act," Meyer told the *Washington Post*. "For me personally, the sexual orientation is perhaps a little disturbing. But this action certainly has no bearing on his office." Paul Weyrich, however, seeing more clearly the threat Bauman could pose to the cause, called on him to resign immediately.

Bauman lost the vote by 4 percent. Voters may have rejected him not only for his two-facedness over the issue of homosexuality, but also because of FBI charges that he had misused his office, reportedly agreeing to request an honorable discharge for the son of a constituent after she threatened to publicly expose his homosexuality. The actions of his former friends and colleagues probably did not do much to help him, either.[62]

L'affaire Bauman indicated just how ruthless the New Right leadership could be. Neither old friendship nor the forgiveness by others of Bauman in the face of his remorse could dissuade them from the course they thought would bring the country a conservative voting majority.

The alliance of the right-to-life movement with the "winning coalition" eventually afforded them ten new seats in the Senate and twenty-five in the House, according to *Lifeletter*'s triumphant reporting.[63] The win gave them an enormous sense of accomplishment and a feeling of security, knowing that they could expect more consideration out of the next Congress than ever before. For the grass-roots activists, it was a historic moment, just as Sandra Faucher's voter-identification booklets had prognosticated. As banner headlines in the next *National Right to Life News* suggested, it looked as if they might, indeed, come away with their cherished Human Life Amendment.[64]

Their victory had been something of an illusion, however, and achieved at quite some cost. They had won their races only as the result of a tiny swing vote in the absence of an aroused electorate, and in some cases simply because of the nonvoters alone. Whether this small group could reduplicate its efforts to maintain its balance in Congress, and improve upon it, depended upon a number of factors, not the least of which was the other side. The artificial inflation of the importance of abortion was sure to bring out the pro-choice supporters in 1982, maybe in force enough to topple the right-to-life voting bloc.

Their fate was now irrevocably bound up with that of the evangelicals, the New Right, the Republican Party and those elements of the business community that had supported them, as well as the new President, Ronald Reagan. If any of those should fail them, or get into a quarrel, or shut them out, the original right-to-lifers would be in big trouble. Additionally, the right-to-lifers would have to take responsibility for the apparent achievement of the coalition in helping to move the entire country, if only temporarily, to the right.

This brought up another question. The unholy alliance meant that right-to-lifers had traded moral for strategic planning. In the future, every decision would become a trade-off between their values and their chance to win on abortion. The right-to-life movement, in joining the "winning coalition," may just have lost its soul.

IX.

The Facts of Life

On Friday morning, August 12, 1982, Hector Zevallos and his wife, Rosalie Jean, did not show up for work. The Zevalloses were owners of the Hope Clinic for Women, Ltd., an obstetrical- and gynecological-care facility that did abortions. Located in the economically depressed town of Granite City, the clinic served the farm country of southern Illinois. When the Zevalloses were reported missing, sheriff's deputies went to their house to investigate. The rear doors were unlocked. Lights and a television set were on, and near the TV set was a bowl of popcorn. Authorities said there was no sign of a struggle, but also no clue as to what had happened to the couple.

The following Sunday, a man called the FBI office in St. Louis, Missouri, just over the state line. Identifying himself as a member of "the Army of God," he claimed he was holding the Zevalloses for ransom. His demand was not for money, however, but for President Ronald Reagan to publicly denounce abortion and call for an end to it. The caller also threatened the Zevalloses with death if the demand was not complied with by Wednesday. He then told the

FBI that taped inside a chimney in a rest room in a town park was an envelope in which they would find more information.

Agents found the envelope, and inside, just as the caller had promised, was a long letter and a cassette tape with a message purportedly from Hector Zevallos. The letter was entitled "The Epistles." It was forty-three pages long, and, according to an inside source, it rambled, sometimes incoherently. It was written in what the source described as "biblical style." The writer referred to himself as "I, God."

The Wednesday deadline passed, and still no word. Reagan had declined comment, according to White House deputy press secretary Larry Speakes, because the situation was too critical for the President to intervene.

That night, a man phoned the nearby *Collinsville Herald* and talked to news editor Ed Gurney. He too used "biblical" language. He never spoke of Zevallos by name, but at one point, referring to "the man from the abortion clinic," the caller stated, "The man's evil" or "Man is evil"—Gurney couldn't quite make out which. Later the caller informed Gurney, "The end is near."

As part of its investigation, the FBI swarmed out over the countryside taking samples from typewriters of people who might have had any relationship with the crime. One whom they approached was the Reverend Edwin Arentsen of Okawville, a Roman Catholic priest who had led demonstrations against the Hope Clinic. The priest, in fact, had served two terms of ten and eleven days respectively in jail for trespassing on clinic property. The FBI reportedly got no help there.

Another whom law-enforcement officials called on was the Reverend Peter Donohoe, pastor of Sts. Peter and Paul Catholic church in neighboring Alton. Donohoe told the press afterward that the officials had asked for the names of anti-abortion leaders in the area. "Somebody else here gave out the names," Donohoe admitted, "but I would have had reservations in doing so. These are legitimate, honest, good people; there is nothing lunatic about them."

After eight days of captivity, the Zevalloses were released. They were shaken, and authorities told them not to talk much about what had happened. It did come out that their abductors had kept them in an abandoned bunker used for storing ammunition during World War II. A concrete structure rising a few feet above the ground, the

sweltering bunker was located in the middle of a cornfield where
the fully eared stalks concealed it from the outside world. The Zevalloses had been fed peanut-butter sandwiches and soda and forced
to use a large bucket as a toilet. The kidnappers had harassed Hector
Zevallos to denounce abortion, and had threatened both him and
his wife with death if they refused to close down their clinic.

The FBI finally caught the kidnappers, Don Benny Anderson,
forty-two, of Pearland, Texas, Wayne Moore, eighteen, and his
brother Matthew, twenty. Because they had not taken the Zevalloses
across state lines, the abductors could not be charged with kidnapping. Anderson was indicted with obstructing interstate commerce,
and all three of them with conspiring to do so. [*1]

This was not the first instance of violence from right-to-lifers.
Incidents had occurred in Omaha, Nebraska, Cleveland, Ohio, and
Hempstead, New York, among other places. The perpetrators were
obviously deadly serious about their mission. Only hours after the
firebombing at the Omaha Ladies Clinic, for instance, the local
newspaper received a letter reportedly concluding, "You'd bomb a
concentration camp—why not an abortion clinic?" In some places,
the assaults just would not stop. The Planned Parenthood clinic in
St. Paul, Minnesota, for instance, spent a nightmarish year of threats,
harassment and intimidation. It started in February 1977, when
unknown persons set fire to the administrative offices after having
tried to penetrate the area below that housed the clinic. The entire
administrative wing was destroyed, and the clinic suffered water and
smoke damage. Altogether, the estimated cost of repair was a quarter
of a million dollars. During the following year, the clinic lived
through more insidious vandalism. For several weeks, one member
of the board of directors required police protection twenty-four hours
a day. Other directors received threats that their children would be
kidnapped. One child had to be taken out of school because of
warnings that his life was in jeopardy. A year later, a bomb was
thrown through the window, but, fortunately, it never exploded. [2]

Right-to-life leaders adamantly denied any knowledge of or part
in the incidents. Regardless of their disclaimers, the terrorism put
a chill on the climate surrounding abortion rights, traumatizing

---

*Anderson was convicted of the charges on January 28, 1983. As of this writing,
the other two men were awaiting trial.

abortion-clinic operators and patients alike. "The thought that exercising a legal right can make you a target of some strange group is absolutely terrifying," Uta Landy, executive director of the National Abortion Federation, an umbrella group with 240 member clinics, told *Ms* magazine soon after the Zevallos kidnapping. "There is no doubt that the violence is escalating. We're talking about a nationwide reign of terror."[3]

The Zevallos kidnapping came at a point at which wiser heads among the right-to-lifers were beginning to lapse into despair. The activists had tried all the conventional tactics, using the courts, the legislatures, the Congress; marching through the streets; beseeching everyone from the Pope to the President to help them; praying. Nothing was promising to carry them beyond the flush of immediate newsworthiness. The 1980 election had seemed a great victory, but it quickly became apparent that most of the gains at the polls were an illusion. This exposed the "winning coalition" for what it really was, the wishful thinking of the New Right; and the New Right for what it really was, Richard Viguerie, Howard Phillips, Paul Weyrich and Terry Dolan. Period. A nonexistent victory coupled with a nonexistent coalition did not bode well for the future. Terrorism came at that critical juncture when the right-to-lifers were in the process of realizing they'd been had.

Perhaps even more discouraging to them was the strengthened position of the other side. In a few short years, the feminist movement had been able to engineer almost a complete reversal in American attitudes about women.*[4] As part of this trend, public-opinion polls revealed steadily increasing support for abortion. Even conservatives, according to a poll published in 1981 by the neoconservative journal *Public Opinion,* were against a constitutional amendment banning

---

*A Harris survey, for example, found in 1971 that 62 percent of American women were against "efforts to strengthen and change women's status in society," but by 1976, only five years later, 65 percent supported such efforts. Once secured, that support did not fade. Just before the ill-fated drive to pass the Equal Rights Amendment in Congress, another Harris survey, conducted in April 1982, found overwhelming backing for that supposedly controversial measure. Men and women across the country favored ERA ratification by 63 to 34 percent, with major pluralities even in the more conservative South (55 to 41 percent) and Midwest (60 to 36 percent).

abortion, by a margin of 57 percent to 43 percent.[5] As for the general public, a *Life* magazine poll of November 1981 showed that 67 percent of those questioned felt that a woman who wanted an abortion ought to be able to obtain it legally, and an astonishing 90 percent felt that having an abortion could be "the right thing" for them.[6] The majority of Catholics, those supposedly staunch upholders of the anti-abortion cause, consistently proved themselves pro-choice as well.

The irony was that for so long the pro-choice movement had appeared weak when it was really strong, while the right-to-life movement had appeared strong when it was really weak. The explanation for this was that up through the end of the decade the right-to-lifers had been able to use their considerable public-relations skills to generate a misleading impression of their strength. After the 1980 election, the pro-choice movement revitalized itself and started to present the real picture. Once the truth was out, the right-to-lifers had the dilemma of having somehow to prove the polls wrong or find another gimmick.

Not only was this a next-to-impossible task, but their most valuable supporter of all was wavering. Ronald Reagan could read the polls. * However much he may have believed in the cause, he was a politician and a Republican before he was a right-to-lifer or a conservative. His symbiosis with the right-to-life movement and the New Right was based on the assumption that they could deliver votes, not only for him but for a conservative Republican Congress. When that did not pan out, Reagan would go the way of many politicians, to where the votes actually were. While the President would still declare his anti-abortion allegiance, he would avoid follow-up.

As a result of all this, right-to-life activists felt isolated, confused as to where to go from there. Rather than banding together for support, they responded by attacking not only their opponents but also each other. These mutual hostilities threatened the very existence of the "winning coalition" and made their goal of consolidating right-to-life support in the Congress appear all the more unattainable.

The first display of antagonism came when the right-to-lifers began

---

*Irony upon irony: the President used the same pollster as the National Abortion Rights Action League, Richard Wirthlin's Market Opinion Research.

to distance themselves from the New Right. Sandy Faucher, for example, the NRLC political-action committee head, went to great lengths to point out the few electoral races they had targeted in 1980 that were different from those of NCPAC, and the one in which they had taken the opposite side. The prize instance was Missouri Senator Thomas Eagleton, whom NRLC-PAC had successfully supported because of his stand against abortion, and whom NCPAC had opposed because of his progressive stands on almost everything else.

Then, too, the right-to-lifers were less than satisfied with President Reagan's performance in office, and they did not hesitate to let him know it. They had expected firm anti-abortion leadership at every turn, and instead they had encountered waffling. Reagan did meet with leaders of the right-to-life movement promptly after the election. He did appoint a number of openly right-to-life sympathizers to his administration, among them Marjory Mecklenburg, the Reverend Robert Billings and a former Viguerie colleague, Morton Blackwell. None of these really represented mainstream right-to-life, however. Nor did Reagan provide the leadership to get a constitutional amendment off the drawing board. His only partially satisfactory excuse for this was that the first order of business was the economy. Moreover, he could point to the confusion within the movement as keeping him from favoring a particular approach. To the right-to-life way of thinking, however, Reagan had absolutely no excuse for his choice of Supreme Court Justice Sandra Day O'Connor.

The traditionalists within the right-to-life movement were disturbed enough by the appointment of Marjory Mecklenburg, because of her liberalism on matters of contraception, but at least Mecklenburg, as one of the founders of the movement, was unequivocally against abortion. They were not so sure about Sandra Day O'Connor. According to them, O'Connor was in fact a leading pro-abortionist during her days in the Arizona state legislature, and her appointment was yet another "betrayal."*[7]

---

*As with many other things about this movement, their accusations were based on somewhat flimsy information. O'Connor had been on the State Senate Judiciary Committee in 1970 when that body considered whether to make a recommendation to the full legislature to repeal Arizona's restrictive abortion law. Interestingly, there

As if that weren't humiliation enough, the Reagan appointment was a double embarrassment to movement leader Carolyn Gerster. In the spring of 1980, Gerster had had an audience with Ronald Reagan right after he was badly beaten by George Bush in the Iowa presidential caucuses. According to her account of the meeting, Reagan told Gerster that if he were elected President he would appoint an anti-abortion judge to the Supreme Court. He asked in exchange for Gerster's support in the election, to which she publicly agreed. Afterward, in July 1981, one Marie Craven of Chicago, identifying herself as a longtime right-to-lifer, a Catholic and a Democrat who had voted for Reagan because of his stand on abortion, wrote to tell the President that she was "sickened by witnessing once again the broken promises of the politician." Forthwith, in August, Reagan replied. In his response, which *The National Right to Life News* printed, Reagan explained away the charges against O'Connor and then added an aside: "I believe that most of the talk about my appointment was stirred up principally by one person in Arizona. I have done a great deal of checking on this and have found this person has something of a record of being vindictive." Whomever Reagan was referring to, right-to-lifers universally assumed he meant Gerster, and they termed his insult a gratuitous display of insensitivity.[8]

As the right-to-lifers drifted away from the New Right and the President, the New Right leaders began to respond in kind. Paul Brown was particularly guilty of taking unnecessary potshots at the right-to-life leadership. He called Jack Willke, for instance, an "egotistical maniac" and "a somewhat dubious guy." Brown also faulted

---

is no extant record of which way committee members voted—just the vote, six to three in favor of repeal. The only confirmation of her supposed stand came from right-wingers and Christian Republic promoter John Conlan, who was serving with O'Connor at the time of the committee. According to right-to-lifers who claimed to have spoken with him after O'Connor's nomination to the Supreme Court, Conlan declared that after the repeal vote he and the two other right-to-lifers identified themselves as such but O'Connor did not, thus proving that she must have been on the other side—at best, a somewhat dubious charge. O'Connor also took the unacceptable position in a couple of tangential votes, which appear to have reflected more her strict-constructionist feelings about the Constitution, law and government rather than any sympathy for abortion. In one case, she refused to support a "right to life memorial" that called on Congress to extend constitutional protection to the unborn. In another, she sponsored a family-planning measure that she reportedly thought would not allow abortion, if properly interpreted.

Willke for getting angry when *People* magazine interviewed the Browns instead of Willke and his wife as examples of a right-to-life couple. "The lady [reporter for *People*] chose Judie," Brown asserted in an interview, "because Judie is such a go-getter and so capable, so intelligent, yet still a wife and a mother, and enjoys doing it. And the other thing the reporter said was that the Willkes—they were just too old."

Brown was also furious with the Florida branch of the NRLC for having published in its newsletter that the NRLC had spent a full 92 percent of its own political-action committee's money on an election in 1980 whereas LAPAC had spent only 9 percent. Brown didn't exactly deny the charge, but he explained the difference by pointing out that the National Right to Life PAC, with all its incidental charges picked up by the parent NRLC, doesn't need to pay salaries, overhead or expenses, as LAPAC must. Comparing the two, he claimed, was an unfair distortion.

Brown had trouble maintaining cordial relationships with his religious allies as well. He regularly made statements condemning the bishops. "They could stop abortion tomorrow," Brown claimed, "if they really wanted to." In June 1980 he even brought a lawsuit against the church for not allowing LAPAC to distribute leaflets in church parking lots.[9] The flap was soon over—cooler heads prevailed and Brown withdrew the suit—but a bad taste remained. Brown also ridiculed the fundamentalists. "Jerry Falwell couldn't spell abortion five years ago," Brown liked to say.

The right-to-lifers' problems became even more complicated as other elements within the "winning coalition" began, too, to squabble. The first evidence of this came with the very public rift between the New Right and the Republican Party. New Right dissatisfaction with the GOP had surfaced almost immediately after the new administration took office. In the spring of 1981, Republican National Committee chairman Richard Richards lashed out at the "damned independent expenditure system" that could "create all kinds of mischief." In a not-so-disguised swipe at the New Right, Richards complained that such groups were "not responsible to anyone" and suggested that they created the same sort of problem that brought about the Watergate scandal. This characterization understandably did not please the New Right. Terry Dolan countered with his usual candor, "I'm sorry Dick Richards spends more time attacking his friends than he does his adversaries." The confrontation in print was followed by one in person, about which neither side would comment. Everybody came out of the summit apparently lovey-dovey, but the damage clearly had been done.

This was not immediately apparent to outsiders. Conservatives were creating organizations as fast as ever, many of them with impressive boards of directors. Viguerie's Council for National Policy, for instance, which was put together about the time of the Richards-Dolan flap, included Robert Billings, Bill Bright, Joseph Coors and his wife, Cullen Davis and his wife, Terry Dolan, Senator John East, Jerry Falwell, Senator Jesse Helms, Nelson Bunker Hunt and his brother, Tim LaHaye and his wife, Ed McAteer, Howard Phillips, Pat Robertson, James Robison, William Rusher, Phyllis Schlafly, Richard Viguerie, Paul Weyrich and a few other lesser mortals—although not a single representative from a traditional Republican background. Similarly a special coalition to "defund the left" had many of the organizations represented by the same names, along with the Council of State Chambers of Commerce and a couple of businesses, but, again, no one from the GOP. [10]

At the same time, as a part of this antagonism, New Right distrust extended to Ronald Reagan. Reagan turned out to be hardly the conservative that Viguerie and his New Right associates would have liked. The full force of Viguerie's wrath against the President would come out in the July 1982 *Conservative Digest*. The entire forty-eight-page volume was devoted to a broadside against the President's policies and included invective from some of the forty-five conservative members of Congress, including Senator Jesse Helms. The magazine listed forty issues on which Reagan had supposedly "deserted the conservatives," among them the proposed $122 billion tax increase over the next three years, the $110 billion budget deficit, the appointment of too many moderates to key government positions, the failure to abolish the Departments of Energy and Education, the signing of the Voting Rights Act, and the lack of leadership in pursuing constitutional amendments allowing prayer in the public schools and banning busing and, of course, abortion.

Nor did the religious right feel entirely comfortable with the President. The Reverend Jerry Falwell, for instance, told *The New York Times* that he still had "personal confidence" in the President's commitment to stopping abortion. "But," he added, "I'm a little anxious that we haven't had some aggressive support." [11]

The most serious weakness of the coalition, however, was the New Right's failure to mitigate tensions within its own ranks. Restless, eager to exert their own control, the Browns, for instance, began attacking other members of the coalition, and Paul Brown complained that they did not give him enough proper support. "There are a lot of conservative groups that are more interested in the military than anything else. The American Security Council [a conservative pro-military advocacy group] is one. The day I see some checks for $1,000 or $2,000 or $3,000 arriving from the military establishment might be the day I start believing a little bit more in defense. In other words, I simply feel they're taking advantage of the situation today, the vote we can give, proclaiming on one side of their mouth to be pro-life, and I don't know if they really are."[12]

The internal bickering eventually led to the two forces that really sustained the right-to-life movement—the Catholic Church and the New Right—facing off in Congress on two entirely different and ultimately conflicting proposals to stop abortion. The church and the conservatives each hoped not only to get their initiatives passed but also to assume leadership of the movement once and for all. Their ever more public rift further jeopardized the future of the right-to-lifers. Moreover, they both made mistakes—big mistakes—which only exacerbated matters.

The church favored the proposed constitutional amendment known as the Hatch Amendment, after Utah Republican Senator Orrin Hatch. First introduced in 1980, the Hatch Amendment, essentially a countermeasure to the Supreme Court abortion decision, would permit Congress and the states once again to pass their own laws against abortion. Holding to a purist line, many right-to-lifers preferred the amendment strategy over any other approach, for a number of reasons. Some, like James McFadden and his colleagues at the Ad Hoc Committee in Defense of Life, appreciated it because it was a direct attack on the Supreme Court decision, which they saw as not only immoral but also an unreasonable exercise of judicial power. Others, like the action faction behind Jack Willke at NRLC, believed it would provide the quick victory they needed, allowing them actually to stop abortion at the state level, if only for a while. Both camps, forever pragmatic, felt that the Hatch Amendment was the measure most likely to survive the inevitable court challenge. They may indeed have been correct about all this. Their big mistake

228   The Facts of Life

was in ignoring the fact that there was no way that the Hatch Amendment could get the necessary two-thirds endorsement of the United
States Congress. Orrin Hatch himself admitted that he just didn't
have the votes.

The New Right thrust came from the formidable Senator from
North Carolina, Jesse Helms. Helms introduced his measure in the
form of a statute rather than a constitutional amendment. Unlike
Hatch, Helms attacked the problem by having the bill state right off
that life begins at conception, thus effectively making abortion "murder." Helms's bill also would have banned all federal monies for
abortion, and it anticipated a legal challenge by stating that abortion
was beyond the jurisdiction of the courts.

This was the first of three big mistakes by Senator Helms. The
bill had the virtue of needing only a simple majority to pass, but it
did not sit right with many legislators, conservatives among them,
who felt that such a measure would weaken the court system and
could be used as an all too unfortunate precedent in other types of
situations. What was called the "court-stripping" aspect of it eventually brought out the big guns of the American Bar Association.

Even so, the bill was backed by Helms's old friend Richard Viguerie and his New Right colleagues, including Paul and Judie
Brown. More surprising, Helms also received the support of some
within NRLC who simply didn't like Jack Willke. But that would
come later.

Helms quickly brought his bill to the public eye with hearings in
the spring of 1981. The hearings were supposed to include everyone
of the right-to-life persuasion, even Orrin Hatch. They were conducted by another freshman Senator, North Carolina Republican
John East. East is widely viewed on Capitol Hill as a Helms protégé.
He even looks and sounds like his patron, with the same balding
pate and mid-South drawl. East was originally elected in part because
of big bucks given to his campaign by Helms's Congressional Club.
The junior Senator is confined to a wheelchair, and thus he is
sometimes referred to—in that cruel jocular way they have on the
Hill—as "Helms on wheels" for his loyal support of the conservative
line, especially the social issues.

The hearings were Helms's second big mistake. Something of a
sideshow, they had been packed by East with his own kind, giving
those on the pro-choice side only one opportunity to testify. Then

one day in the middle of the hearings Orrin Hatch suddenly and unexpectedly withdrew his support, and from that point on he was conspicuously absent from the hearing-room chair which bore his name. Hatch's abandonment of the proceedings allowed pro-choice forces to exploit their one advantage, access to the press. The word went out that the right-to-life movement was disintegrating, with the now public Helms–Hatch feud as proof.

Right-to-lifers were acutely conscious of how damaging all this might be. "We are a movement in disarray," Paul Brown admitted to *The New York Times* in September 1981, "and we better get our act together and restore our credibility and do it fast, or we're going to be in real trouble."[13] That November, accordingly, the Browns held what they called a "unity" convention, the hidden agenda of which was to bring the movement around to Helms. Featured prominently among the speakers and guests were Richard Viguerie, Paul Weyrich, Howard Phillips, Mildred Jefferson and Henry Hyde, as well as a representative from James McFadden's Ad Hoc Committee, Robert Sassone, Murray Norris, Jaynann Payne and numerous state leaders. Notably missing were the Reverend Edward Bryce and Ernest Ohlhoff, the Catholic institutional representatives. The Browns did try valiantly, however, to include grass-roots Catholics, offering mass every morning. They invited a host of fundamentalists too, and they organized regular religious services for them as well. All in all, it was a rousing right-to-life event, the hallways cluttered with display tables and literature and the main conference room festooned with a ten-foot-long full-color painting of a bloody baby in fetal position.

Despite the attention to detail, the convention revealed, among other things, the schism that had been developing between Catholics and fundamentalists in the movement. One workshop conducted by Onalee McGraw of the Heritage Foundation left many right-to-lifers baffled. McGraw tried to show that right-wingers had properly removed books from local libraries around the country, and that the American Library Association in response was mounting a vicious attack against them, using innuendo and falsehood to smear these well-meaning citizens. The basis of McGraw's argument was a point-by-point rundown of an ALA analysis of book-banning, the only ostensible purpose of which was to show that the ALA had overestimated the number of such incidents. At the end of another workshop, in which the group leader excoriated "secular humanism," a Catholic priest stood up and reminded the audience angrily that "humanism," anyway, had a long and proud tradition in the church. [14]

The Unity Convention was a noble effort, but perhaps was doomed from the start. At the banquet Sunday night, the Browns introduced virtually every member of the right-to-life movement who had a recognizable name—and a few who did not—in an effort to give them each an award. The only problem was that more than half of them had decided not to come—a not so subtle hint of their disagreement with the Browns' strategy.

If Paul and Judie Brown had been unsuccessful in getting the movement to arrive at consensus on the Helms approach, Jack Willke was still trying to convince them of the wisdom of Hatch. Willke's manipulations, while having short-term success in the form of an NRLC vote backing the constitutional-amendment strategy, would ultimately damage the solidarity of his organization, the breach having serious ramifications throughout the movement. Not only was the "winning coalition" falling apart, and the New Right attacking the Republicans, the President, the Catholic Church and the original right-to-lifers, as well as bickering among themselves, but now the grass roots were about to split right down the middle.

Under Willke's leadership, the National Right to Life Committee finally accepted the Hatch Amendment as its official position in December 1981 by a vote of only thirty to twenty-four with one abstention, awfully close for a major strategic—and as it turned out, by implication, ideological—decision. NRLC might have been hopelessly mired but for Willke, who had played power politics all the way through to get the vote. When the Hatch Amendment and the Helms bill came up again in the spring of 1982, Willke, clearly identifying himself as president of NRLC, sent a letter to everyone of importance on Capitol Hill urging them to support not the bill, but rather the constitutional amendment. The maneuver put the NRLC office staff, not all of them in agreement with Willke about the wisdom of the amendment strategy, in a difficult predicament. It was especially embarrassing for Chuck Donovan, NRLC lobbyist, who from then on couldn't even talk to the Helms people without repudiating his own president. With his wife six months pregnant, Donovan was finally forced to resign. Willke's strong-arm tactics infuriated Donovan's already impatient colleagues on the staff.

Willke then sent around another letter, this one to NRLC board members, telling them, despite what they might have heard, that the staff was happy, hard-working and content. As one staffer later described their reaction, "That was partly true. We were working hard." Willke's action further angered the staff, who felt that they were now being used in a bid by him for reelection to the presidency. "We didn't want to be used as a pawn in Willke's campaign," explained one staffer, "particularly when the way in which he was using us was a lie." John Cavanagh O'Keefe, then assistant editor of *The National Right to Life News*, sent around his own letter to board members saying as much. Accused of having gone over the heads of his superiors, O'Keefe was summarily fired. The editor of the paper, who had taken the job on the understanding that he could hire and fire his own staff, subsequently resigned in protest.[15]

Willke also used his now considerable prestige to bring some of the state affiliates into line, according to Paul Brown. In Missouri, for instance, Willke edged out longtime and quite liberal right-to-lifer Ann O'Donnell as president and installed a new crew who were more loyal to him. He similarly strong-armed the leadership in Louisiana and Kansas.

Willke then went on to try to consolidate support on Capitol Hill. When the Congressional Pro-life Caucus, a group of congressmen who met regularly to discuss the abortion issue and to plan common strategy, held a closed-door session in order to try to determine exactly what it was that the movement wanted, Willke showed just how shrewd he really was. NRLC had not yet declared its position, so he couldn't very well promote his own opinion under the auspices of the organization, considering that it was involved in a heated three-way split. So, according to accounts of those present, Willke testified first as president of NRLC, reading a resolution the board had drafted saying that the Hatch Amendment was worthy of exploration. Then, explaining that he was taking off his hat as president of the national group and putting on another as the delegate from the state of Ohio, he made his real feelings clear. He told the congressmen that his state organization was planning to print two million leaflets before the 1982 elections, advertising how they voted on the Hatch Amendment. He did not need to say much more.

Civil war finally broke out within the movement over Willke's moves. Several of the NRLC state affiliates indicated to the Browns that they wanted to quit NRLC and join up with them, according to Paul Brown. The Browns urged them to wait at least until close to a majority of the NRLC board was willing to do the same, so that they could form one powerful entity that would be truly competitive with NRLC.[16]

The National Right to Life convention in June came off without a hitch despite all the warfare. The year before, in a spirit of confrontation, the Browns had arrived in matching T-shirts with a LA-PAC emblem and, sitting in on the political-organizing workshop, had made snide comments at appropriate moments. This year they didn't even bother to come. While that made for more peaceful proceedings, their absence clearly was noted. At the traditional roast for the president, the big joke against Jack Willke was that somehow Paul Brown would get on the board of Willke's money-making Hayes Publishing Company. NRLC even made a bid at establishing the "unity" the Browns had been trying for. The board invited Marjory Mecklenburg to be the keynote speaker, in an attempt to heal those very old wounds. They also managed to get old Viguerie associate Morton Blackwell to give an address introducing a pre-videotaped speech from none other than President Ronald Reagan. In his message, Reagan offered his warm and congenial, if vague, blessings. With all of that, the convention was not a roaring success. Ordinarily it did not attract much attention; in this critical election year, the coverage was mostly of the pro-choice demonstration across the street.[17]

Two months later, Jesse Helms again introduced his anti-abortion measure, the debate over which would reveal to the world the chaos existing within the right-to-life ranks. The Helms proposal came this time in the form of an amendment to the debt-ceiling act that was paired with an amendment on school prayer. The debate began on August 18. Among those blasting the measure were Senator Daniel Patrick Moynihan of New York and Lowell P. Weicker, Jr., of Connecticut. Moynihan began his contribution by shouting from his desk at the back of the Senate, "We have before us the greatest constitutional crisis since the Civil War!" He contended that Congress would be guilty of an "abomination" if it were to direct its "rage and irresponsible fury" against the Supreme Court.* "If the Court

---

*The Helms anti-abortion amendment actually did not have the "court-stripping" provision in it throughout the deliberations, but since the companion prayer amend-

is to be a subordinate branch of the U.S. Government, of the U.S. Congress," Moynihan expostulated, according to a *New York Times* report, "then we are no longer the Republic founded at Philadelphia in 1787." Weicker then offered a proposal which would have reaffirmed the authority of the federal courts. Helms countered by moving to kill the Weicker proposal. Helms lost this crucial vote by fifty-nine to thirty-eight.[18]

During the debate, the senators on both sides apparently had engaged in a little back-room bargaining which ultimately was to divide right-to-lifers even further. All of those concerned about the issue of abortion were negotiating for some kind of agreement that would allow both the Hatch and Helms measures to be debated on the floor. "We were within ten seconds of a unanimous consent agreement," Senator Robert Packwood told a reporter, but at the last minute the agreement was sabotaged by none other than Jesse Helms.[19] This was the third big mistake from the stubborn Senator, revealing before the Congress of the United States and the world his readiness to embarrass his own kind and throw the right-to-lifers into even more disarray. As a miffed Orrin Hatch was later to observe, "I've learned not to wait for anybody else, to make my own arrangements for getting something on the floor, whether Helms or anybody else likes it."

The next day in another part of the country, the Zevalloses were released. This bizarre incident did nothing to encourage Congress to act on abortion. Consideration of the Helms amendment extended well into September. On September 15, conservative California Senator S.I. Hayakawa offered an amendment to table the amendment on abortion. A week later, Senator Barry Goldwater, the dean of American conservatives, offered the same for school prayer. The abortion portion was finally tabled by only one vote, forty-seven to forty-six. Coming that close to victory might have indicated considerable strength on Helms's side, except that by the time the amendment came down to a vote it had been effectively emasculated. Helms had been forced to take out the wording that declared the fetus to be a person and allowed "court-stripping," leaving only the provision stopping federal funds for abortion. In a time of austerity, many could suport that. Right to

_____

ment did, many of those debating the package viewed it as possibly applicable to both.

234 The Facts of Life

life, the New Right and Jesse Helms had been soundly repudiated.[20]

Helms had justified all his actions by touting the vote on his amendment as a device for right-to-lifers to use during the upcoming midterm elections. It didn't work out that way. Much like the amendment vote, the election did not prove much more than that the right-to-life movement was every bit as weak as intelligent observers might have seen two years earlier had they chosen to look.

Media coverage before the election barely even mentioned abortion one way or the other. Most of the analysis afterward was devoted to the impact of the economy, although right-to-lifers were still regarded as a formidable voting bloc. The comment of Curtis Gans of the Committee for the Study of the American Electorate was typical: "Very few pro-choice women will vote pro-choice above everything else, but right to lifers will vote only on that." The phenomenon would hold, the thinking went, whatever the other factors in a race, giving right to life generally the margin.

This was apparently sometimes true and sometimes not. In a specific targeted race in which the right-to-lifers engaged in a diligent get-out-the-vote campaign, they could occasionally win against their opponents. However, right-to-lifers wisely tended to select only the more conservative areas in which to mount their efforts; their victories thus gave a distorted impression of their strength. Moreover, if the pro-choice side teamed up with its own "winning coalition"— that is, a broad-based liberal drive—they too could win, and win big.

Typically optimistic, *Lifeletter* in its postelection edition crowed:

> We predict that the political pollsters and pundits—wrongheaded and off base as they were in "predicting" how Americans would vote Tuesday—will take it all in stride and churn out a new stream of stories explaining what didn't happen. They're off and running already: the lead morning-after story in the New York *Daily News* . . . trumpeted "Voters across the nation gave liberal Democrats a far stronger hand in the House and cut Republican command of the Senate in a stern protest against Reaganomics"—a too-early dream of what they *wanted* to happen, maybe, but hardly a description of what *did* happen.
> Hours later, it was clear that the billions spent in the too-long months of frantic campaigning had produced topsy-turvy results that added to a virtual dead-heat finish in which *both* parties

were defeated and the liberal/conservative split only marginally shifted. . . .

For anti-abortionists, whose "single-issue" was largely ignored by the major media . . . , the results mainly paralleled the political ones—some sad losses in the House (e.g. Marge Heckler in Massachusetts) balanced by some potentially-important gains in the Senate, which should now have *two more* anti-abort votes.[21]

National Right to Life Political Action Committee head Sandy Faucher estimated even more cheerfully that right-to-lifers had won "two and a half" seats in the Senate. Right-to-lifers definitely had helped Republicans Chris Hecht in Nevada and Paul Trible in Virginia, Faucher claimed, and probably had given some assistance to California's upset Republican victor, Pete Wilson. What she meant by the odd number of votes was that Hecht and Trible were both staunch advocates of a constitutional amendment banning abortion, but Wilson opposed only federal funding for it.[22] Of the House of Representatives Faucher wasn't so sure, although a preliminary analysis in the postelection issue of *The National Right to Life News* was hopeful of the movement's having held its own.[23]

The National Abortion Rights Action League completed a much more comprehensive analysis that offered an entirely different picture of the election outcome. Improving on its organizing techniques used in 1980, NARAL had worked long and hard in 1982 to establish an affirmative presence at the polls. By its reckoning, the activity had paid off. Abortion had become an important issue in gender-gap voting. Not only was the pro-choice position no longer a stigma for candidates, but single-issue voting on their side was now benefiting them in some cases. Moreover, pro-choice PACs had given more money to more effect than the right-to-lifers'. Furthermore, the preelection maneuvering around the Helms amendment, according to the NARAL accounting, had backfired miserably, with twenty-two of thirty-three senators up for reelection voting against it, and none of them who were targeted afterward on NCPAC hit lists changing their minds. Finally, by comparison with pro-choice electioneering, NARAL claimed, right-to-life efforts were trifling and confused.* Jesse Helms's Congressional Club lost all the races

_____

*Specifically, Americans for Life as of June 30, 1982, had raised $37,653 and spent $48,623. LAPAC as of August 1 had raised $311,080, spent $320,000 and

in which it put money, including two with avowedly right-to-life
candidates. The once feared Americans for Life, the PAC of Stop
the Babykillers, supported only one candidate. Paul Brown's LAPAC
was all over the map, targeting candidates and then retracting its
threat, and going after some politicians in situations clearly detri-
mental to the right-to-life cause.[24]

LAPAC put Republican Lowell Weicker on its hit list, for instance, although Weicker's political fall would have meant the rise
of the even more pro-choice Democrat Toby Moffett. Even more
damaging was the Browns' brief flirtation with the opponent of Senator Orrin Hatch, Salt Lake City Mayor Ted Wilson. "He was
playing with us," explained Brown of why he finally dropped Wilson.
"He said he was pro-life but we finally got definite evidence that he
was a friend of Planned Parenthood. When we discovered that, I
sent Orrin a letter of endorsement and a hundred dollars."[25]

One race that Brown tried hard to influence was that against
Senator Edward M. Kennedy of Massachusetts. The LAPAC campaign, conducted in conjunction with NCPAC, was reminiscent of
Stop the Babykillers. The front organization for it was called Citizens
to Replace Kennedy (CORK), which as of September 1, 1982, had
raised $251,530.[26] This was an extraordinary amount to spend on
what was essentially a warm-up. LAPAC never intended to support
Kennedy's opponent, millionaire Ray Shamie, whom Brown called
"inept." As Brown admitted, "I never had any visions that we were
going to beat Kennedy." The campaign instead was an effort to make
it more difficult for the Senator to run for President in 1984.[27]

The centerpiece of the campaign was a comic book sent to registered voters in Massachusetts. Entitled "Every Family Has One,"
the comic book featured a cartoon of the Senator as a black sheep
hopping through thirty-six pages of examination of his character,
which dredged up his cheating at Harvard, a very old speeding offense

---

supported three candidates in the primary, two of whom lost. The National Right
to Life PAC, Faucher's committee, raised $320,726 and spent $218,484; NRL-PAC
supported 15 candidates in the primary, won 9 and lost 6, and supported 32 candidates in the general election, won 18 and lost 14. By comparison, NARAL raised
almost twice as much money, $564,695, spent $428,349, supported 21 candidates
in the primary election, won 18 and lost 3; by the time of the general election,
NARAL had raised more than $100,000 more, and, of 186 candidates supported,
won 70 percent.

and, of course, Chappaquiddick. Interestingly, the comic book was also one of the first times that LAPAC did not concentrate just on abortion; it went after Kennedy's record on all the New Right bugaboos, including the Panama Canal, busing, defense spending and the nuclear freeze. One particularly biting feature was a series of boxes spread out through the book and headlined "Time Out for a Teddyquiz." The quiz on the Senator's stand on national health insurance—what the comic book dubbed "compulsory government health care"—read as follows:

- Who in the world is going to pay for the BILLIONS of dollars this crackpot idea would cost?
- Who would REPLACE all of our doctors who would go to another country, where free enterprise still exists?
- Would TEDDY'S FAMILY go down to the government clinic and take a number?... And wait their turn?... After YOU? Don't hold your breath.[28]

Kennedy, of course, eventually did announce his decision not to run for President, but neither the comic book nor the right-to-life movement was among the reasons he gave for it.

Except for isolated races, the NARAL analysis seemed to hold. A *New York Times* article confirmed that right-to-lifers had done abysmally. A postelection *Times*/CBS poll found that whereas members of the House in the Ninety-seventh Congress had opposed by 54 to 46 percent the passage of a constitutional amendment allowing individual states to prohibit abortion, members of the new Ninety-eighth Congress by comparison opposed it by a much larger 58 to 42 percent. Freshman members felt even more strongly, opposing it 74 to 26 percent.[29] This was hardly a ringing victory for the right-to-lifers.

Analysts predicted that the "social issues" were dead. *The New York Times* foresaw an eclipse for the New Right, using NCPAC as an example.[30] Terry Dolan did not agree with the assessment. "The conservative movement is stronger than it ever was," Dolan insisted in an interview after the election. As Paul Brown put it, "The pro-life movement has been declared dead many times. They've buried us before. Hopefully, the lesson we learned will help us to be more successful."[31]

Regardless of their diminishing credibility, there was no question in the minds of the right-to-lifers that they would go back to Congress to try to stop abortion. The only problem was how. Hatch or Helms; Helms or Hatch. Or maybe another approach altogether. The election had not helped clarify what would be the best way, and the disagreements over the conflicting approaches were just as debilitating as ever, if not more so.

Dr. Jack Willke continued to support the Hatch Amendment and urged right-to-lifers to "organize, grow, organize, teach, lecture, grow, work and grow" in a typically down-home *National Right to Life News* editorial. Willke's assessment was that the priority should be on preparation for the 1984 elections, particularly voter identification.[32]

Juli Loesch, representative of the "progressives" of the movement, felt that right-to-lifers should make a drastic change in course. "If the right-to-life movement aligned itself with the human-needs agenda of the left, it would be a whole different ball game," Loesch argued. "We want fertility education, free medical care, guaranteed annual income, job education and opportunity, affirmative action—and we want to stop abortion. It would make sense politically because it's a program that is saying that if the law binds upon the woman the obligation to carry the pregnancy to term, then it must also support the woman in a really comprehensive fashion."[33]

Paul Brown had no compunction about trumpeting his thoughts on the future, too, although, typically, he was careful not to pin himself down to any particular course of action. "My feeling is that we are a large growing movement that's still wandering," he mused. "We're being romanced by the conservatives. We're still being spurned by the middle-of-the-road Jerry Ford and Howard Baker–type Republicans. The Democrats have left us out. Yet a lot of our people are still Democrats. My feeling is that somewhere along the road, somebody in one of the parties—it could very well be the Democrats—is going to be smart enough to put this all together. The only person smart enough to do it so far is Paul Weyrich. He's very smart. I don't know if the Republicans are very smart. Right now, the Democrats are really stupid." For the time being, Brown was content to stick with his alliance with the New Right, and to support Helms.

At the same time, Brown was finally making his bid to capture the NRLC affiliates. He claimed that he had about half of them interested in joining him, maybe more. As of fall 1982, his game plan was to create an organization again along federalist lines, but without the cumbersome democratic voting system. The state affiliates would run their show in their territories, and the Browns would serve as information and consultation services for them out of Washington. Brown even got his attorneys to look into the legality of claiming the Right to Life name and tax perks. Brown had already scheduled meetings around the country with various interested leaders. "I think there's great demand for this among the grass-roots people," Brown explained. "They want somebody they can contact in Washington. We want somebody we can contact in the states. But we don't want to dictate to them what to do, nor in turn do we want them to dictate to us."[34] The face-off between the Browns and NRLC would start to occur at the worst possible time—just as Congress started to deliberate the fate of Hatch versus Helms again.

The only one who didn't seem to have a particularly strong opinion on all this was NCPAC's Terry Dolan. As a matter of fact, Dolan did not appear to care much for the right-to-lifers at all anymore. "I'm angry at the right-to-life activists because the spirit was not there." Dolan felt that Ronald Reagan's waffling on abortion had "disheartened" right-to-lifers and conservatives as well. "I don't think the fire was there for the conservative grass-roots organization in 1982 the way it was in 1980," he admitted. However, while he saw "exponential growth" on the horizon for the New Right, NCPAC included, he sensed that the right-to-lifers' poor showing sent a message to at least some in Congress that the movement was a "paper tiger."[35]

In short, it looks as if abortion is losing its usefulness to the Republicans, the President and the New Right, and, by association, the fundamentalists. Where the politicos go, the business community is sure to follow. This does not mean that the "winning coalition" might not regroup at some point, but only that the prospects do not look good. The bleak outlook leaves the right-to-lifers nowhere to run to except back where they started. The others having failed them, they are likely to end up at the bosom of the Roman Catholic Church.

They are certainly no paper tiger, even so. Their ferociousness may have been tamed, but the church has virtually unlimited resources to carry on the fight and is not likely to abandon it for expediency. Indeed, the renewed energy that comes of having added anti-war to anti-abortion may make the Pastoral Plan even more formidable than before.

Back under the protection of the church, the right-to-lifers still have a shot at a statute banning abortion. Short of that, they will undoubtedly continue attempts to harass or defund abortion providers. By the end of fiscal year 1981–82, for instance, they had managed to have audited thirty-one affiliates and seven abortion clinics of Planned Parenthood. The right-to-lifers also will probably draft new laws in order to limit abortion.

This is the favored strategy of Thomas Marzen, chief counsel for Americans United for Life, a Chicago-based legal think tank. Marzen wants to "chip away" at *Roe v. Wade* while waiting on the day that the Supreme Court overturns it. This will occur, he predicts, when medical advances have moved back the age at which the fetus can survive outside the womb and have thus made the current definition of viability obsolete. However, the rejection on June 15, 1983, by the Supreme Court of an Akron, Ohio, ordinance restricting abortion makes the success of this strategy seem remote. The legislation that Marzen's group helped draft required, among other things, that a doctor tell a woman seeking an abortion that "the unborn child is a human life from the moment of conception" and provide a detailed description of its "anatomical and physiological characteristics." Ruling in his majority opinion that these requirements seemed designed to dissuade women seeking abortions, Justice Lewis F. Powell, Jr., explicitly reaffirmed *Roe v. Wade* and rejected a dissenting argument about viability.

As for a constitutional amendment banning abortion, the right-to-lifers probably will not get the necessary votes. Their ability to do that depends not on the New Right and its associates, not even on the church. Ultimately, they can't get what they really want unless the American public suddenly and inexplicably reconsiders ten years of support for abortion and decides that the right-to-lifers are right after all.

X.

Life Under the Twenty-sixth Amendment

The right-to-life movement has been in existence for more than a decade. The Catholics' Pastoral Plan and the fundamentalists' plan for the Christian Republic have been in operation for more than half a decade. The New Right's plan to join them together into a "winning coalition" has been around for three or four years. None of them has stopped abortion, but together they have come awfully close.

The right-to-lifers have put abortion back on the national agenda, and along with it the issues of sexuality, birth control, and family and the proper roles of its members, birth defects and population control. They have raised moral, theological, scientific and legal questions about when life begins and when it should be protected and by whom. They have won local elections and even helped provide the small margin of victory in national races. In one state, they have created a Right to Life Party. They have caused the passage of laws that restrict government funding for abortion for the poor, as well as prohibiting federal money for abortion appropriated through bills covering nurses' training, the Legal Services Corporation, the Peace Corps and the Defense Department. Additionally, if unintentionally, the right-to-lifers have raised the profile of the Roman Catholic Church and of fundamentalism in America.

With other members of the "winning coalition," the movement has prompted heated controversy about the nature of government control over personal morality, government payment for social programs and, in general, the relationship between the public and private sectors.

The right-to-lifers have also helped bring about, if only temporarily, a basic realignment in American politics. In addition to being partially responsible for the Republican Party moving to the right and the Democratic Party to the left, right-to-lifers also lined up those of their persuasion with the Republicans and those not with the Democrats. In some cases, this involved realignments that did not always come easily.

In all of this, the movement has come head to head with some of the most powerful forces in the society, the Democrats, the liberals, the media, the courts, the women's movement, and won, or almost so. This is no mean feat.

Consideration of some of these questions was overdue. Approximately one million abortions performed each year is a staggering number and certainly does not bode well for the health of American women. Abortion itself is unpleasant and sometimes dangerous and— no matter what the personal moral conviction about it—invariably calls up some measure of ambivalence, both from the woman having it and from her mate. Such an enormous number of unwanted pregnancies indicates as well a deep and abiding inability of the nation's people to deal comfortably with their sexuality, and with the possibility of having children. The lack of risk-free, convenient, widely available and inexpensive contraception makes decisions about sexuality all the more difficult, particularly for the young.

Similarly, the American family is definitely in trouble. Regardless of how much traditionalists may protest otherwise, the family has changed and probably will keep doing so dramatically over the next ten years or so. Projections from *The Nation's Families: 1960–1990*, a study published in 1980 under the auspices of the respected Joint Center for Urban Studies of MIT and Harvard, indicate four trends that will most likely occur within the next decade. They are that

1. Low marriage, high divorce and low fertility rates will probably be common for today's generation of young adults, consistent with long-term trends but not consistent with the experience of their parents.

2. Households made up of married couples will probably increase only slightly, while other types (singles, friends, relatives living together) will rise a lot.

3. Fewer households are likely to have children present.

4. Although more wives are presently working, their contribution to family income is small. However, a revolution in women's work may be on the horizon, which will see more women working full time and continuously. If this does occur, it may bring about changes in consumption, time use and mobility patterns of families, and could drastically alter family life.[1]

On paper, all this seems unremarkable, but making such transitions never is. Inevitably, some of the existing nuclear families will break up painfully and others will stay together when they should not, while some of the alternative families will be insecure, hapless or dull.

The question of how society deals with defective fetuses is also not open to easy answers. During the testimony at the hearings on the Human Life Statute chaired by the crippled Senator John East, some of those of the pro-choice persuasion were inattentive. Finally annoyed, East at one point rose up to his full height in his wheelchair, leaned out over the horseshoe-shaped committee table as far as he could, and thundered, "You know, if my mother had had amniocentesis, I probably wouldn't be here today!"[2]

Likewise the movement brought a valuable perspective—if not always precise documentation—to the population question. The Erlichs had vastly overestimated the danger of the Population Bomb. Responsible demographers had been shifting their estimates downward ever since. Researchers at the Population Information Program at Johns Hopkins University, for instance, have been guardedly optimistic. The results of a seven-year study there showed that the population would stabilize early in the next century at about eight billion—double the present number but only half what was originally estimated.[3]

Moreover, right-to-lifers were correct in their concerns about the coming responsibilities for the elderly. The UN World Assembly on

Aging in 1982 reported that people aged sixty and over are the most rapidly growing sector of the world population. As global population goes up threefold, the report estimated, the aging population will soar, with over-sixties increasing fivefold and over-eighties, sevenfold in the next half century. Only 23 percent of the men and 6 percent of the women will be receiving pensions—a real challenge to Social Security.[4]

All of these are matters of profound importance both for present generations and for those to come. All of them can in one way or another involve abortion. None admits to quick answers. Certainly fanatic right-to-lifers cannot contribute solutions by simply ignoring the problems and having abortion banned. Indeed, this might aggravate the conditions that caused the trouble in the first place.

This is where the real fault of the right-to-life movement lies, not just in agitating over a single issue, allying itself with one church or another, attempting to influence the political process or even using underhanded tactics—right or wrong, those things, frankly, are done all the time in American politics—but rather in trying to turn back a historical clock with one-way hands.

Women are changing, having fewer children and spending less time in the home. The decline in birth rates comes about not because of some perverse, selfish refusal on the part of women to reproduce, but as a legitimate, rational response to their situations. The function of mothers, children and the family has changed. Where historically children were an integral part of the economic unit that was the extended family, the changing nature of society and work has created nuclear families with fully dependent children who have no suitable social niche. Contemporary families that are thriving financially can afford the luxury of the stay-at-home Mom, but the less fortunate cannot. As the economy worsens, many more women may have to go to work to supplement their husbands' incomes. The demands of the women's movement for things like abortion rights are really an effect, not a cause, of these long-term social changes, an acknowledgment of what is actually going on in women's lives.

Ever more sophisticated studies are showing what the women's movement has maintained all along—that large numbers of women will probably get abortions no matter what the law. According to a 1974 study of Catholic countries such as Spain and Portugal in which abortion was completely prohibited, illegal abortions occurred at a high rate and so did deaths as a consequence. *Worldwatch* reported three years later on an estimate of the Bolivian Ministry of Health that the treatment of complications from illegal abortions accounted for more than 60 percent of that country's obstetrical and gynecological expenses. Even more to the point, one study of prac· tices in Rumania, where abortion was legal for many years and then banned by the government, showed an initial surge of the birth rate following the ban, and then a decline—partly due to more or better use of contraception, and partly to illegal abortion.[5]

If the right-to-life movement were successful, and abortion were banned in the United States, the consequences might be disastrous. More than likely, women would continue to get abortions, regardless of the law. Some of them would have complications, possibly serious ones, possibly fatal. All of them would be outlaws. Having once had the freedom to choose, they would probably be angry outlaws. This sense of lowered expectations and diminished opportunities could have far-reaching effects both on women and on the culture. Additionally, those who would have more babies would probably be disproportionately the poor. Then, too, the lack of access to abortion might conceivably lead to greater family tension and a higher incidence of divorce and child abuse. Society might also be overwhelmed by a sudden mini-population explosion of defective infants who would grow up into totally dependent adults. The birth rate might take off again, outstripping the earth's capacity to provide for the increasing numbers of people. Life under the Twenty-sixth Amendment could be catastrophic. Overcrowding might lead to war, famine, the plague—or worse.

Or nothing. Nobody knows.

As Christopher Jencks has observed, demographers are about as reliably able to predict the future as, say, weathermen the weather.[6] And that is exactly the point. Doomsday scenario or not, is the risk worth it?

With this in mind, it is tempting to ponder the ultimate fate of another populist movement. The Prohibitionists were finally able to pass a constitutional amendment. After the teetotalers had had their day for a while, something happened. A critical mass of people started to change their minds. Leading the way were the giants of industry—several du Ponts, John J. Raskob of the General Motors fortune and even John D. Rockefeller—who for a while had been on the other side. Everyone began to realize that Prohibition had a number of unintended consequences. Prohibition was unenforceable, and it had created a nation of crooks. Prohibition was ineffective, and it had not helped prevent the development of a nation of drinkers. Perhaps most important of all, Prohibition made the federal government into a national cop overseeing people's private lives. Nobody liked that. Prohibition was repealed.

Acknowledgments

My warmest thanks and admiration go to three rare individuals without whom this book would never have been possible: Arthur H. Samuelson for his clarity of reason, sensitivity, skill and patience; James Silberman for his gracious understanding and early belief in the idea; and Kathy Robbins for her invaluable intelligence, energy and friendship at critical moments.

I am also indebted to Sidney Blumenthal for his insightful help in the inception and planning; Cathy Cramer and Marie Urciuoli for their tireless, expert research and technical assistance; Sarah Flynn, Robert Lovinger, Ted Kaynor, John Reinstein, Susan Phillips, Rochelle Lefkowitz, Larry Kramer and Jackie Jordan for the unselfish lending of their time to read the manuscript and offer incisive suggestions; Kerry Gruson for having kept me going at a difficult time in my career; Wesley McCune for having afforded me the use of his vast and meticulously kept library; Tish Stein, Lorraine Parent and Elisa Karnofsky for their kind offer of a place to stay and child care; Brian McMenimen and Thomas Heffernon for their generous aid and suggestions; the partners and staff of the offices of Homans, Hamilton, Dahmen and Marshall for their cheerful toleration of my use of their facilities.

I would also like to thank my friends in the pro-choice movement too numerous to name, whose spirit and drive have helped raise the stature of women everywhere.

Finally, I would most of all like to thank my family, Lauren and Jim for their good-natured sufferance of my schedule, my mother, Virginia, for her unflagging support, my best friend, Jim, for his constant affection, help and encouragement, and my son, Chapin, for his mature understanding and love.

Appendix A

The New Right's Money Tree

A PARTIAL LISTING OF CORPORATE AND FOUNDATION DONORS TO NEW-RIGHT CAUSES*

CORPORATIONS:

Weyerhaeuser
Ford
Reader's Digest
Potlatch
Mobil
Coca-Cola
Consolidated Foods
Ashland Oil
Tennessee Gas Transmission
Firestone
Pizza Hut
Castle & Cook

*From "'Hearts and Minds': The Conservative Network," *Washington Post*, Jan. 4, 1981.

Hershey
Exxon
Citibank
Republic Steel
General Motors
Morgan Guaranty Trust
IBM
and others

FOUNDATIONS:

Bechtel Foundation (Construction)
Assets: $7 million. Public-affairs grants: $40,000/year.
Adolph Coors Foundation (Brewing)
Assets: $73 million. Public-affairs grants: $328,000/year, foreign affairs, free-market economics, media, anti-environmental legal defense.
Fred C. Koch Foundation (Energy, Real Estate)
Assets: $4.2 million. Public-affairs grants: about $75,000/year mainly to libertarian groups.
Lilly Foundation (Pharmaceuticals)
Assets: $699 million. Public-affairs grants: vary. $1 million committed to American Enterprise Institute.
Samuel Noble Foundation (Oil and Drilling)
Assets: $238 million. Public-affairs grants: $500,000+/year. $750,000 to Heritage Foundation in 1979.
John M. Olin Foundation (Agricultural Chemicals, "Sporting Weapons")
Assets: $11 million. Public-affairs grants: $280,000/year, public-policy think tanks, media, libertarian groups, anti-environmental legal defense.
J. Howard Pew Freedom Trust (Sun Oil)
Assets: $184 million. Public-affairs grants: $2.5 million/year, libertarian groups, public-policy think tanks, anti-union organizations. Includes $1 million to American Enterprise Institute.
Sarah Mellon Scaife Foundation (Gulf Oil)
Assets: $97 million including 1,254,621 shares of Gulf Oil. Public-affairs grants: $955,000/year, defense, foreign policy, government regulation, free market. Includes $400,000 to Law and Economic Center, $300,000 to Institute for Contemplary [sic] Studies.
Smith-Richardson Foundation (Vicks Vaporub)
Assets: $73 million. Public-affairs grants: $650,000/year, national-defense-policy think tanks.

Appendix B

Fundamentalist Donors

DONORS AND CONTRIBUTIONS TO THE PRINCIPAL U.S. EVANGELICAL ORGANIZATIONS, 1970–80*

By Deborah Huntington and Ruth Kaplan

Recipient/Donor	Amount	Year	Background on Donor
CAMPUS CRUSADE:			
Pew Memorial Trust, Philadelphia, PA	$100,000	1976	One of five trusts of the J. Howard Pew billion-dollar family fortune derived mainly from holdings in Sun Oil (32%). This trust is largest ($400 million in assets). Pew was longtime friend of Robert Welch, founder of John Birch Society, was on its Editorial Advisory Board.

*Compiled by Deborah Huntington and Ruth Kaplan for *Press-On!* (Winter, 1979–80, Volume 1, No. 4 and Volume 2, No. 1). Information was drawn from: I.R.S. 990 AR annual reports; *Who's Who in America*; *Who's Who in Finance*; *Who's Who* (regionals); *Stock Ownership Directory Series* (No. 1–4)

Recipient/Donor	Amount	Year	Background on Donor
Atkinson (Myrtle L.) Fdn., La Canada, CA	73,900	1976	Fdn's purpose: "To teach . . . the gospel of Jesus Christ throughout the world and to unite in Christian Fellowship the large number of Christians in the various evangelical churches . . ."
Christian Workers' Fdn., Montgomery, AL	5,000	1976	Fdn's purpose: "To train Christian workers planning evangelistic or mission work and to support Christian evangelical institutions . . ."
Berry (Lowell W.) Fdn., Oakland, CA	1,900 2,200 1,750 2,400 200	1976 1977 1977 1978 1979	Fdn. gives primarily to religious programs. (1977 and 1979 donations to Here's Life campaign.)
Ahmanson Fdn., Los Angeles, CA	10,000	1977	Ahmanson family interests hold 48.7% of H. F. Ahmanson Savings & Loan, Los Angeles, the largest home savings-and-loan association in the nation (donation was to San Bernardino chapter).
DeVos (Richard & Helen) Fdn., Grand Rapids, MI	12,000 2,500	1977 1978	DeVos is co-founder and president of AMWAY, a home products company, which also owns the Mutual Broadcasting System. Fdn. gives primarily to evangelistic causes, with particular support for Radio Bible Hour, Garden Grove Community Church, and Gospel Films.
World Evangelism & Christian Education Fund	NA*	NA	Subsidiary of Billy Graham Evangelistic Assn.
Pepsico Fdn., Purchase, NY	10,000	1977	(To Here's Life in Greater New York.)
Coors (Adolph) Fdn., Denver, CO	10,000	1976	Family foundation of the owners of Coors Brewery, now headed by son Joseph. Both father (now de-

---

*Not available.

Recipient/Donor	Amount	Year	Background on Donor
			ceased) and son have been supporters of the John Birch Society and contributors to numerous ultraconservative groups. (Donation to Here's Life, Denver.)
Nelson Bunker Hunt	5.5 mill. 10 mill.	1979 1980	Chief fund-raiser for campaign, with goal of $1 billion by 1982. Hunt family fortune has alternately cornered the soybean, silver and other commodity trading; John Birch supporter. (1979 to film, *Jesus*, 1980 to Here's Life.)
Wallace Johnson	NA	NA	International Division chairman. Founder of Holiday Inn chain. (To Here's Life.)
W. Clement Stone	NA	NA	Stone is insurance executive, including chairman of board of Combined America Insurance Co.; trustee of Religious Heritage of America, Inc., Washington, DC, and donor to same. (To Here's Life.)
Roy Rogers	NA	NA	Fund-raising committee. Roy Rogers Family Restaurants are franchised by Marriott Corp.; Marriott interests donate to evangelical causes (see Billy Graham Evang. Assn.). (To Here's Life.)
Walter Burke	NA	NA	Retired president of McDonnell Douglas Corp. (To Here's Life.)
Mobil Fdn., New York, NY	NA	NA	Gave to Here's Life.
Coca-Cola Corp.	NA	NA	Gave to Here's Life.

CHRISTIAN ANTI-COMMUNISM CRUSADE:

Recipient/Donor	Amount	Year	Background on Donor
Pew Memorial Trust, Philadelphia, PA	25,000 45,000 50,000	1972 1974 1977	The Pew Trust also gave $30,000 in 1969. For description of the Pew Memorial Trust see Campus Crusade.
Berry (Lowell W.) Fdn., Oakland, CA	200 400 300	1976 1977 1978	The Berry Fdn. also gave $500 in 1969.

Recipient/Donor	Amount	Year	Background on Donor
Pew (J. Howard) Freedom Trust, Philadelphia, PA	50,000 15,000	1977 1978	One of the Pew family trusts. Fdn.'s purpose is to give to certain organizations which "uphold the free enterprise system as a matter of public policy."
Patrick Frawley	NA	NA	Frawley is owner of a major, unidentified razor and ballpoint-pen firm.
CHRISTIAN CRUSADE:			
H. L. Hunt	NA	1962	H. L. Hunt is the founder of the Hunt family fortune; father of Nelson Bunker Hunt of Campus Crusade.
Mrs. Grover Herman	5,000	1979	
CHRISTIAN EMBASSY:			
Warren Hodgedon	50,000	1976	Hodgedon is an investor.
Claude Brown	50,000	1976	
Ed Flato	NA	1976	The exact sum of money is not known. He is a wealthy, very conservative oilman from Texas.
Austin Pryor	NA	1976	The exact sum of money is not known.
Arlis Priest	NA	1976	The exact sum of money is not known. He is a fund-raiser and board member of Campus Crusade.
Lt. Col. Paul Miller	NA	1976	The exact sum of money is not known. He is also on the boards of Christian Freedom Foundation and Third Century Publishers.
CHRISTIAN FREEDOM FOUNDATION:			
Pew (J. Howard) Freedom Trust, Philadelphia, PA	300,000	1974	J. Howard Pew gave $50,000 in 1950 to start the Christian Freedom Fdn. For description of Pew Freedom Trust see Christian Anti-Communism Crusade. Between 1962 and 1969 the various Pew trusts donated a total of $2,150,750.

Recipient/Donor	Amount	Year	Background on Donor
Richard DeVos	25,000	1974	DeVos is a co-founder of Amway.
Curran Fdn.	3,000	1975	1967–1969 the Curran Fdn. do-
	3,000	1976	nated $5,000 each year to Christian Freedom Fdn.
Elizabeth Trust, WI	750	1975	
	250	1976	
Berry (Lowell W.) Fdn., Oakland, CA	1,000	1975	For description of the Berry Fdn.
	500	1976	see Campus Crusade.

CHURCH LEAGUE OF AMERICA:

Recipient/Donor	Amount	Year	Background on Donor
Curran Fdn.	10,000	1975	In 1969 the Curran Fdn. also gave $2,000.
Elizabeth Trust	200	1975	
	500	1976	
Ahmanson Fdn., Los Angeles, CA	100/yr.	1975-1979	For description of the Ahmanson Fdn. see Campus Crusade.
Hearst (William Randolph) Fdn., New York, NY	5,000	1978	Publications-empire magnate; donor to numerous ultraconservative causes.
Coors (Adolph) Fdn., Denver, CO	500	1978	For description of the Coors Fdn.
	500	1979	see Campus Crusade.
Gen Robert E. Wood			Wood was the former chairman of the board, Sears, Roebuck & Co.
Sewell Avery			Avery has been chairman of the board, Montgomery Ward and U.S. Gypsum Corp.

FELLOWSHIP OF CHRISTIAN ATHLETES:

Recipient/Donor	Amount	Year	Background on Donor
Pew Memorial Trust, Philadelphia, PA	5,000	1972	The Pew Memorial Trust also donated $10,000 in 1969. For description of Trust see Campus Crusade. All donations went to the office in Kansas City, MO.
	10,000	1974	
	15,000	1977	
	15,000	1978	
Stone (W. Clement & Jessie V.) Fdn., Chicago, IL	12,000	1973	Donation was to train group leaders for summer conference. Stone is a donor to Campus Crusade, active in its Here's Life campaign.
Mabee (J. E. & L. E.) Fdn., Tulsa, OK	30,000	1975	The Mabee Fdn. "aids Christian religious organizations, charitable organizations, education and
	800,000	1978	
	2,000	1979	

Recipient/Donor	Amount	Year	Background on Donor
			medicine." Fdn. is 16th largest private foundation in U.S. (1978 to construction of national headquarters in Kansas City.)
Kresge Fdn., Troy, MI	50,000 100,000	1975 1978	1975 donation was for construction of a chapel at their National Resource Center; 1978 donation was for their National Resource Center.
Berry (Lowell W.) Fdn., Oakland, CA	1,000 250	1976 1978	Donations were to the office in Kansas City, MO.
Christian Workers Fdn., Montgomery, AL	500	1976	Donation was to the office in Kansas City, MO. For description of the fdn. see Campus Crusade.
Butt (Howard E.) Fdn., Corpus Christi, TX	1,000	1977	Donation was to the office in Kansas City, MO. The fdn. primarily supports "camps related to lay theological education and mental health." H. E. Butt is a millionaire supermarket executive (H.E.B. Food Stores) in Texas.
Butler Mfg. Co. Fdn., Kansas City, MO	10,000	1977	Donation was to the office in Kansas City, MO.
Crowell (Henry P. & Susan C.) Trust, Chicago, IL	7,500	1977	Donation was to the office in Kansas City, MO. The fdn. "aids evangelical Christianity by supporting organizations... which evangelize at home and abroad." Henry is chairman of the board at Quaker Oats and is a founder of the Church League of America.
Lilly Endowment, Indianapolis, IN	27,500 150,000 75,000	1977 1978 1979	Donation was to the office in Kansas City, MO. Endowment is one of several funds handling the EH Lilly family fortune derived from the pharmaceuticals business.
Pew (J. Howard) Freedom Trust, Philadelphia, PA	15,000	1978	Donation was to the office in Kansas City, MO. For descrip-

Recipient/Donor	Amount	Year	Background on Donor
			tion of the Pew Freedom Trust see Christian Anti-Communism Crusade.
World Evangelism & Christian Education Fund	NA	NA	Donation was to the office in Kansas City. The fund is a subsidiary of the Billy Graham Evangelistic Assn.
Coors (Adolph) Fdn., Denver, CO	25,000 2,000	1978 1979	Donation was to the Denver, CO, chapter. For description of the Coors Fdn. see Campus Crusade.
Conn Memorial Fdn., Tampa, FL	7,500	1978	Donation was to the Orlando, FL, chapter.
Harper (Phillips S.) Fdn.	500 500	1978 1979	Donation was to the Orlando, FL, chapter.
Pitcairn-Crabbe Fdn., Pittsburgh, PA	5,000	1978	Donation was to the Pittsburgh, PA, chapter. Family has major holdings in steel, coal and chemicals.
Hillman Fdn., Pittsburgh, PA	9,000	1978	Donation was to the Pittsburgh, PA, chapter. Hillman family has major holdings in coal, steel and chemicals.
Mabee (J. E. & L. E.) Fdn., Tulsa, OK	20,000	1978	Donation was to the Oklahoma chapter.

FULL GOSPEL BUSINESSMEN'S FELLOWSHIP:

Recipient/Donor	Amount	Year	Background on Donor
Berry (Lowell W.) Fdn., Oakland, CA	5,500 250 250	1976 1976 1978	For description of the Berry Fdn. see Campus Crusade.

FULLER THEOLOGICAL SEMINARY:

Recipient/Donor	Amount	Year	Background on Donor
Berry (Lowell W.) Fdn., Oakland, CA	18,000 34,000 12,500	1976 1978 1978	Between 1967 and 1969 the Berry Fdn. gave a total of $46,000. For description of the fdn. see Campus Crusade
Butt (Howard E.) Fdn., Corpus Christi, TX	1,100	1977	Donation was tuition for one student. For description of the Butt Fdn., see Fellowship of Christian Athletes.

GARDEN GROVE COMMUNITY CHURCH:

Recipient/Donor	Amount	Year	Background on Donor
Berry (Lowell W.) Fdn.,	1,100	1977	$1,000 of the 1977 donation went

Recipient/Donor	Amount	Year	Background on Donor
Oakland, CA	1,000	1978	to the *Hour of Power*. For description of the Berry Fdn. see Campus Crusade. In 1977 the Lowell W. Berry Fdn. gave $212,000 and in 1978 $25,036 to the Schuller Institute for Successful Church Leadership. It is assumed to be connected to the Garden Grove Community Church.
DeVos (Richard & Helen) Fdn., Grand Rapids, MI	50,000	1978	For description of the DeVos Fdn. see Campus Crusade.
W. Clement Stone	$1 mill. pledge	1977	Donation was toward the building of Schuller's $12.5 mill. Crystal Cathedral. For a description of Stone see Campus Crusade.

BILLY GRAHAM EVANGELISTIC ASSOCIATION:

Recipient/Donor	Amount	Year	Background on Donor
Pew Memorial Trust, Philadelphia, PA	100,000	1974	The trust also gave $85,000 in 1969. For description of the Memorial Trust see Campus Crusade.
Pew (J. Howard) Freedom Trust, Philadelphia, PA	100,000	1975	For description of the Freedom Trust see Christian Anti-Communism Crusade.
Berry (Lowell W.) Fdn., Oakland, CA	45,000 22,000 15,000 70,000 35,000 15,000 40,000	1975 1975 1976 1977 1979 1977 1977	The Berry Fdn. gives $110,000–$125,000 each year to the various parts of the Graham organization; it also gave $198,812 from 1967 to 1969. For description of the fdn. see Campus Crusade. The 1975 and 1977 gifts were directed to LCMI—it is assumed to be Graham-related, as it first appeared in connection with Graham organizations.
Atkinson (Myrtle L.) Fdn., La Canada, CA	4,000	1976	For description of the fdn. see Campus Crusade.
Richardson (Sid W.) Fdn., Fort Worth, TX	25,000/yr.	1975-78	Sid Richardson had several Texas oil and gas interests. Estate was managed by John Connally when Richardson died.

Recipient/Donor	Amount	Year	Background on Donor
Marriott (J. Willard) Family Fdn., Washington, D.C.	2,500 2,500 2,500	1975 1978 1977	Marriott family fortune is derived from Marriott Corp., controlling nearly 20% of stock. Family donates to numerous ultraconservative and business causes.
Butler Mfg. Co. Fdn., Kansas City, MO	2,500	1978	For description of the fdn. see Fellowship of Christian Athletes. Donation was to Graham's Mid-America Crusade.
Fred R. Esty	NA	1970	Esty was chairman of the board, U.S. Banknote Corp. in 1970 and is now chairman emeritus. He is also on the board of *Christianity Today*, chairman N.Y. Bible Society, member of committee Religion in American Life, member Gideons (general industry chrmn). He was head of Graham's N.Y. Crusade at Shea Stadium.
George Champion	NA	1969	Champion was a director at Chase Manhattan Bank in 1969. He was a member of the N.Y. Crusade General Committee.
Roger Hull	NA	1969	Chairman, Mutual Life Insurance Co., N.Y., in 1969. Hull was a member of the N.Y. Crusade General Committee.
Elmer W. Engstrom	NA	1969	Chairman of Executive Committee of the Board, RCA, in 1969. Part of N.Y. Crusade.
Maxey W. Jarman	NA	1969	Head of Genesco Inc., in 1969. Treasurer of N.Y. Crusade.

INTER-VARSITY CHRISTIAN FELLOWSHIP:

Recipient/Donor	Amount	Year	Background on Donor
Kresge Fdn., Troy, MI	20,000 100,000	1973 1979	Donation was to the Ann Arbor chapter. The 1979 donation was for a training center, Madison, WI.
Pew Memorial Trust, Philadelphia, PA	5,000	1972	The Pew Memorial Trust also gave $5,000 in 1969. For a description of the trust see Campus Crusade.

Recipient/Donor	Amount	Year	Background on Donor
Crowell (Henry P. & Susan C.) Trust, Chicago, IL	5,000 4,000	1976 1977	For description of the Crowell Trust see Fellowship of Christian Athletes.

MORAL MAJORITY:

Mrs. Holly Coors	5,000	1979	Wife of brewer Joseph Coors. Coors family supports numerous business and right-wing causes. Donation was for the Political Action Committee.
Mr. & Mrs. Bob Perry, TX	10,000	1979	Donation was for Moral Majority PAC. Mr. Perry is a building contractor in Texas.

NATIONAL ASSOCIATION OF EVANGELICALS:

Pew (J. Howard) Freedom Trust, Philadelphia, PA	5,330 4,700	1976 1978	Donations were to the Wheaton, IL, office. For description of the Pew Freedom Trust see Christian Anti-Communism Crusade.
Pew Memorial Trust, Philadelphia, PA	150,000 100,000 3,000	1972 1974 1974	1972 donation was to the office in King of Prussia, PA; the $100,000 donation was for their World Relief Mission, and the $3,000 donation was for the office in Washington, D.C. For description of the Pew Memorial Trust see Campus Crusade.

ORAL ROBERTS EVANGELISTIC ASSOCIATION:

Berry (Lowell W.) Fdn., Oakland, CA	250	1976	For description of the Berry Fdn. see Campus Crusade.

ORAL ROBERTS UNIVERSITY:

Kazanjian (Calvin F.) Economic Fdn.	10,000 10,000 10,000	1973 1974 1975	
Noble (Samuel Roberts) Fdn., Ardmore, OK	10,000 10,000 10,000	1973 1974 1975	For description of the Noble Fdn. see Campus Crusade.
Berry (Lowell W.) Fdn., Oakland, CA	1,000 100	1975 1977	For description of the Berry Fdn. see Campus Crusade.
Amoco Fdn., Chicago, ILL	9,331	1977	Donation was a matching grant. For description of the Amoco Fdn. see Heritage Fdn.

Recipient/Donor	Amount	Year	Background on Donor
General Electric Fdn., Bridgeport, CT	6,091	1977	Donation was a matching grant. The GE Fdn. gives institutional grants primarily to education.
Gulf Oil Fdn. of Delaware, Pittsburgh, PA	8,221	1977	Matching grant. Fdn. gives primarily to education.
Mabee (J. E. & L. E.) Fdn., Tulsa, OK	150,000 500,000	1977 1977	Donations were to the School of Business and expansion of the library, respectively. For description of the Mabee Fdn. see Fellowship of Christian Athletes.

WORLD EVANGELISM & CHRISTIAN EDUCATION FUND:

			The fund is a subsidiary of the Billy Graham Evangelistic Assn.
Davis (Edwin W. & Catherine M.) Fdn., St. Paul, MN	2,000 2,000	1977 1978	Donations were to the Bellevue, WA, office for staff salaries. From 1966 to 1969 the fdn. gave an additional $25,000.
Scaife (Sarah) Fdn., Pittsburgh, PA	5,000 25,000 50,000	1974 1976 1977	Donations were to the Pittsburgh, PA, office. Foundation is part of the Mellon family interests.
Berry (Lowell W.) Fdn., Oakland, CA	1,000 1,300 2,000 1,700 500 180	1975 1976 1977 1978 1979 1979	The 1975 donation was to the office in Colorado Springs, CO; the 1979 donations were to the Oakland and San Francisco, CA, offices, respectively. For description of the Berry Fdn. see Campus Crusades.
Pepsico Fdn., Purchase, N.Y.	300	1976	For description of the fdn. see Campus Crusade.
Crowell (Henry P. & Susan C.) Trust, Chicago, IL	5,000	1976	For description of the fdn. see Fellowship of Christian Athletes.
Murdock (M. J.) Charitable Trust, Vancouver, WA	45,000	1977	
Hearst (William Randolph) Fdn., New York, N.Y.	10,000 5,000	1977 1978	For description of the fdn. see Church League of America. 1978 donation was to the Pittsburgh, PA, office.
Lilly Endowment,	140,000	1977	For description of the endow-

Recipient/Donor	Amount	Year	Background on Donor
Indianapolis, IN			ment see Fellowship of Christian Athletes.
Heinz (Howard) Endowment, Pittsburgh, PA	14,000	1978	Donation was to the Pittsburgh, PA, office.
Pitcairn-Crabbe Fdn., Pittsburgh, PA	7,600	1979	For description of the fdn. see Fellowship of Christian Athletes.
Conn Memorial Fdn., Tampa, FL	20,000 27,500 31,500	1977 1978 1979	Donation was to the Tampa, FL, office. For description of the fdn. see Fellowship of Christian Athletes.
Pittsburgh Fdn., Pittsburgh, PA	7,600	1979	Donation was to the Pittsburgh, PA, office.
Mabee (J. E. & L. E.) Fdn., Tulsa, OK	5,000	1979	Donation was to the Tulsa, OK, office. For description of the fdn. see Fellowship of Christian Athletes.

WORLDWIDE CHURCH OF GOD:

Recipient/Donor	Amount	Year	Background on Donor
Bobby Fischer	94,000	NA	Fischer is a chess champion.

YOUNG LIFE:

Recipient/Donor	Amount	Year	Background on Donor
Mabee (J. E. & L. E.) Fdn., Tulsa, OK	1,900	1977	Donation was to the office in Colorado Springs, CO, for Camp Malibu. For description of the Mabee Fdn. see Fellowship of Christian Athletes.
Pew Memorial Trust, Philadelphia, PA	10,000 10,000	1977 1979	Donation was to the office in Colorado Springs, CO. For description of the Memorial Trust see Campus Crusade.

YOUTH FOR CHRIST:

Recipient/Donor	Amount	Year	Background on Donor
Crowell (Henry P. & Susan C.) Trust, Chicago, IL	10,000	1977	For description of the trust see Fellowship of Christian Athletes.
Berry (Lowell W.) Fdn., Oakland, CA	1,000	1979	For description of the fdn. see Campus Crusade.

Source Notes

Chapter I

1. *Commonwealth v. Kenneth Edelin*, 371 Mass. 489; also transcripts from the trial itself and personal attendance at most court sessions.
2. *Boston Globe*, Feb. 3, 1975.
3. *Newsweek*, March 3, 1975.
4. *Boston Globe*, May 18, 1982; also an interview with Kenneth Edelin.
5. I conducted numerous investigations into conditions at Boston City Hospital for articles in Boston's two weekly newspapers, *The Boston Phoenix* and *The Real Paper*, from which I culled this information.
6. Interview with Joseph Reilly, then chairman, Massachusetts Citizens for Life.
7. *Boston Globe*, June 2, 1974; *New York Times*, Feb. 17, 1975; also an interview with Thomas Connelly.
8. I conducted an investigation into the behavior of the Suffolk County sheriff, some of the background for which and the results of which were printed in *The Real Paper*.
9. *Boston Globe*, June 2, 1974.
10. *New York Times*, March 1, 1976.
11. *New England Journal of Medicine*, June 7, 1973; also interviews with the doctors who did the research, for an article in *The Boston Phoenix*, April 21, 1974.
12. *New England Journal of Medicine*, June 7, 1973; *Boston Globe*, June 2, 1974; also William A. Nolen, *The Baby in the Bottle* (New York: Coward, McCann and Geoghegan, 1978), pp. 35–39, 51–53.

13. *Boston Globe,* June 2, 1974.
14. Interview with Newman Flanagan.
15. Transcripts from the trial; also Nolen, *op. cit.*, pp. 148–51; also *Boston Globe,* Feb. 1, 1975.
16. *Commonwealth v. Kenneth Edelin.*
17. Interview with William Homans.
18. *Commonwealth v. Kenneth Edelin.*
19. Trial transcripts.
20. *Ibid.*
21. *Ibid.*
22. I conducted an investigation into this case for an article in *The Boston Phoenix.*
23. Trial transcripts.
24. *Ibid.*; also Nolen, *op. cit.*, pp. 144–51.
25. *Commonwealth v. Kenneth Edelin.*
26. *New York Times,* Feb. 16, 1975.
27. *Newsweek,* March 3, 1975.
28. *New York Times,* Feb. 19, 1975.
29. *Boston Globe,* Feb. 19, 1975.
30. *New York Times,* Feb. 17, Feb. 21, March 16, 1975.
31. *Newsweek,* March 3, 1975.
32. Interview with William Delahunt.
33. William Safire, "What's with Boston?," *New York Times,* March 10, 1975.
34. *Newsweek,* March 3, 1975.
35. *Time,* July 9, 1979.
36. Fund-raising appeal from Faye Wattleton for Planned Parenthood, undated.
37. Fund-raising appeal from Archibald Cox for Common cause, undated.
38. Interview with William Homans.

Chapter II

1. Linda Gordon, *Woman's Body, Woman's Right* (Penguin Books, 1977), pp. 1–46.
2. David Feldman, *Birth Control in Jewish Law* (New York: New York University Press, 1968), *passim.*
3. John T. Noonan, "An Almost Absolute Value in History," in *The Morality of Abortion: Legal and Historical Perspectives* (Cambridge, Mass.: Harvard University Press, 1970).
4. Daughters of Saint Paul, *Yes to Life* (St. Paul, Minn.: St. Paul Editions, 1977), pp. 41–45.
5. *Documentation of the Right to Life and Abortion* (Washington, D.C.: United States Catholic Conference, 1974), pp. 35–38.
6. Gordon, *op. cit.*, p. 54.
7. James C. Mohr, *Abortion in America: The Origins and Evolution of National Policy, 1800–1900* (New York: Oxford University Press, 1978), pp. 46–85, 93–94, 107, 111, 120–29, 184–97.
8. Dennis Pettibone, "The Christian Voice," *Liberty,* January–February 1981.
9. Mohr, *op. cit.*, p. 240.
10. Gordon, *op. cit.*, pp. 48–53.

11. "Culture and Population Change" (Washington, D.C.: American Association for the Advancement of Science, 1974).
12. Lawrence Lader, *Abortion II: Making the Revolution* (Boston: Beacon Press, 1973), p. 42; also *New York Times*, Feb. 25, March 12, April 30, May 21, May 22, 1967; May 17, June 26, June 29, 1970; June 3, June 4, June 19, June 30, 1971.
13. Bob Woodward and Scott Armstrong, *The Brethren* (New York: Simon and Schuster, 1979), pp. 165–77, 182–89, 218, 229–40, 413–16.
14. John T. Noonan, *A Private Choice* (New York: Free Press, 1979), p. 29.

Chapter III

1. Interview with Phyllis Deroian, Chuck Benke, Marie Damiano and Andra Deroian.
2. "Abortion Politics and the American Catholic Church," *Conscience*, Catholics for a Free Choice, July 1981.
3. Mary Daly, "Women and the Catholic Church," in *Sisterhood Is Powerful: An Anthology of Writings from the Women's Liberation Movement*, ed. Robin Morgan (New York: Vintage Books, 1970), pp. 137–52.
4. "Political Responsibility: Reflections for an Election Year," United States Catholic Conference, Washington, D.C., Feb. 12, 1976.
5. Mary T. Hanna, *Catholics and American Politics* (Cambridge, Mass.: Harvard University Press, 1979), p. 20.
6. Daly, *op cit.*
7. Andrew H. Merton, *Enemies of Choice* (Boston: Beacon Press, 1981), pp. 20–22.
8. Msgr. John McCarthy, *In Defense of Life* (Houston: Lumen Christi Press, 1970); also Frederick S. Jaffe, Barbara L. Lindheim and Philip R. Lee, *Abortion Politics: Private Morality and Public Policy* (New York: McGraw-Hill, 1981), p. 92; also John H. Wright, "An End to the Birth Control Controversy?," *America*, March 7, 1981.
9. Merton, *op. cit.*, p. 43.
10. Lawrence Lader, *Abortion II: Making the Revolution* (Boston: Beacon Press, 1973), pp. 69, 140.
11. "Abortion Politics and the American Catholic Church," *loc. cit.*
12. *Cora McRae, et al., v. Secretary, United States Department of Health, Education and Welfare, Defendant, and Senators James L. Buckley, et al., Intervenor-Defendants*, 76 C 1804.
13. "Abortion Politics and the American Catholic Church," *loc. cit.*
14. Interview with Father Paul Marx.
15. *Foundation Directory*, 1980, 1981 (New York: Foundation Center), for data on the Dan Murphy and De Rance Foundations; also *Supplement: The Profiles*; also IRS 990 AR annual reports.
16. *New York Times*, Feb. 18, 1973.
17. *Ibid.*, Sept. 7, 1974.
18. *Ibid.*, April 9 and 14, 1975.
19. *Ibid.*, Aug. 10, 14, 15 and 22, 1973.
20. "Documentation on the Right to Life and Abortion," United States Catholic Conference, Washington, 1974.

21. "Abortion and the Law," *New Republic*, May 18 and June 22, 1974.
22. *New York Times*, May 21, 1974.
23. "Abortion Politics and the American Catholic Church," *loc. cit.*
24. Interview with Rev. Edward Bryce.
25. Interview with Patricia Driscoll.
26. Letter from the late Michael Cardinal Browne, Rome, March 5, 1970.
27. Interview with Susan Brindle.
28. Interview with Pam Cira.
29. Interview with Juli Loesch.
30. Hanna, *op. cit.*, p. 167; also Frederick S. Jaffe, Barbara L. Lindheim and Philip R. Lee, *Abortion Politics: Private Morality and Public Policy* (New York: McGraw-Hill, 1981), p. 106.
31. Lader, *op. cit.*, p. 187.
32. *New York Times*, March 3, 1978.
33. *Pastoral Plan for Pro-Life Activities*, United States Catholic Conference, Nov. 20, 1974.
34. "Respect Life! A Catholic Community Experience," National Conference of Catholic Bishops, Washington, D.C., 1980.
35. George Higgins, "The Prolife Movement and the New Right," *America*, Sept. 13, 1980.
36. Interview with Rev. Edward Bryce.
37. *Catholics United for Life*, May 1981 and June 1982.
38. Interviews with Mark Drogin and Marguerite Stearns.
39. Interview with Marguerite Stearns.
40. Melshisedek Barton, *The Secret of the Universe: The Third Order* (CUL Publications, 1981), pp. 5–16.
41. *Catholics United for Life*, Christmas 1981.
42. "National Day of Rescue," CUL press release, June 26, 1981.
43. Interview with Jack Pelikan.

Chapter IV
1. Interview with Carolyn Gerster.
2. *National Right to Life News*, Jan 12, 1981.
3. *New York Times*, March 1, 1976; also an interview with Paul and Judie Brown.
4. Interview with Paul and Judie Brown.
5. *Washington Star*, April 23, 1981.
6. Paul and Judie Brown interview.
7. Gerster interview.
8. Helen Epstein, "Abortion: An Issue That Won't Go Away," *New York Times Magazine*, March 30, 1980.
9. Gerster interview.
10. Conversation between Naomi Braine and the Gans sisters, taped by the author.
11. Daughters of Saint Paul, *Yes to Life* (St. Paul, Minn.: St. Paul Editions, 1977), pp. 41–45.
12. "Diary of an Unborn Child," undated.
13. Leo Alexander, "Medical Science Under Dictatorship," *New England Journal of Medicine*, No. 241, pp. 39–47, reprinted in Dennis J. Horan and David Mall, eds., *Death, Dying and Euthanasia* (Frederick, Md.: Aletheia Books,

University Publications of America, 1980), pp. 571–92. I conducted an investigation into Dr. Alexander's hospital and several others like it in the Boston area in conjunction with a series of articles on electroshock treatment for *The Boston Phoenix*.

14. Gerster interview; also Carolyn Gerster, "Will the Real Adolph Hitler Please Stand up?," *National Right to Life News*, March 1980.
15. John T. Noonan, *A Private Choice* (New York: Free Press, 1979), p. 190.
16. Colin Clark, *Population Growth: The Advantages* (Santa Ana, Calif.: Life Quality Paperbacks, 1972), p. 34.
17. Robert L. Sassone, *Handbook on Population* (Santa Ana, Calif.: Robert L. Sassone, 1978), pp. 3, 75, 99, 147.
18. Randy Engel, speech on Planned Parenthood before the National Right to Life Annual Convention, Cherry Hill, N.J., 1982.
19. *New York Times*, May 28, 1975.
20. Myre Sim, "Abortion and Psychiatry," in Thomas W. Hilgers, Dennis J. Horan and David Mall, eds., *New Perspectives on Human Abortion* (Frederick, Md.: Aletheia Books, University Publications of America, 1981), pp. 159–60.
21. *New York Times*, Jan. 21, 1974.
22. Stanislaw Z. Lembrych, "Fertility Problems Following Aborted First Pregnancy," in Hilgers *et al.*, *op cit.*, pp. 128–34.
23. Richard A. Watson, "Urologic Complications of Legal Abortion," in Hilgers *et al.*, *op cit.*, pp. 135–44.
24. Matthew J. Bulfin, "Complications of Legal Abortion: A Perspective from Private Practice," in Hilgers *et al.*, *op cit.*, pp. 145–50.
25. Sim, *op. cit.*, pp. 151–63.
26. Thomas W. Hilgers and Dennis O'Hare, "Abortion Related Maternal Mortality," in Hilgers *et al.*, *op. cit.*, pp. 69–91.
27. *Boston Globe*, Sept. 9, 1982.
28. *New York Times*, March 1, 1976.
29. Noonan, *op. cit.*, p. 67.
30. *National Right to Life News*, Aug. 18, 1980.
31. Margot Hentoff, "Let's Stop Deceiving Ourselves About Abortion," *Village Voice*, March 1975, reprinted in *Human Life Review*, Spring 1975.
32. Marshall McLuhan, "Death and the Mechanization of Man," in Horan and Mall, *op. cit.*, p. 32.
33. Eugene Ionesco, "On Euthanasia," in Horan and Mall, *op. cit.*, p. 33.
34. Richard Neuhaus, keynote speech before the National Right to Life Annual Convention, Cherry Hill, N.J., 1982; also an interview with Pastor Neuhaus.
35. Interview with Burke Balche.
36. Interview with Pam Cira.
37. Jeremy Rifkin, keynote speech before the National Right to Life Annual Convention, Omaha, 1981; also an interview with Jeremy Rifkin.
38. Loesch, *op cit.*

Chapter V
1. *New York Times*, Jan. 23 and Feb. 16, 1979; *Washington Post*, Feb. 16, 1979; also fund-raising letter from Carolyn Gerster, undated.
2. Letter from Burke Balche to Eleanor Smeal, Feb. 17, 1979.

3. "Statement [from participants to press] for February 15, 1979 National Dialogue on Abortion," Feb. 14, 1979; *ACCL Update*, March 1979.
4. Gerster, *op. cit.*
5. National Right to Life Committee press release, February 15, 1979.
6. *National Right to Life News*, March 1980.
7. *New York Times*, Jan. 7, Feb. 26 and Feb. 27, 1972.
8. James Bopp, workshop on laws concerning abortion at the National Right to Life Annual Convention, Cherry Hill, N.J., 1982.
9. *New York Times*, July 1, 2 and 3, 1979.
10. *Ibid.*, March 24, 1981.
11. *Ibid.*, March 6, 1979.
12. *Ibid.*, July 1, 1980; also Michael Barone and Grant Ujifusa, *The Almanac of American Politics*, 1982 (Washington, D.C.: Barone & Co.), pp. 304–5; also *Lifeletter*, July 21, 1976.
13. *New York Times*, July 1, 1980; also interview with David Fine, former clerk to Justice John Dooling.
14. *New York Times*, Feb. 24, Feb. 27, March 2 and Nov. 14, 1976; also *Lifeletter*, March 3, March 22 and Sept. 8, 1976.
15. *Lifeletter*, April 6, 1976.
16. *New York Times*, Aug. 11 and 14, 1976; also *Lifeletter*, Aug. 23, 1976.
17. *New York Times*, June 23, 1977.
18. *Ibid.*, Oct. 7, 1977.
19. *Ibid.*, Feb. 3, 1978.
20. *Ibid.*, July 17, Sept. 12, 1977.
21. *Ibid.*, May 17, July 29, Nov. 10, 24 and 25, 1978.
22. *Cora McRae, et al., v. Secretary, United States Department of Health, Education and Welfare, Defendant, and Senators James L. Buckley et al., Intervenor-Defendants*, 76 C 1804; also Anne Nelson, "God, Man and the Reverend Moon," *The Nation*, March 31, 1979; also Barone and Ujifusa, *op. cit.*, pp. 570–71; also *Wall Street Journal*, Aug. 15, 1978.
23. *National Right to Life News*, June 16, 1980.
24. John T. Noonan, *A Private Choice* (New York: Free Press, 1979), p. 183.
25. *Ibid.*, p. 25.
26. *Ibid.*, p. 186.
27. David N. O'Steen, "The Case for a New Pro-Life Strategy—Two Amendments," undated.
28. Andrew H. Merton, *Enemies of Choice* (Boston: Beacon Press, 1981), p. 12; also interviews with Dr. John Willke and Father Paul Marx.
29. Dr. & Mrs. J. C. Willke, *How To Teach Children the Wonder of Sex* (Cincinnati: Hayes Publishing Co., 1964).
30. Interview with Paul and Judie Brown.

Chapter VI

1. Richard Viguerie, speech on the New Right and abortion before the Unity Convention, Washington, D.C., 1981.
2. Viguerie, *The New Right: We're Ready to Lead* (Falls Church, Va.: Viguerie Co., 1980), pp. 19–22. Unless otherwise indicated, the biographical information on Richard Viguerie comes from this book.

3. Nick Kotz, "King Midas of 'The New Right,'" *Atlantic Monthly*, November 1978.

4. Viguerie, *The New Right*, pp. 21–24.

5. "Barry Goldwater and the Organized Right Wing," Group Research Special Report No. 17, Oct. 12, 1964.

6. *Group Research Reports*, 1965 (Washington, D.C.: Group Research, Inc.), p. 23, and 1972, p. 39.

7. Viguerie, *The New Right*, pp. 25–27.

8. George F. Gilder and Bruce K. Chapman, *The Party That Lost Its Head* (New York: Knopf, 1966), *passim*.

9. Clifton F. White and William J. Gill, *Why Reagan Won* (Chicago: Regnery Gateway, 1981), *passim*.

10. *Democratic Congressional Campaign Committee Report, August–September 1978*, ed. Diana Fairbank (Washington, D.C.: Democratic Congressional Campaign Committee).

11. Viguerie, *The New Right*, pp. 25–27.

12. Alan Crawford, *Thunder on the Right* (New York: Pantheon Books, 1980), pp. 62–63; also Alan MacRobert, "Moon Cult's Future Hangs on Korea Power Struggle," *The Real Paper*, Nov. 24, 1979; also Fairbank, *op. cit.*

13. Kotz, *op. cit.*

14. Viguerie, *The New Right*, p. 5.

15. Morton Blackwell, lecture as part of the series "A New Right Perspective on America's Future," Kennedy School, Harvard University, fall 1981.

16. *Group Research Reports*, 1966, pp. 13, 87–88; 1967, pp. 34–35; 1968, pp. 58, 75; 1969, pp. 32, 36, 86.

17. *Dem. Congr. Comp. Report, August–September 1978*; also Thomas J. McIntyre, *The Fear Brokers* (Boston: Beacon Press, 1979), p. 73.

18. Unless otherwise indicated, the biographical information on Paul Weyrich comes from an interview with him.

19. *Conservative Digest*, June 1979 and October 1981.

20. *Ibid.*

21. *Foundation Directory*, 1980, 1981 (New York: Foundation Center); *National Review*, Dec. 20, 1980; *Washington Post*, Jan. 4, 1981.

22. *Foundation News*, March–April 1979.

23. *Group Research Reports*, 1972, p. 39; 1973, p. 26; 1974, pp. 17–18.

24. *Ibid.*, 1980, p. 33.

25. Unless otherwise indicated, the biographical information on Howard Phillips comes from an interview with him.

26. McIntyre, *op. cit.*, p. 71.

27. Viguerie, *The New Right*, p. 53.

28. *Congressional Digest*, June 1979; also McIntyre, *op. cit.*, pp. 232–59, 278–97.

29. Burton Yale Pines, *Back to Basics* (New York: Morrow, 1982), pp. 286–88.

30. "TCC Leadership Manual," The Conservative Caucus, Vienna, Va., 1979.

31. McIntyre, *op. cit.*, p. 79.

32. Crawford, *op. cit.*, pp. 23–24.

33. Unless otherwise indicated, the biographical information on John "Terry" Dolan comes from an interview with him.

34. *Miami Herald*, March 30, 1980; *New York Times*, May 31, 1981.
35. *Washington Post*, Aug. 10, 1980; also McIntyre, *op. cit.*, p. 61.
36. William A. Rusher, *The Making of a New Majority Party* (New York: William A. Rusher, Sheed and Ward, Inc., 1975); also Kevin P. Phillips, *The Emerging Republican Majority* (Garden City, N.Y.: Doubleday Anchor Books, 1970).
37. *Washington Post*, Feb. 22, 23 and 24, 1981.
38. Viguerie, *The New Right*, pp. 32–33.
39. *Washington Post*, July 26, 1981.
40. *Group Research Reports*, 1977, p. 42.
41. Foundation Directory, 1980, 1981.
42. Unless otherwise indicated, the biographical information on and anecdotes about Paul and Judie Brown come from an interview with them.
43. *Washington Star*, April 23, 1981.
44. Robert L. Sassone, "Changing Congress—How?" (Washington, D.C., undated).
45. Paul and Judie Brown interview.
46. Michael Kramer, "The Trials of the New Right: From Abortion to Island Park," *New York*, Feb. 16, 1981.
47. Viguerie, speech before the Unity Convention, 1981.
48. Paul and Judie Brown interview.

Chapter VII

1. Interview with Ed McAteer.
2. Jim Wallis and Wes Michaelson, "The Plan to Save America," *Sojourners*, April 1976.
3. "Study Guide," Public Affairs Department, Dow Chemical USA, Midland, Mich., undated.
4. *imprimis*, Bulletin of Hillsdale College, Hillsdale, Mich., June 1981.
5. Thomas Mechling, "Patriotism, capitalism and positive thinking," *Commonweal*, Aug. 29, 1980.
6. Michael Barone, Grant Ujifusa and Douglas Matthews, *The Almanac of American Politics*, 1978 (New York: Dutton), p. 34.
7. Wallis, *op. cit.*
8. Richard Quebedeaux, *The Worldly Evangelicals* (San Francisco: Harper & Row, 1978), pp. 55–59.
9. Wallis, *op. cit.*; also McAteer interview.
10. Quebedeaux, *op. cit.*, p. 58.
11. Michael Barone, Grant Ujifusa and Douglas Matthews, *The Almanac of American Politics*, 1980 (New York: Dutton) p. 872; also Barone and Ujifusa, *The Almanac of American Politics*, 1982 (Washington, D.C.: Barone & Co.), p. 1099.
12. Wallis, *op. cit.*
13. Edward E. Plowman, "Is Morality All Right?," *Christianity Today*, Nov. 2, 1979.
14. Jim Stenzel, "A Stronger Voice for the American Way," *Sojourners*, November 1977.
15. Quebedeaux, *op. cit.*, pp. 3–5.

16. McAteer interview; unless otherwise indicated, all biographical information comes from this interview.
17. *Washington Star*, March 11, 1981.
18. Jerry Falwell, *Listen, America!* (Garden City, N.Y.: Doubleday, 1980), p. 13.
19. *Democratic Congressional Campaign Committee Report, April 30, 1980*, ed. Diana Fairbank (Washington, D.C.: Democratic Congressional Campaign Committee).
20. Falwell, *op. cit.*, pp. 166, 179.
21. Interview with Murray Norris.
22. *New York Times*, Aug. 13, 1975, and April 2, 1981.
23. Interview with Jaynann Payne.
24. *Group Research Reports*, 1980 (Washington, D.C.: Group Research, Inc.), p. 20.
25. *Ibid.*, p. 27; *ibid.*, 1968, p. 63; 1978, p. 31.
26. Tim LaHaye, *The Battle for the Mind* (Old Tappan, N.J.: Fleming H. Revell Co., 1979), pp. 163–64; also Quebedeaux, *op. cit.*, pp. 78–79.
27. LaHaye, *op. cit.*, pp. 197–206; also *Dem. Congr. Camp. Report, July 2, 1980*; also *Newsweek*, July 6, 1981.
28. *New York Times*, Aug. 4 and 5, Nov. 26, 1976; April 14, Aug. 21 and 23, Nov. 13 and 18, 1977; Aug. 21, 22, 23, 25 and 30, Nov. 6, 12, 15, 17 and 18, Dec. 18, 20, 29 and 30, 1978; Jan. 4, 10, 13, 23, April 21, May 25, Nov. 10, 1979.
29. *Group Research Reports*, 1980, p. 27.
30. Milton Moskowitz, Michael Katz and Robert Levering, *Everybody's Business: An Almanac* (San Francisco: Harper and Row, 1980), p. 863.
31. *Press-On!* (Winter, 1979–80, Volume 1, No. 4 and Volume 2, No. 1).
32. *Los Angeles Times*, June 7, 1980.
33. Quebedeaux, *op. cit.*, p. 79.
34. Payne interview.
35. Norris interview.
36. Interview with Jim and Ann Pierson.
37. Interview with Gary Jarmin; also Alan MacRobert, "Moonies in Reagandom," *Mother Jones*, May 1981.
38. Interview with William Billings.
39. *Boston Globe*, July 7, 1980.

Chapter VIII

1. Greg Denier, "A Shift Toward the Right? Or a Failure on the Left?," *Christianity and Crisis*, Dec. 22, 1980.
2. Morton Blackwell, Howard Phillips and Paul Weyrich, lectures as part of the series "A New Right Perspective on America's Future," Kennedy School, Harvard University, fall 1981; also interview with Ed McAteer; also conversations with numerous right-to-life leaders.
3. Interview with Ed McAteer.
4. *Group Research Reports*, 1979 (Washington, D.C.: Group Research, Inc.), p. 6.
5. Sandra Faucher, workshop on right-to-life election plan at National Right to Life annual conventions, Omaha, 1981, and Cherry Hill, N.J., 1982; also

"Voter Identification Program: Phase I: Voter Survey Project," National Right to Life Committee, Washington, D.C., 1977; also "Let's Get Organized," undated; also Robert G. Marshall, *Bayonets and Roses* (Falls Church, Va.: Robert G. Marshall, 1976).

6. Jerry Falwell, *Listen, America!* (Garden City, N.Y.: Doubleday, 1980), pp. 245–66; also "A Program for Political Participation of Church-Going Christians," undated.
7. *U.S. News and World Report*, Sept. 24, 1979.
8. *New York Times*, April 30, 1980.
9. *Washington Post*, Aug. 24, 1980.
10. "Congressional Report Card," Christian Voice, undated.
11. *Washington Post*, Oct. 5, 1980.
12. Michael Barone, Grant Ujifusa and Douglas Matthews, *The Almanac of American Politics*, 1978 (New York: Dutton), pp. 790–93; *ibid.*, 1980, p. 23.
13. *Group Research Reports*, 1977, pp. 13, 25; *ibid.*, 1978, p. 11.
14. Alan Crawford, *Thunder on the Right* (New York: Pantheon, 1980), pp. 23–24; also interview with Mary Crisp, former co-chair of the Republican National Committee.
15. *New York Times*, Feb. 6, 1978.
16. Barone *et al.*, *op. cit.*, 1980, pp. 303, 306.
17. Thomas J. McIntyre, *The Fear Brokers* (Boston: Beacon Press, 1979), pp. 138–142.
18. Howard Phillips, lecture at Kennedy School, Harvard University, fall 1981.
19. Richard A. Viguerie, *The New Right: We're Ready to Lead* (Falls Church, Va.: Viguerie Co., 1980), pp. 83–91.
20. Interview with New Right leader who asked to remain anonymous.
21. Viguerie, *op. cit.*, p. 91.
22. *Washington Post*, Dec. 25, 1980.
23. *New York Times*, Jan. 13, 1980; *Washington Post*, Nov. 1, 1980.
24. Myra MacPherson, "The New Right Brigade," *Washington Post*, Aug. 10, 1980; Mark Shields, "Running with NCPAC," *Washington Post*, April 17, 1981.
25. *Washington Post*, Dec. 26, 1980, and Jan. 27, 1981; *Miami Herald*, March 29, 1981.
26. *Washington Post*, July 9, 1981.
27. *National Journal*, Aug. 9, 1980.
28. Burton Yale Pines, *Back to Basics* (New York: Morrow, 1982), p. 289; also McIntyre, *op. cit.*, p. 61; also an interview with John "Terry" Dolan; also *New York Times*, May 31, 1981.
29. *National Journal*, Aug. 9, 1980.
30. *Ibid.*, also *Group Research Reports*, 1980, pp. 5–6.
31. *Wall Street Journal*, Aug. 15, 1978.
32. Jane Stone, "Have Calumny, Will Travel," *The Nation*, Oct. 10, 1981.
33. *Miami Herald*, March 29 and 30, 1981.
34. "The anti-abortion movement and the right wing," unpublished report, Group Research, Inc., Washington, D.C., April 1981.
35. Barone *et al.*, *op. cit.*, 1980, p. 303; also Michael Barone and Grant Ujifusa, *The Almanac of American Politics*, 1982 (Washington, D.C.: Barone & Co.), pp. 281, 342–45.

36. Barone and Ujifusa, *op. cit.*, pp. 280–81.

37. "The anti-abortion movement and the right wing."

38. *Group Research Reports*, 1979, p. 28.

39. Letter over the signature of Buz Lukens, undated.

40. *Miami Herald*, March 30, 1981.

41. Interview with George Cunningham.

42. Letters over the signature of Dale Bell, Dec. 1, 1978, and Jan. 1, 1979.

43. NCPAC letter, July 27, 1980; the funds raised by Americans for Life appeared in *The Nation*, Oct. 10, 1981.

44. Interview with Paul and Judie Brown and Ellen Dempsey; also Faucher workshop.

45. Cunningham interview.

46. Barone and Ujifusa, *op. cit.*, 1982, pp. 1018, 1021.

47. *National Right to Life News*, Oct. 27, 1980.

48. Letter over the signature of Sen. Jesse Helms, June 22, 1979; letters from the South Dakota Senatorial Research Committee, July 1979, and from the Republican State Central Committee of South Dakota, July 1979. FEC File No. 1231.

49. Interview with Don Todd, former chairman of Anybody But Church (ABC) and NCPAC consultant; also *Boston Globe*, June 15, 1980.

50. *New York Times*, March 25 and Oct. 27, 1980; *Wall Street Journal*, Sept. 11, 1980.

51. Associated Press report of *Chicago Sun-Times* article, June 30, 1980.

52. *New York Times*, March 25, 1980; also interview with Tom Connaughton, campaign director for Birch Bayh.

53. Barone and Ujifusa, *op. cit.*, 1982, pp. 372–73, 375; also interview with Park Rinard, aide to former Sen. John Culver.

54. Interview with Cleve Corbett, campaign director for Frank Church.

55. Interview with John "Terry" Dolan.

56. Interview with Lucy Denney, campaign aide for Rep. Joseph Fisher; also *Group Research Reports*, 1980, p. 33.

57. Interview with Bruce Wright, aide to Rep. Morris Udall.

58. Interview with Rosa Delauro, aide to Sen. Christopher Dodd.

59. Interview with Sen. Patrick Leahy.

60. Interview with Gary Jarmin.

61. *Miami Herald*, Nov. 23, 1980.

62. Barone and Ujifusa, *op. cit.*, 1982, pp. 466–67; also *New York Times*, Oct. 16, 1980, and *Washington Post*, Oct. 6, 1980.

63. *Lifeletter*, Dec. 5, 1980.

64. *National Right to Life News*, Nov. 10, 1980.

Chapter IX

1. *New York Times*, Aug. 19, 20 and 23, 1982, and Jan. 2, 1983; *St. Louis Post-Dispatch*, Aug. 15 and 31, 1982.

2. *New York Times*, Feb. 16, 1979.

3. Lisa Cronin Wohl, "Rise in Antiabortion Terrorism," *Ms*, November 1982.

4. *Boston Globe*, May 6, 1982; also Sara Evans, *Personal Politics* (New York: Vintage Books, 1980), p. 221.

5. "Conscience of a Conservative," *Public Opinion*, February–March 1981.
6. "Abortion: Women Speak Out: An Exclusive Poll," *Life*, November 1981.
7. *Time*, July 20, 1981.
8. *National Right to Life News*, July 13 and 27, Aug. 10 and 24 and Sept. 28, 1981.
9. *Boston Globe*, June 30, 1980.
10. *Congressional Record*, April 30, 1981; *Boston Globe*, July 27, 1982; *New York Times*, Jan. 13 and 22, 1982; *Washington Post*, May 20, 1981; *Human Events*, May 9, 1981.
11. *Newsweek*, July 6, 1981; *San Francisco Chronicle*, May 19, 1981; *New York Times*, Aug. 16, 1982.
12. Interview with Paul Brown.
13. *New York Times*, Sept. 22, 1981.
14. Onalee McGraw, speech on book banning at Unity Convention, Washington, D.C., 1981.
15. Interview with John Cavanagh O'Keefe and other right-to-lifers who preferred to remain anonymous.
16. Paul Brown interview.
17. Personal attendance at National Right to Life annual conventions, Omaha, 1981, and Cherry Hill, N.J., 1982.
18. *New York Times*, Aug. 19, 1982.
19. Chuck Fager, "Dead end for right-to-lifers," *In These Times*, Sept. 29–Oct. 5, 1982.
20. Bill Keller and Nadine Cohodas, "Running Out of Gas?: New Right Lobbying," *Congressional Quarterly*, Oct. 16, 1982.
21. *Lifeletter*, Nov. 3, 1982.
22. Interview with Sandy Faucher.
23. *National Right to Life News*, Nov. 11, 1982.
24. "A Report from the National Abortion Rights Action League," Feb. 24, 1978.
25. Paul Brown interview.
26. Federal Election Commission reports, 1982, of CORK.
27. Paul Brown interview.
28. "Every Family Has One," CORK, 1982.
29. *New York Times*, Nov. 4, 1982.
30. *Ibid.*, Nov. 7, 1982.
31. Interview with John "Terry" Dolan; also Paul Brown interview.
32. *National Right to Life News*, Nov. 11, 1982.
33. Interview with Juli Loesch.
34. Paul Brown interview.
35. Dolan interview.

Chapter X

1. George Masnick and Mary Jo Bane, *The Nation's Families: 1960–1990* (Cambridge, Mass.: Joint Center for Urban Studies of MIT and Harvard University, 1980).
2. Attendance at Senate committee hearings on the anti-abortion amendment.
3. *U.S. News and World Report*, Nov. 26, 1976.
4. "Condensed Background Notes for Journalists Summarising the Essential Facts

on the Subject of Aging Worldwide," United Nations World Assembly on Aging, Vienna, July 26–August 6, 1982.

5. "The Great Abortion Breakthrough," *Internationalist*, June 1977; also Erik Eckholm and Kathleen Newland, "Health: The Family Planning Factor," *Worldwatch*, Paper No. 10, January 1977; also Leslie Iffy, M.D., Garry Frisoli, M.D., and Antal Jakobovits, M.D., "Perinatal Statistics: The Effect Internationally of Liberalized Abortion," in Thomas W. Hilgers, Dennis J. Horan and David Mall, eds., *New Perspectives on Human Abortion* (Frederick, Md.; Aletheia Books, University Publications of America, 1981), p. 95.

6. Christopher Jencks, "Destiny's Tots," *New York Review*, Oct. 8, 1981.

Index

Text copyright © 2012 by Wynton Marsalis
Illustrations copyright © 2012 by Paul Rogers

First edition 2012

Library of Congress Cataloging-in-Publication Data is available.

Library of Congress Catalog Card Number pending

ISBN 978-0-7636-3991-4

SCP 17 16 15 14 13 12
10 9 8 7 6 5 4 3 2 1

Printed in Humen, Dongguan, China

This book was hand-lettered and typeset in Glypha and Caslon 540.
The illustrations were done in ink and finished digitally.
Book design by Jill von Hartmann

Candlewick Press
99 Dover Street
Somerville, Massachusetts 02144

visit us at www.candlewick.com

Squeak, RUMBLE,

WHOMP! WHOMP! WHOMP!

a sonic adventure by

Wynton Marsalis

illustrated by

Paul Rogers

CANDLEWICK PRESS

Our
back
door

squeeeaks.

A nosy
mouse

eeek-eeek-eeeks!

It's also how
my sister's
saxophone
sometimes

Big trucks on the highway *RRRR*

Hunger makes my tummy GRrruMBle.

UMBLE.

The big bass drum goes

Bum!
Brrrum!
BRRRUMBLE!!!!

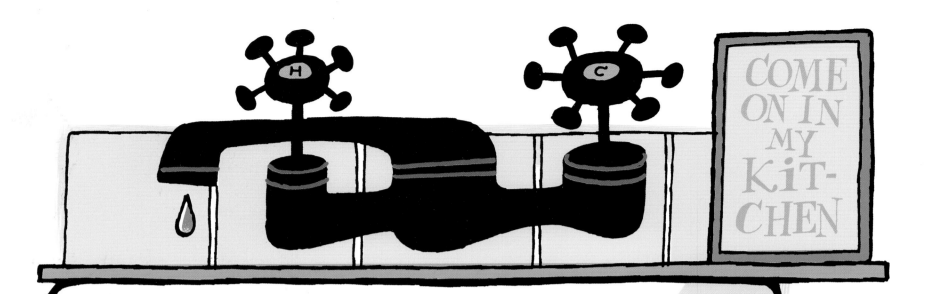

tluck...tlock

tluck...tlock... Our faucet
needs
a fix.

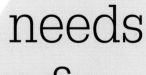
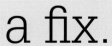

TLICK - TLOCK

TLICK - TLOCK

My alarm
clock ticks.

tlock *tlaack* *tlack* *tlick!*

Pizzicato violinists plick-pluck licks.

WOoo-uuu,
OOoo-uuu

Ambulances say.

MMMrmrmrrr

A motorcycle speeds away.

Brrraaomp!

The trombone
slides down
to play.

I love the wind *whistling* across my face,

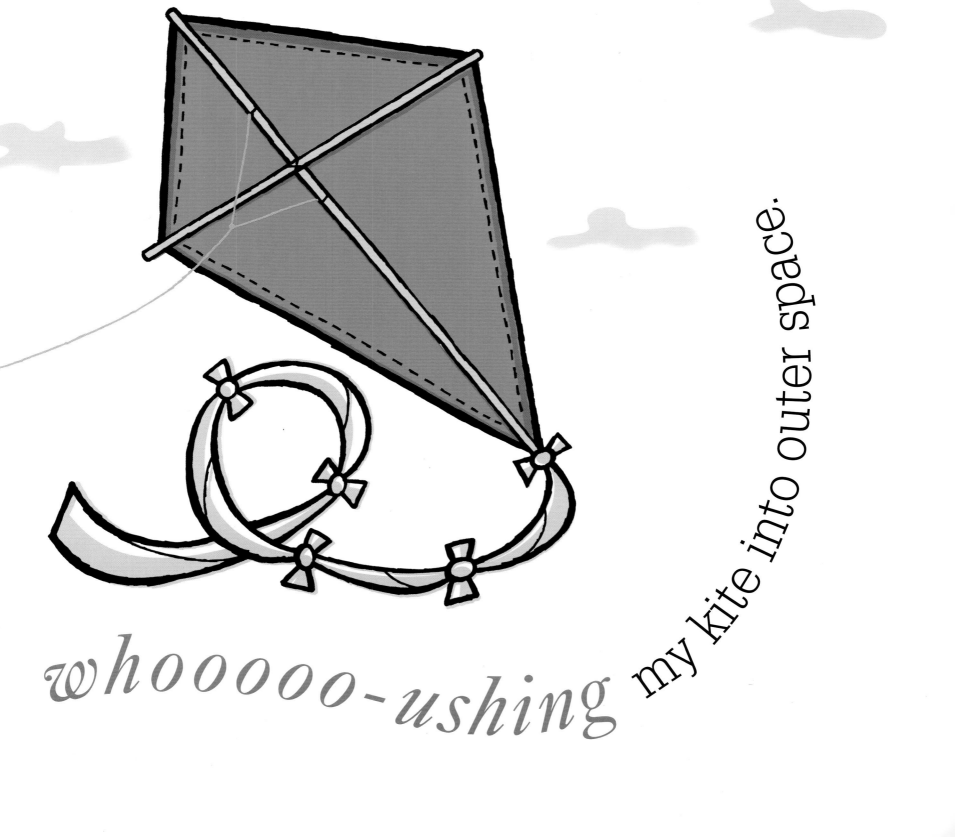

whooooo-ushing my kite into outer space.

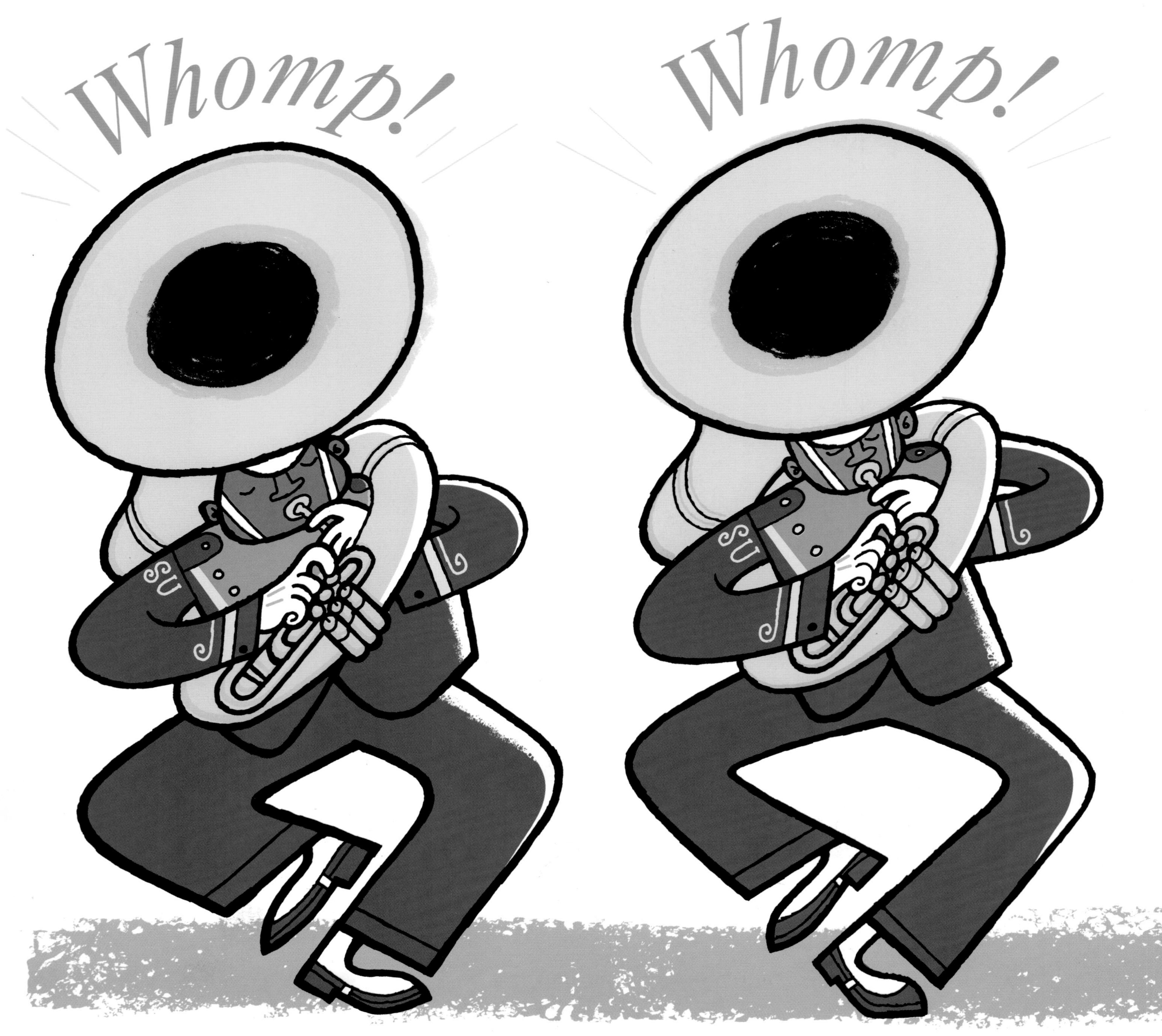
Whomp!
Whomp!
SU
SU

WHOMPING!

Tubas fill up the place.

Chrrrick chrrrick chrrrick chrrrick

—buttering my toast.

Krrrick krrrick krrrick krrrick krrrick

—quick where it itches the most.

Schuk-chuk, schuk-chuk, schuka chuk, sschick.

Hear that washboard boast.

Ting, tink-y, ting, tap!

Flies *bzzz bzzz bzzz* all around my food.

The barber's clippers *Jurrr! Jurrr! Jurrr!* And I'm cool, dude.

I *huz-huzz-huzzz* a kazoo when I gets the mood.

The
Big
Train
rolls
down
the

WAAAA!
BAAAW!
track.

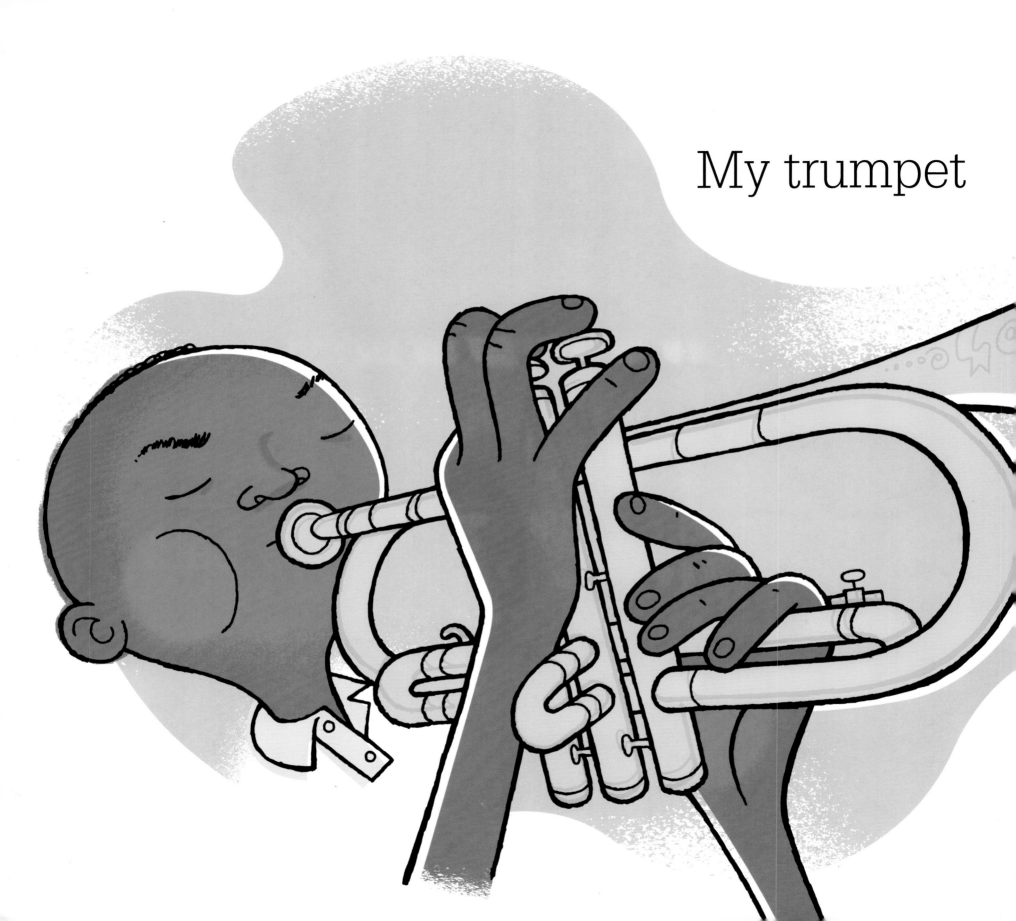

My trumpet

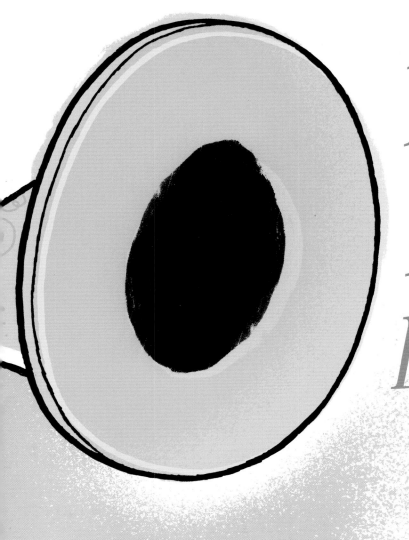

Blaa
BLAA
BLAAARES

with a
BIG OL'
attack!

*Squeak-squeak,
eeeeek-eeeek,*
**RUMBLE
GRUMBLE BRUM.**

*Tlick-tlock,
OOOO-UUU,*
BRUUUM-BRUUM-BRUM.